GETTING UP
FOR THE
PEOPLE

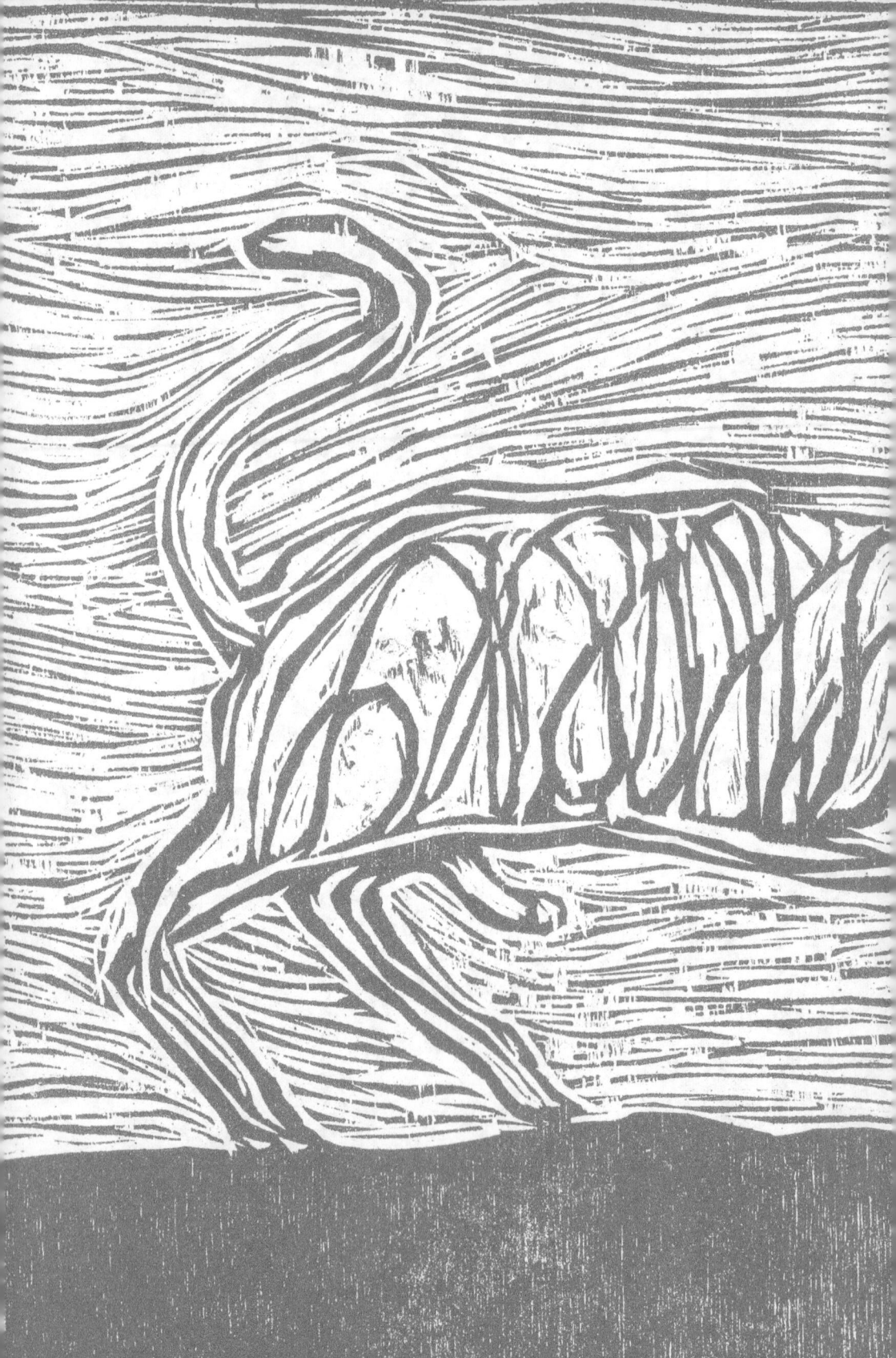

GETTING UP FOR THE PEOPLE
THE VISUAL REVOLUTION OF ASAR-OAXACA

ASARO, MIKE GRAHAM DE LA ROSA, AND SUZANNE M. SCHADL

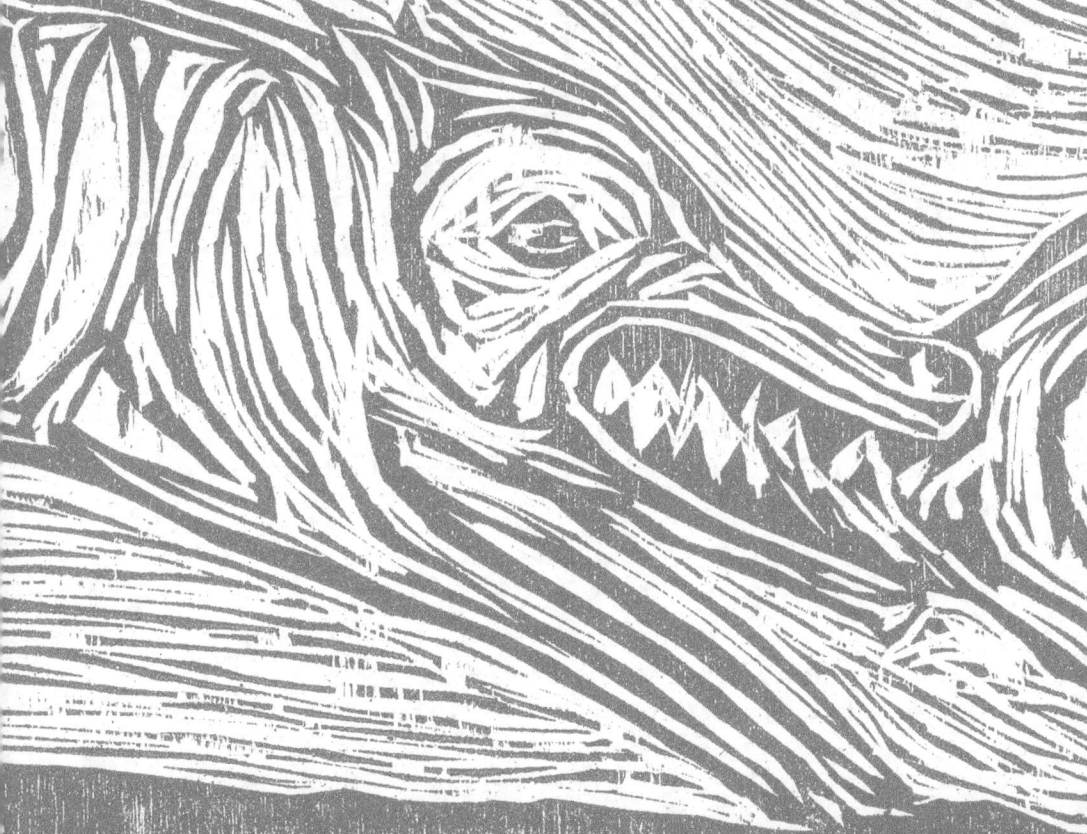

PM
2014

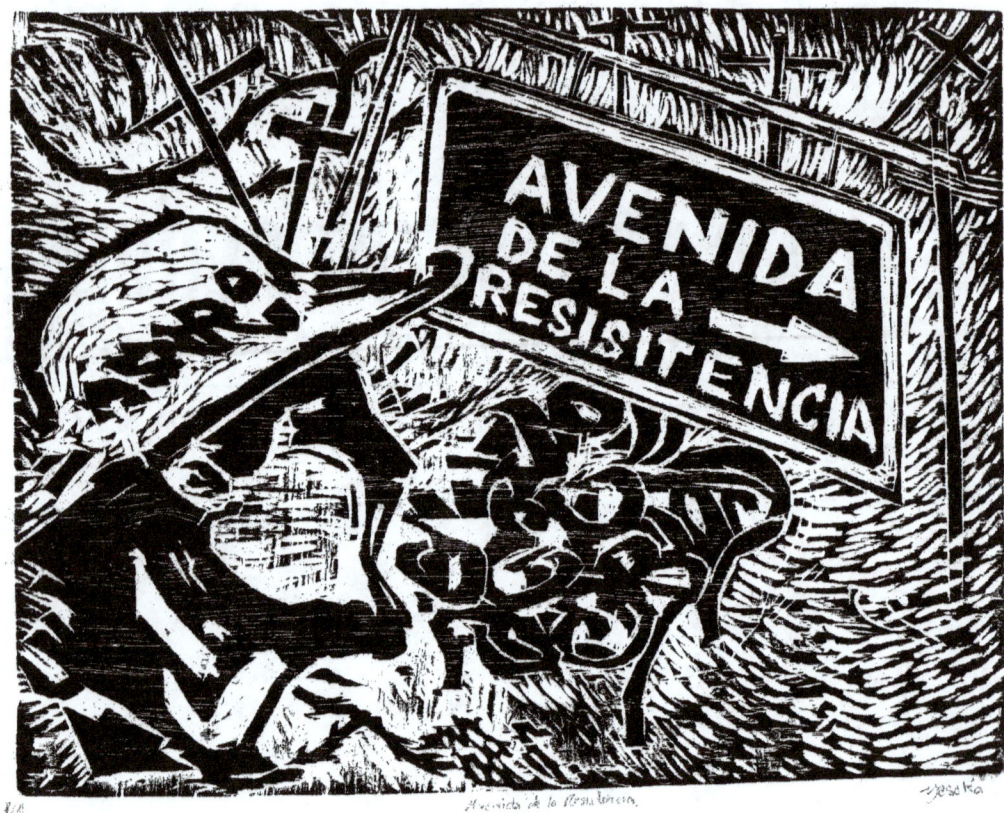

Avenida de la Resistencia, 2010, block print, 18.5" x 15".

Getting Up for the People: The Visual Revolution of ASAR-Oaxaca
ASARO, Mike Graham de la Rosa, and Suzanne M. Schadl
©2014 ASARO, Mike Graham de la Rosa, and Suzanne M. Schadl
This edition ©2014 PM Press

ISBN: 978-1-60486-960-6
LCCN: 2013956915

Cover and interior design: Josh MacPhee/AntumbraDesign.org
Cover image: *La Comuna de Oaxaca 2006*, 2006, block print

10 9 8 7 6 5 4 3 2 1

PM Press, PO Box 23912, Oakland, CA 94623
www.pmpress.org

CONTENTS

Preface   v

Introduction: Manifesting Visual Rebellion   1

Remixing Creative Revitalization—Disrupting the Matrix   17

Peripheral Getting In   28

Multispective and Social Action   44

Counterculture and Consciousness   56

Pa'l Pueblo/For the People   69

Stand Up, Speak Up   92

Acknowledgments   107

Bibliography   110

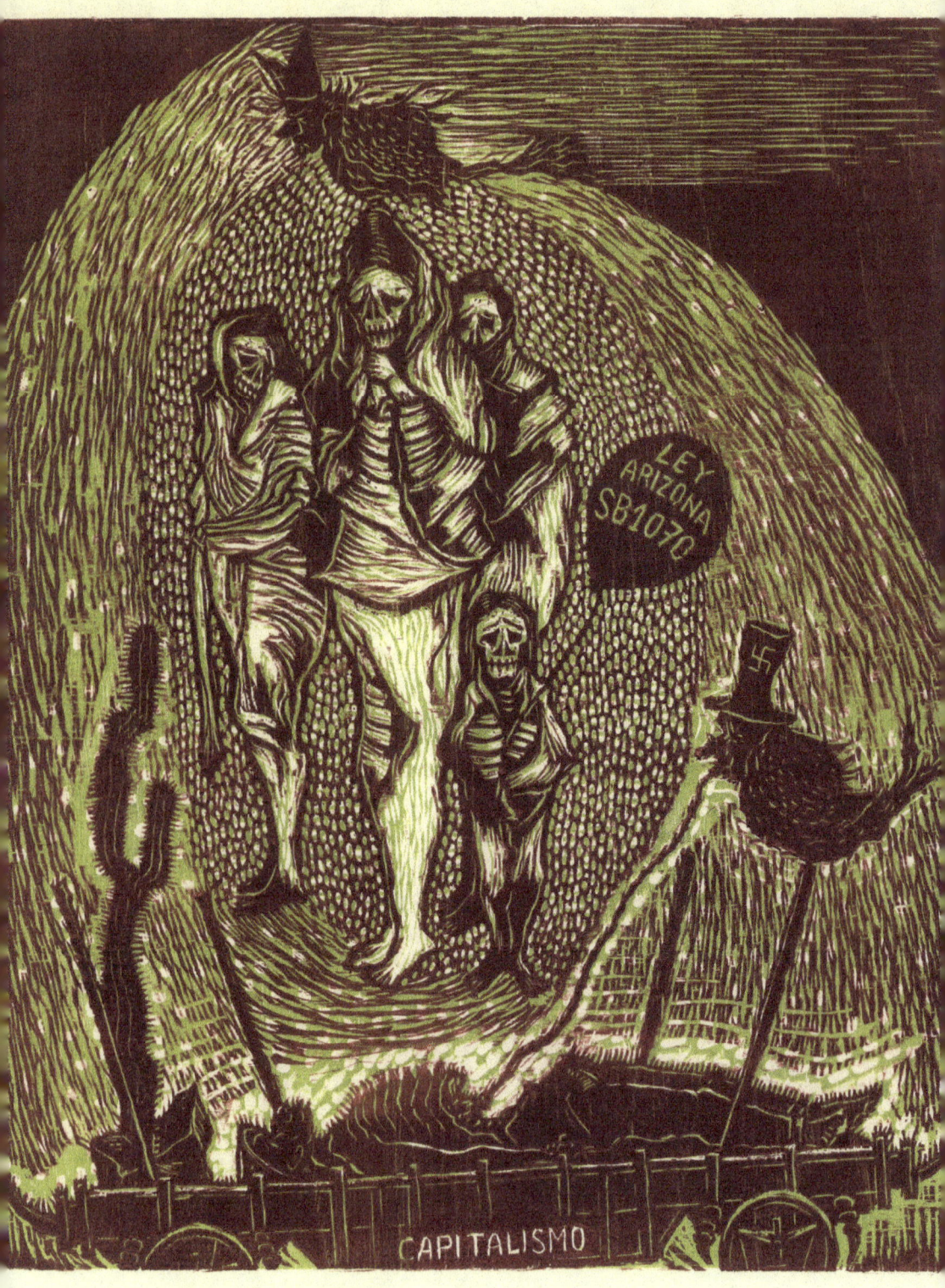

LEY ARIZONA SB1070

CAPITALISMO

PREFACE

This book was possible thanks to ASARO members past and present, many of whom cannot be named. All of the block prints reproduced herein are part of the Asamblea de Artistas Revolucionarios de Oaxaca Pictorial Collection at the Center for Southwest Research in the College of University Libraries and Learning Sciences at the University of New Mexico (UNM). This collection was established in 2010, which is why many of the of the prints have been assigned that date. The photographs were generously provided by Itandehui Franco Ortiz. Unless otherwise noted, the prints depicted throughout this text are ASARO's. Between 2006 and 2008 ASARO included more people than could be counted here, and today only Mario, Cesar, Yescka, Ita, Irving, Chapo, Beta, and Line remain. For this reason, collectivity, community, social context, and articulation through print and image are more important than proper names in *Getting Up for the People: The Visual Revolution of ASAR-Oaxaca*. As ASARO does, this catalog visually remixes the Oaxacan past with its present and exhibits how this contemporary Mexican artists' collective weaves global humanist themes throughout its work. As fliers, posters, and wheat pastes, these images are applied in the streets, inviting people to communicate with them—sometimes by adding a visual twist, or by taking a second glance. Responses can be good and bad; what is important is that they elicit an active dialogue. As collectible prints, these images are paradoxical parts of the outward-looking Oaxacan cultural industry. They invite people outside of Oaxaca to look beyond the veneer of a quaint colonial-like city and to see people struggling, while telling their stories through art and print. *Getting Up for the People* is another vehicle for that important dialogue.

« *Arizona SB 1070*, 2012, block print, 19 ¾" x 25 ½".

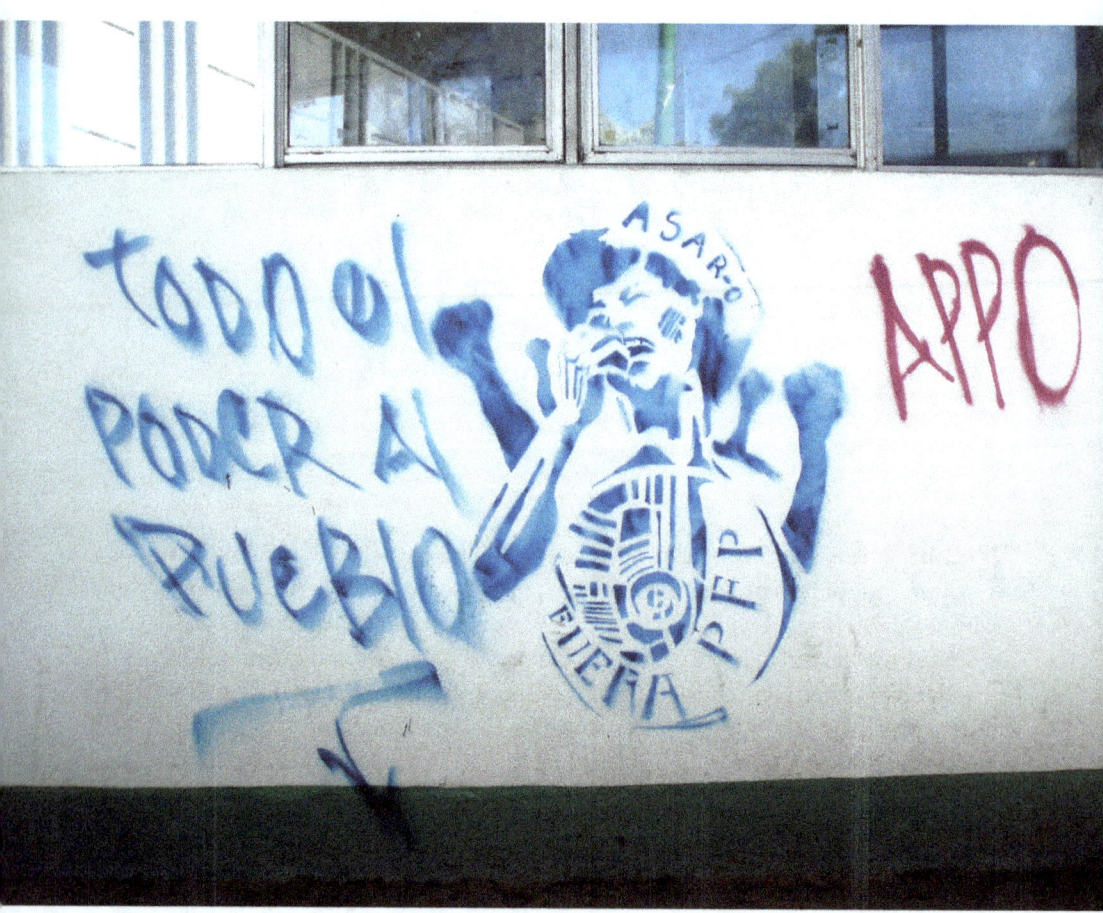

Todo el Poder al Pueblo APPO, 2006, stencil and graffiti.

"I think we first used *arte pa'l pueblo* in 2006, and our language is Western. Sometimes we use that word *art*, and we don't define its meaning. Every individual gives it meaning, and that's what's important. For me, it was essential to communicate with society, the marginalized, who are our neighbors, who we pass every day in the street—the humble working people, not the rich. The rich exploit people, but it's the humble people that make things happen. I think that's what *pueblo* is." —Anonymous

INTRODUCTION: MANIFESTING VISUAL REBELLION

"ASARO is a gathering of artists from various artistic disciplines which creates public art for the purpose of restoring social order." —ASARO Manifesto

This first statement in the manifesto of the Assembly of Revolutionary Artists of Oaxaca (ASARO) does not explicitly state the importance of Oaxaca. The state is intrinsic, however, to ASARO's identity as a community creating "art for the people"—*arte pa'l pueblo*. Written amid the heat of battle against then-governor Ulises Ruiz Ortiz (URO), this statement was intended to express the collective's belief that Ruiz Ortiz's removal was the key to restoring social order. Ruiz Ortiz's success in maintaining his position through 2010 set a steadier flame burning. Eight years later, ASARO now teaches stenciling and printing techniques to young people from Oaxaca's impoverished municipalities and encourages them to translate their histories, perspectives, and social grievances into creative visual exchanges with other Oaxacans and anyone else who circulates through the capital city, Oaxaca de Juárez.

The birthplace of Benito Juárez, Mexico's beloved and only indigenous president from 1858 to 1872, Oaxaca is recognized for its indigenous peoples or *pueblos*. History suggests that Oaxaca's second-largest contemporary indigenous power, the Mixtec, succeeded its largest, the Zapotec, during the postclassical period, only to fall later to the notorious Aztec civilization. Nevertheless, elements from all of these cultures survive today in Oaxaca, each incorporating other cultures. State officials recognize sixteen different indigenous groups with distinct languages, but others remain undocumented by officials. Named for the famous Zapotec president, the state's capital city has long been the central nexus for trading from around the state; many cultures or peoples/*pueblos* converge on the central *mercado*, making it a sensory overload for some and an attraction for others. Tourists from throughout

1

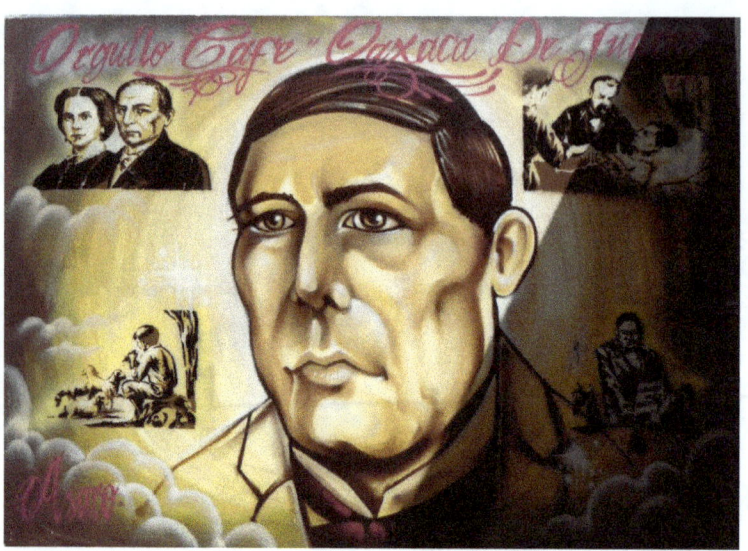

Juárez Pride Café, 2013, graffiti mural.

Mexico and from other countries frequent this space, often because of its indigenous population.

> "The people here are represented as a little savage. Mass media does not reveal the truth; it's always disguised. They show the colors of our pueblos, like they do in celebrations of the communities. It's a way for the state to make money, though and it's a form of exploiting that image of our state and these communities in other states." —Ita, ASARO

For officials in Mexico, the unmarked veneer of Oaxaca de Juárez's historic center attracts visitors by offering them a seemingly authentic confluence of Mexican cultures, past and present. The Oaxacans represented in these contexts are dressed in colorful and intricately woven "costumes" and carry forward enduring, "ancient" traditions. Festivals like July's Guelaguetza, in which indigenous participants from different regions of the state gather around a collective celebration of Oaxaca's diverse cultures, are another highlight for Oaxacan tourism, and people have reclaimed it as their own since Ruiz Ortiz left public office. Disrupting these tourist spaces with contradictory messages of conflict, as in *Ulises Si Cayó* (Ulises Did Fall) reveals the inconsistencies between the state's manufactured bucolic image and the actual experiences of its peoples.

In 2006, Oaxaca de Juárez was turned upside down when the governor, with the support of Mexico's president, sent in riot police to silence teachers' protests against poor pay and inadequate resources. On June 14, the Federal Preventative Police (PFP) at the behest of the Oaxacan governor and the Mexican president

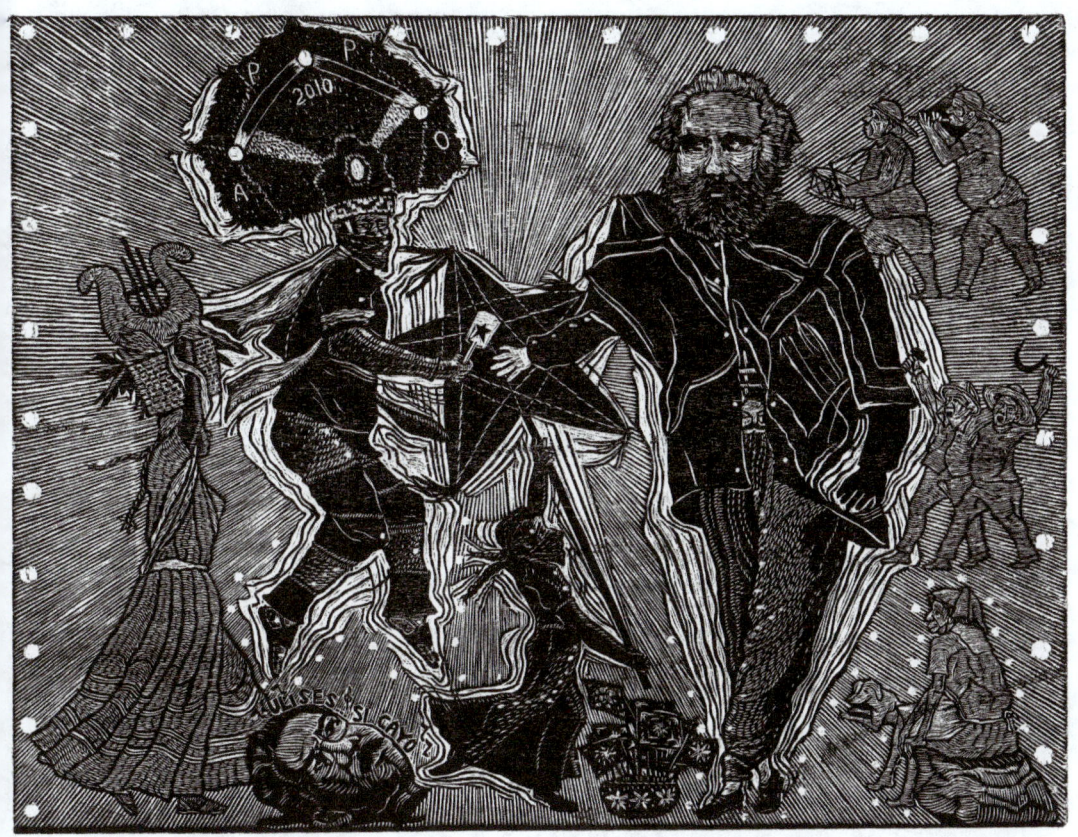

Ulises Si Cayó, 2010, block print, 39" x 27.5".

attacked protesting teachers and supporters with tear gas, and helicopters circled overhead. By the end of the day, ninety-two people had been seriously injured and four unarmed teachers were dead. Shocked and disgusted, city residents joined the teachers the next morning to raise barricades against the police. They also assembled a collective resistance comprised of indigenous organizations, women's groups, rural workers, religious activists, students, human rights organizations, and artists under the umbrella of the Asamblea Popular de los Pueblos de Oaxaca/Popular Assembly of the Peoples of Oaxaca (APPO).

ASARO was born out of these events, a part of APPO to stand united against government repression and economic suppression of Oaxacan peoples. This book is about their work in community and, as such, is essentially about Oaxaca. ASARO manifests and communicates with Oaxacan peoples, through materials that reveal or demonstrate. Their manifesto addresses who they are, what they do, and why they do it. Though things have changed since ASARO wrote its organizational mission statement in 2006, this artists' collective continues to pursue the

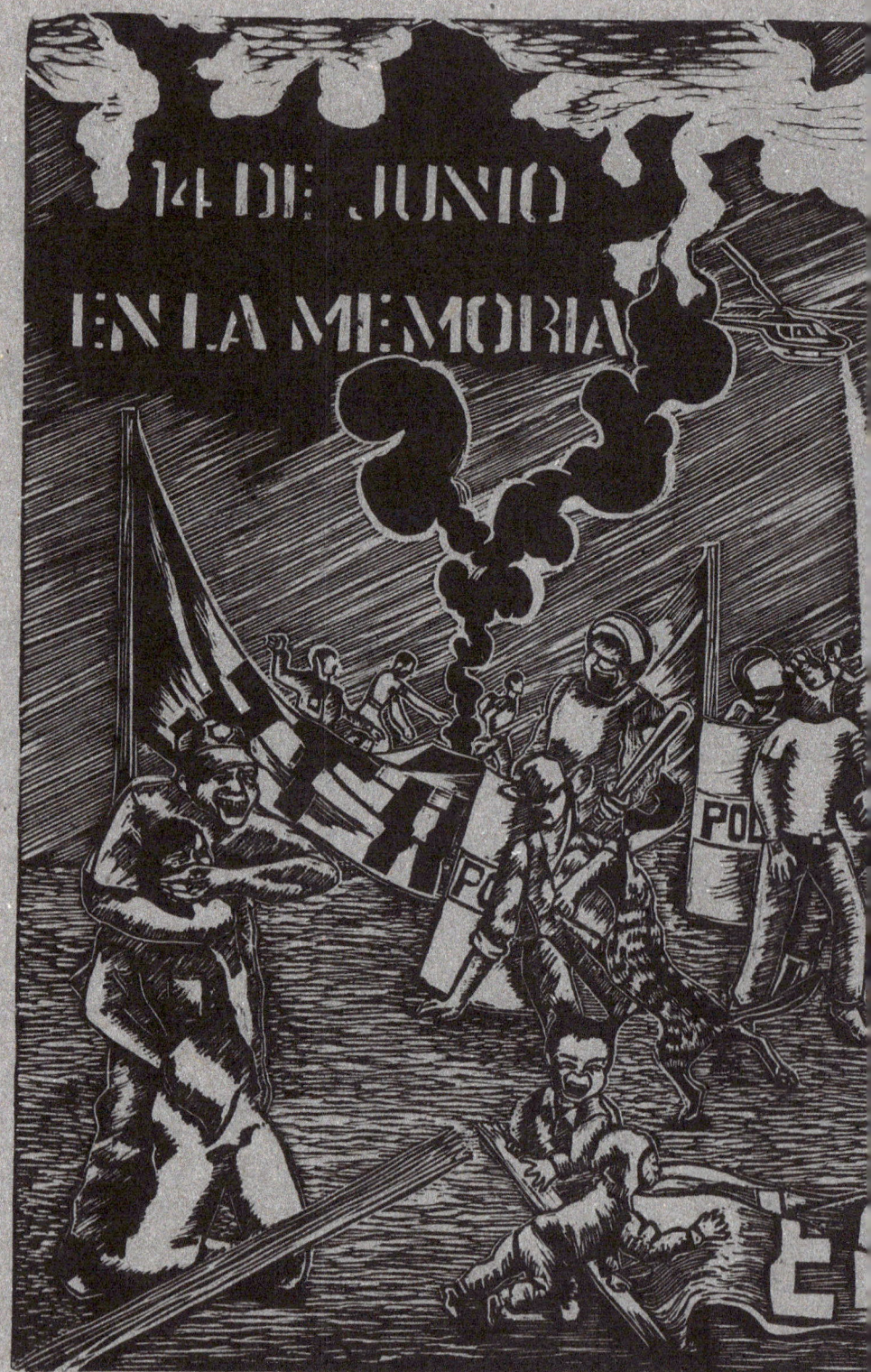

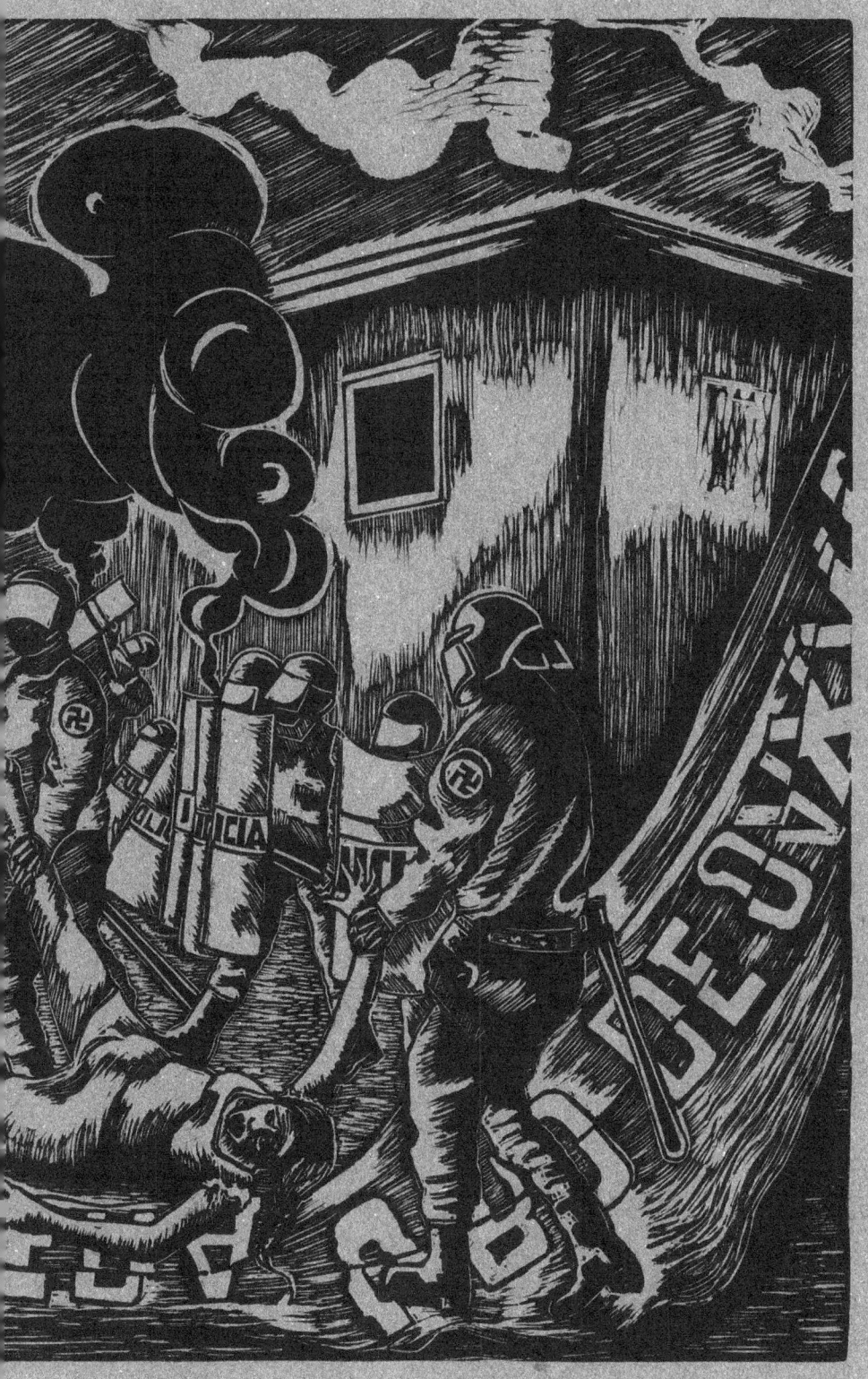

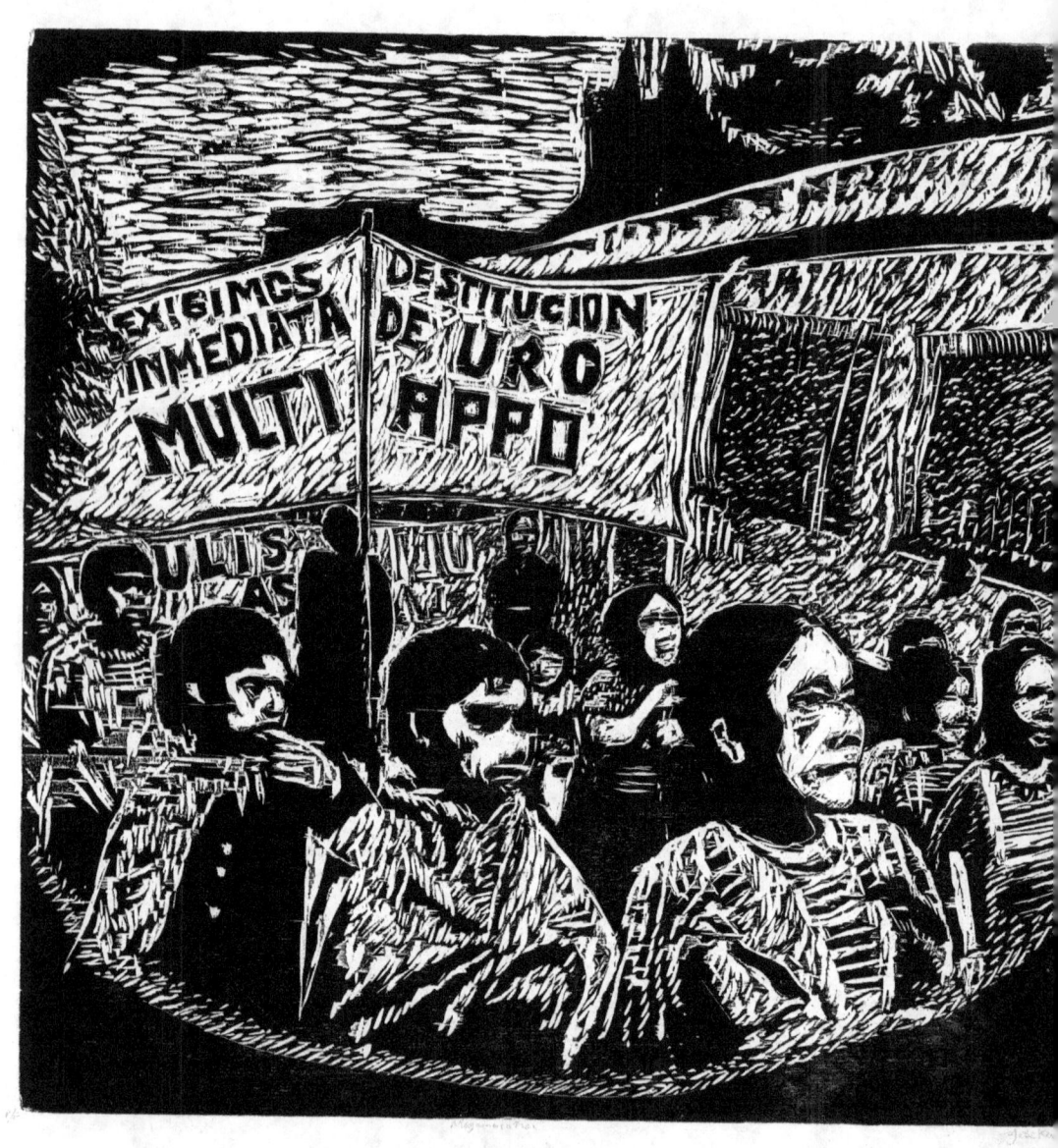

Exigimos Destitución Inmediata de URO Multi APPO, 2010, block print, 27" x 33 ¾".

mission it outlined then within changing conditions and with evolving participation. The document proves a useful compass for organizing this book, which recounts ASARO's journey through political conflict and educational partnering in artists' workshops for the people, pa'l pueblo.

"We promote workshops for the communities. The idea is to unite more people to ASARO, to multiply in small scale including people from different regions to create centers of resistance, and to create workshops in which the youth can visualize their reality in these regions." —Mario, ASARO

"Getting up" is slang for manifesting images repeatedly, often in highly visible spaces through which many people circulate. It is an effective form of protest in places like Oaxaca, where political and economic forces that value stability and profit over democratic process, inhibit legal dissent. Ruiz Ortiz's actions in 2006 were part of a long history of discriminatory practice against Oaxacan interests. ASARO uses this backdrop to remix or visually sample (also known as "assembling") collective social action with Oaxacan history, modern conventions in graffiti, traditional processes in Mexican printmaking, and contemporary communication through social networking. Their work is group-consciously collective, pulling together resources and ideas and working through their paradoxes and differences.

Many of the artists in ASARO have studied art formally at the Benito Juárez Autonomous University of Oaxaca (UABJO). Others have established themselves as graffiti artists. Some joined the collective with little training or established recognition among graffiti artists. Most were involved with the APPO, though some came later. Along with hundreds of other distinct organizations under APPO's umbrella during the months following Ruiz Ortiz's decision to send riot police into teachers' strikes, ASARO organized as a network of individual artists committed to a specific mission: to create publicly enacted art for restorative social purposes.

"Initially our purpose was denouncing, through graphic art, what was happening in the city, but also it was the power of translating a creative and comprehensible language into actions for a society living in conflict." —Chapo, ASARO

Like others within APPO, ASARO calls for all the peoples of Oaxaca to participate. Some ASARO artists voice their grievances in stencils. Others create block prints. Additional members circulate fliers and wheat pastes. Some take photos and video of the group installations. Others maintain related blogs and social networking walls. Generally speaking, most of the artists do all of these; each has connections to additional artists and assemblies. Most importantly, they work as a participatory organization "getting up" against the inequities in their communities by inviting visual exchanges through mutual respect for one another and love of their communities.

"The graffiti artist started to make prints and printmakers started putting their work in the streets." —Yescka, ASARO

ASARO's pieces are meant to be transformative. In some cases, the work itself changes, perhaps as a result of an added or overlaying stencil, or modified perspectives on the same theme. In others, the process converts a block print exhibited on paper to a stencil painted on a public wall. Sometimes it is the venue that changes. ASARO's exhibitions straddle—and are passed back over—divisions between street and gallery exhibitions, asserting artists' presence in all communities' spaces.

"When we put art up on the walls they become public because the streets are where the people, our people, circulate. We take those walls and intervene through them. We take those walls that don't say anything and give them voice. Even the textures, the colors, and the stains of those walls are integrated with the images that capture them." —Mario, ASARO

As a group of artists with different experiences and visions, ASARO pulls together diverse resources and experiences. They address sundry subjects with visual cues expressed in different compositions. They embrace debate, inclusiveness, and difference. They organize their own collective corpus in terms of themes, agreed upon as subjects, and then pursued in series by several artists. The varying styles and compositions ASARO produces are reflective of their collective purpose. ASARO offers no single message because their goal is to encourage public participation in reading, interpreting, reinterpreting, and representing revolution in Oaxaca. As a result, their presentations differ as broadly as the mediums and formats through which they communicate.

"Sometimes artists are very individualistic. . . . Little by little we compromise because really what you do is for love, love of the people and humanity." —Yescka ASARO

In addition to wood and linoleum block prints, large-scale graffiti murals, interventionist stencils, sand sculptures and public performances, ASARO creates digital media. They use electronic networking to facilitate outside access to their messages and to preserve their most ephemeral pieces, such as sand sculptures, or *tapetes*, and public performances. Limited digital access to less-privileged citizens means that traditional forms of alternative media, like fliers and wheat pastes,

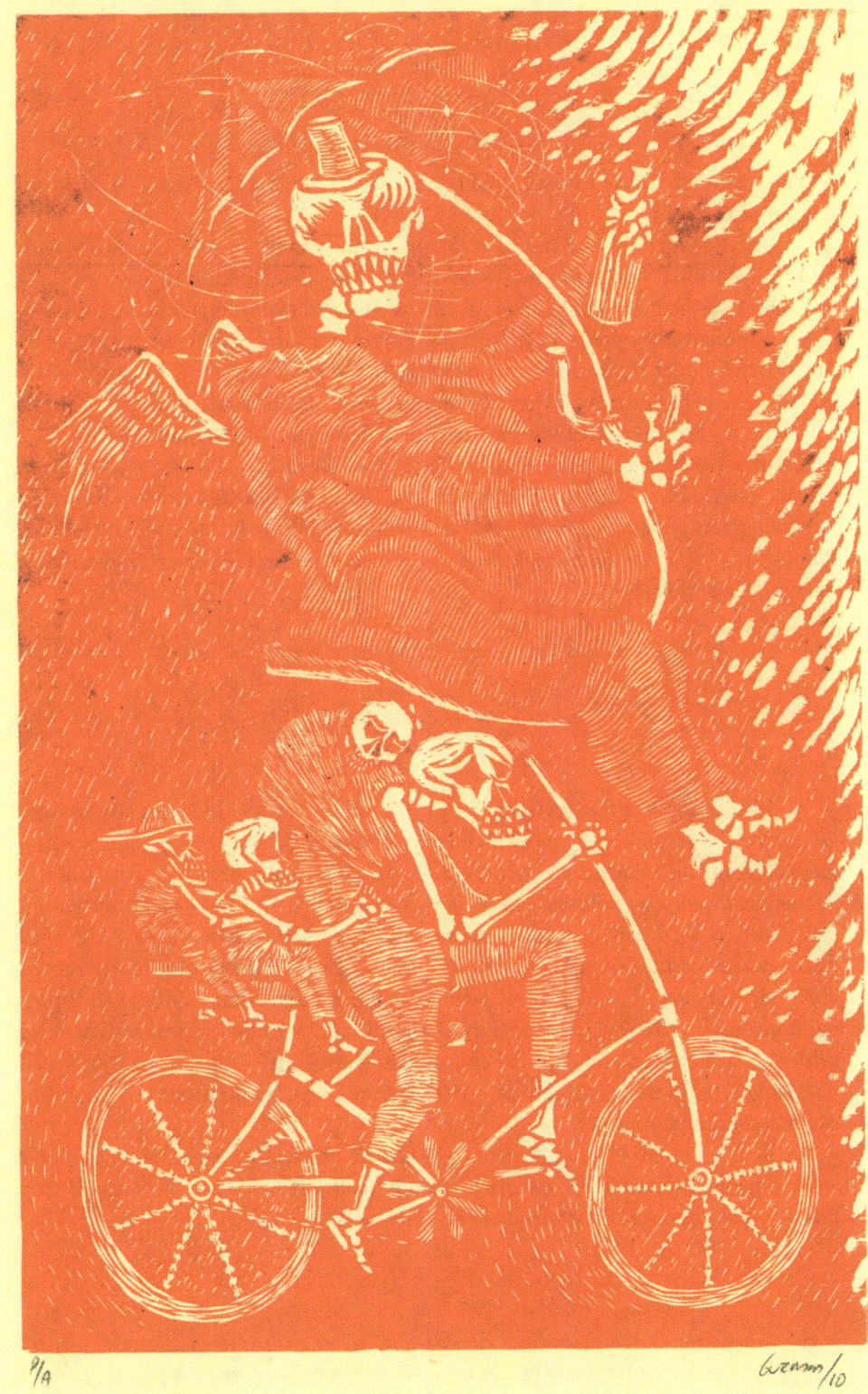

P/A

Guzman/10

Burguesía Calavera on Bike, 2010, block print 19 ¾" x 25 ¾".

remain essential. These formats enable ASARO to remix a rich Mexican tradition in graphic art.

ASARO's use of alternative print media puts them in good company with other revolutionary Mexican artists. Notable examples include Oaxacan brothers Enrique, Jesús, and Ricardo Flores Magón, whose prerevolutionary anarchist newspaper *Regeneración* openly criticized the corruption and repressive measures of Mexican president Porfirio Díaz, also Oaxacan and ironically similar to Ruiz Ortiz. Díaz's dictatorial and pro-expansionist policies ultimately led multiple factions throughout Mexico to revolt during the second decade of the twentieth century. The Mexican prerevolutionary political cartoonist José Guadalupe Posada, known for satirical *calaveras* or skeletons—that can also be found in ASARO's work—generated illustrated pamphlets targeting graft and corruption. Similarly, the Taller de Gráfica Popular (TGP) circulated graphic critiques of corporate inequities in alternative newspapers and fliers.

"We use print techniques because the material can be acquired anywhere. It's inexpensive. You can take it home, work with it, come back to it, and then print it. It is a broadcast medium that gives itself to copy after copy and it reaches many people. It's theirs to take." —Ita, ASARO

In addition to these revolutionary print influences ASARO uses city edifices as canvases to remix the Mexican nationalist tradition of employing muralism as a form of public information and as a means to gain international attention for the arts. Rather than being commissioned to depict cultural patrimony—as Diego Rivera, David Alfaro Siqueiros, and José Clemente Orozco generally were—ASARO has been accused of destroying cultural patrimony with their art until recently, regardless of the veracity of its messages. Participating in a movement to plaster and spray paint images on the walls of a UNESCO World Heritage site like Oaxaca's historic center does elicit attention; it is the epitome of "getting up." This type of action is all part and parcel of the mission to reverse the social order and improve the condition of the Oaxacan people.

Recent attempts on the part of Oaxacan officials to incorporate ASARO workshops into government efforts to ensure quality street art seem contradictory, but they are evidence of a reversal in Oaxaca's social order.

"In the historic center of Oaxaca, paint is not allowed because it is part of the historical patrimony and there are many restrictions, but sometimes people also support us. In more remote parts of the city, we do have support. That's where we want to leave information because it's where people are most marginalized. They don't have the same

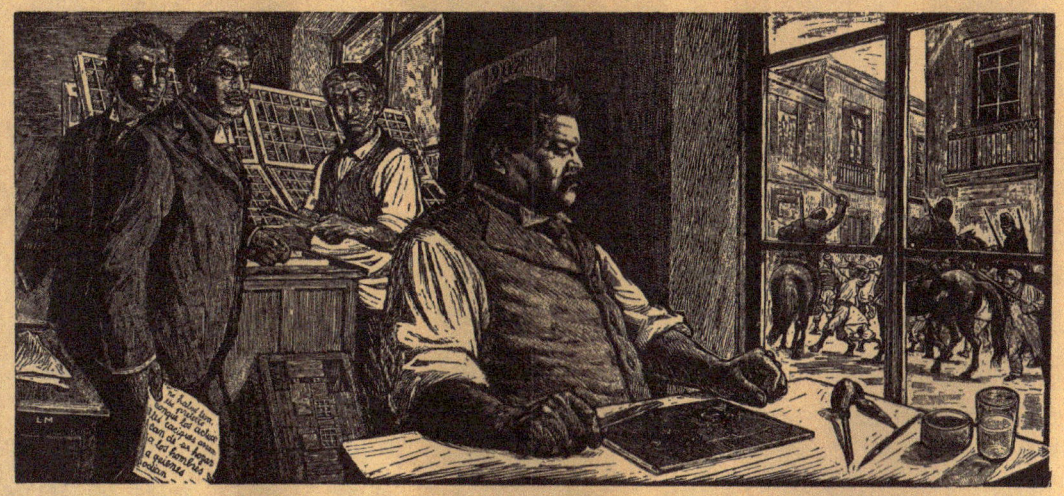

Leopoldo Méndez, *Guadalupe Posada*, 1960, lithograph, 15.75" x 10.6", depicting José Guadalupe Posada in his workshop capturing the scene of military oppression taking place outside of his window. Ricardo Flores Magón stands to Posada's right. Méndez was a lead member of Taller de Gráfica Popular (TGP), and this print is part of their 1960 portfolio, *450 años de lucha: Homenaje al pueblo Mexicano*.

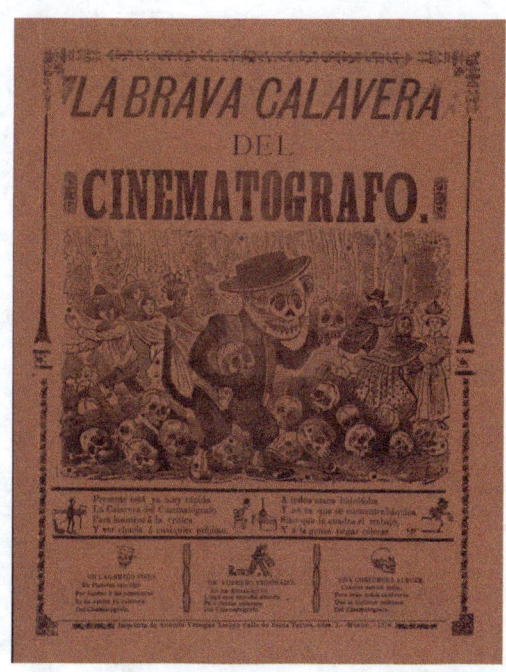

José Guadalupe Posada, *La Bravura Calavera del Cinematógrafo*, 1906, broadside, 5.6" x 9".

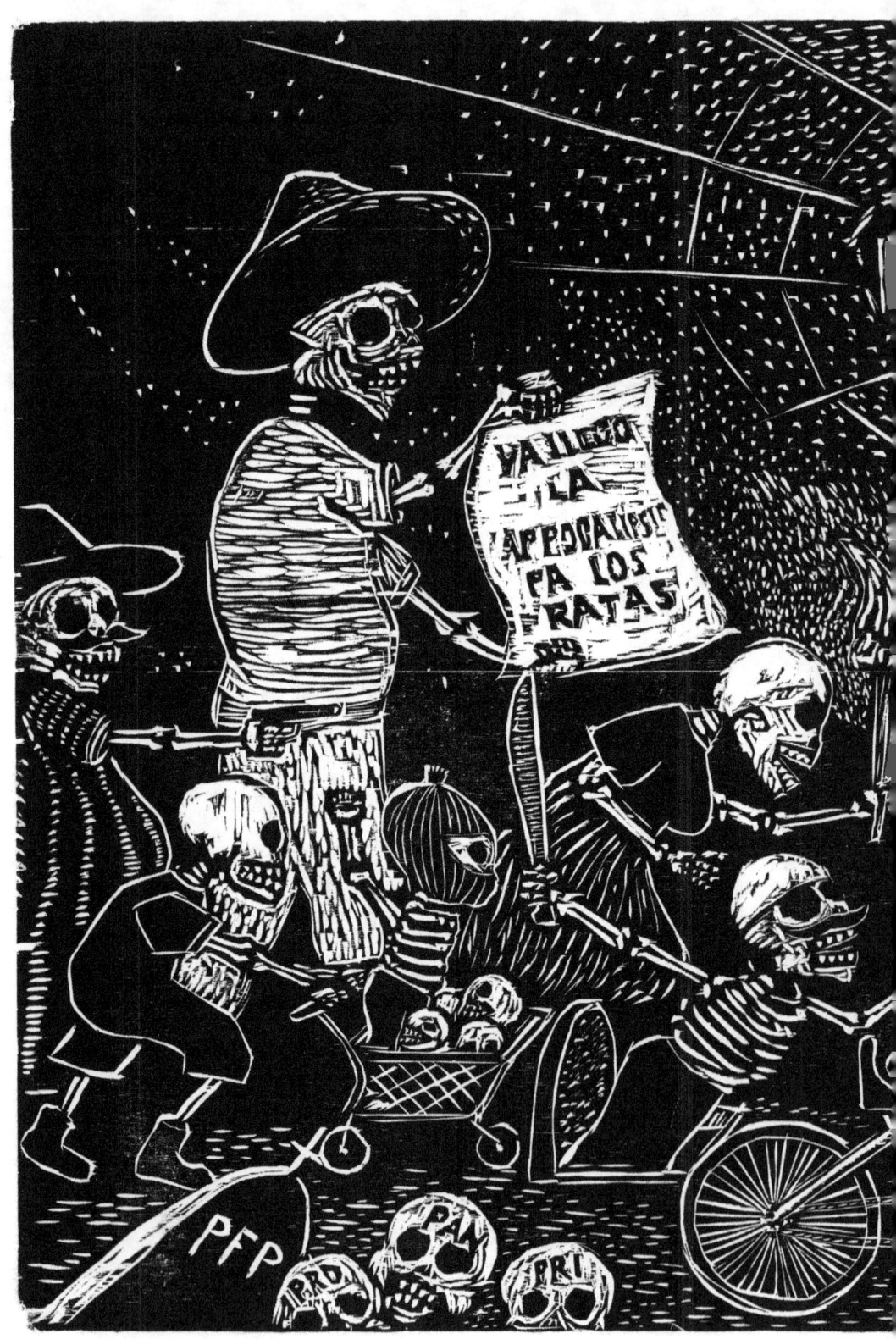

Ya Llegó la Apocalipsis pa' los Ratas, 2006, block print, 39 ¼" x 27 ½".

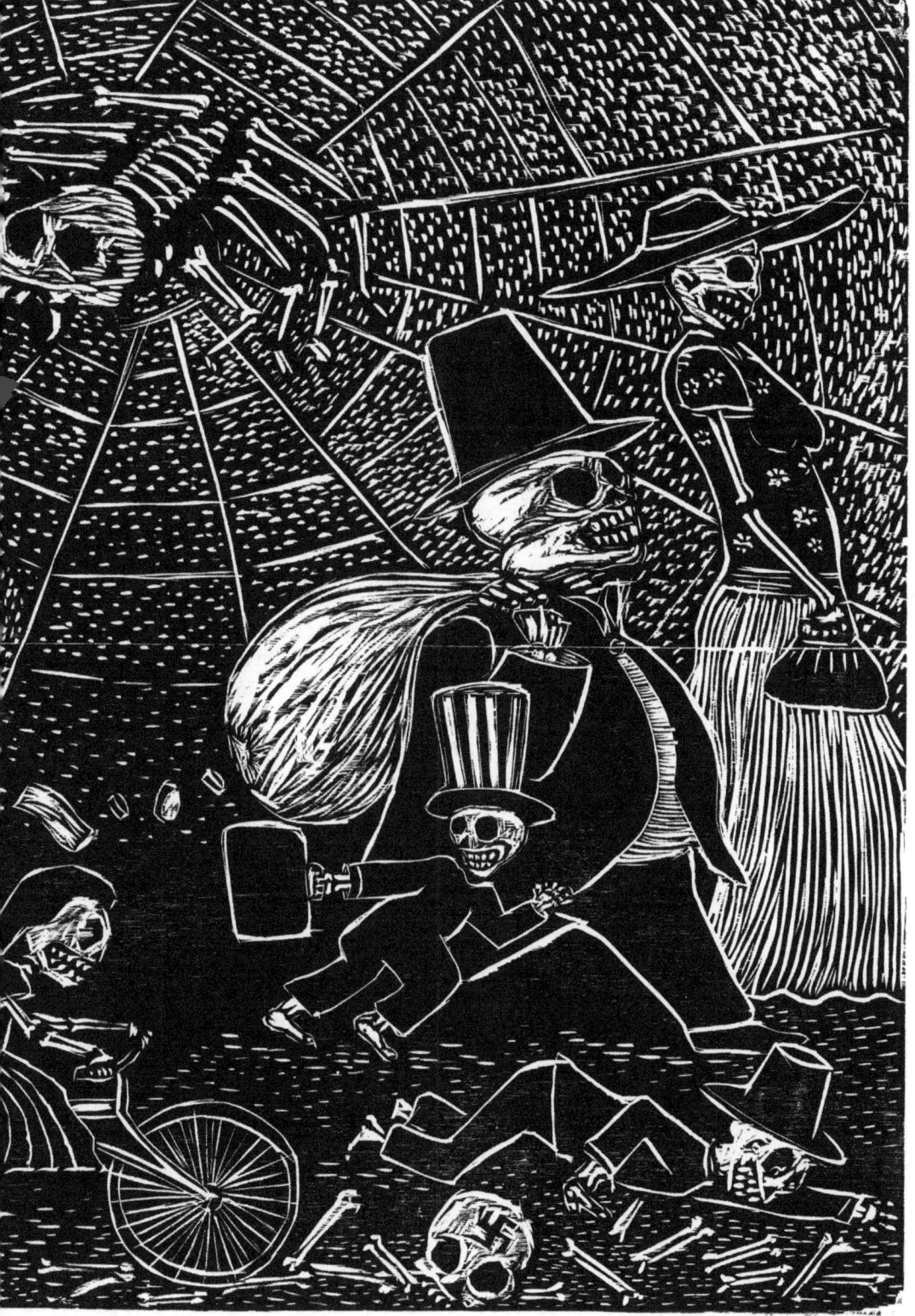

resources that those who live in the historic center have. It's that pueblo, the one living here and now, who gives us means for creating consciousness." —Chapo, ASARO

Instead of being concealed as undesirable stains on Oaxaca's cultural patrimony, young people's work is part of a collaborative project to reinterpret and represent Oaxaca's heritage. There is paradox here, and ASARO is under no illusions about this development, but the relationship does open a dialogue that has been suppressed in Oaxaca for centuries.

Transportation and communication in Oaxaca have always been challenging for residents. The state's terrain is rugged due to the confluence of mountain ranges separated by a Y-shaped valley in its center. Consequently, it is isolated physically from much of the rest of Mexico. Nevertheless, major infrastructural investments in the state facilitate transportation from outside into and out of Oaxaca de Juárez. These infrastructural priorities reflect a historical tendency for industries such as mining to take resources away from Oaxaca, while others, like tourism, circulate people through its historic district and proximal archeological sites. Non-Oaxacan officials like Ruiz Ortiz who envision their positions in state government as springboards onto the national stage, typically supersede local interests in favor of the tourist market. ASARO disrupts this upside down dialogue by taking the city back for Oaxacans and inviting passersby to see what officials have been hiding.

Oaxaca Represión, 2008, wheatpasted stencil on paper. »

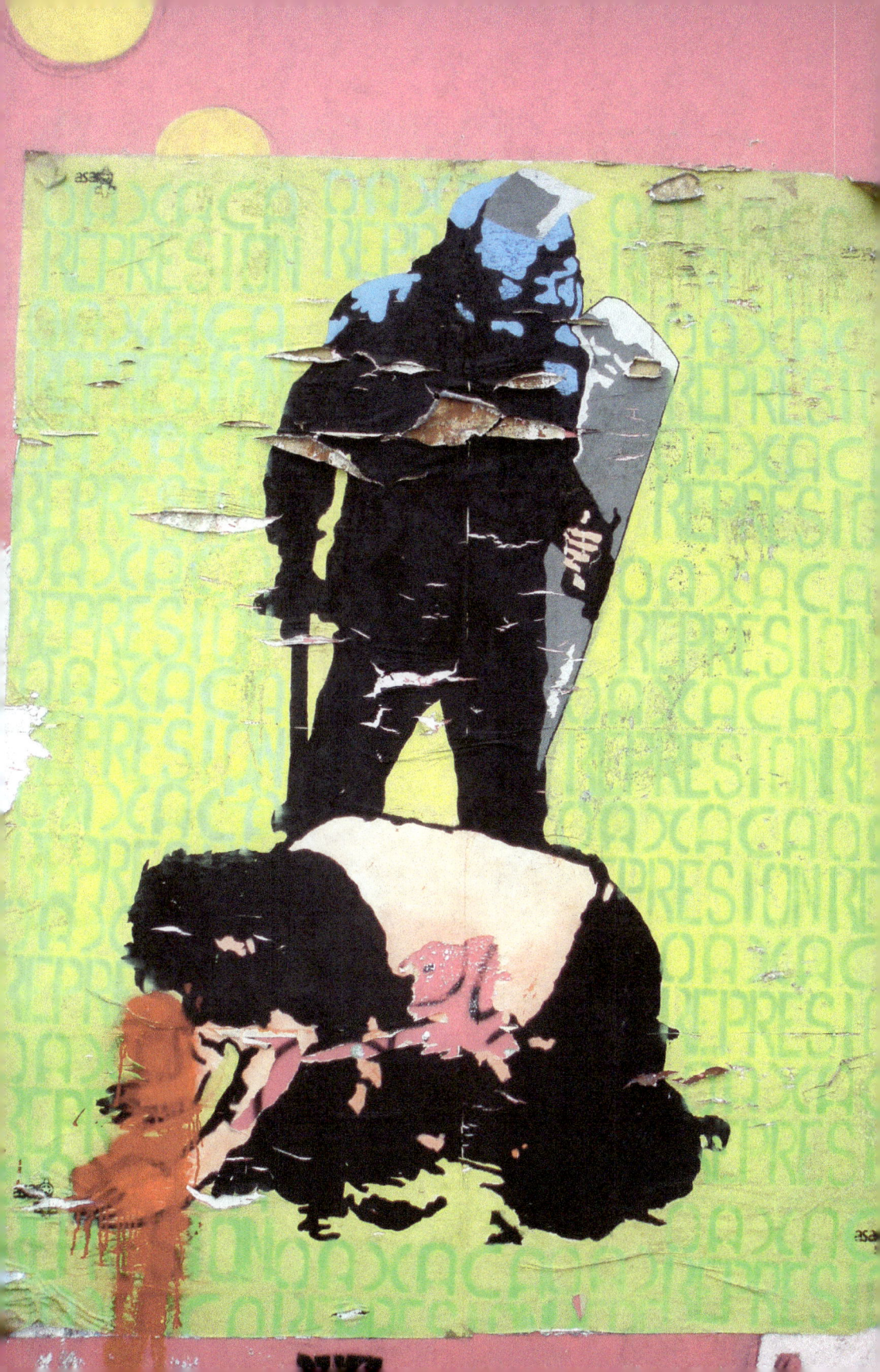

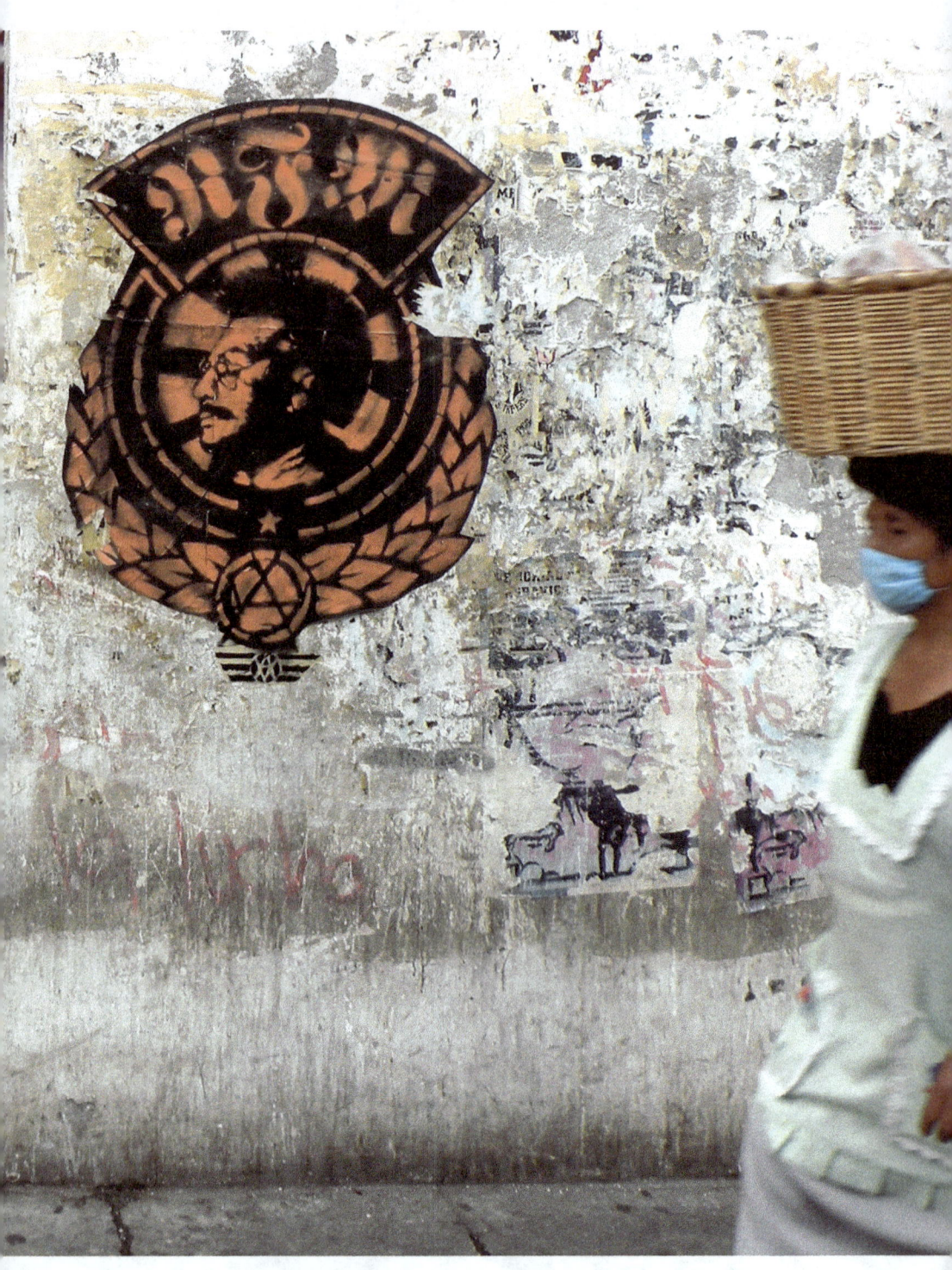

Ricardo Flores Magón, 2009, wheatpasted stencil on paper.

REMIXING CREATIVE REVITALIZATION— DISRUPTING THE MATRIX

"Creative ability is a resource upon which the people of Oaxaca have historically drawn to survive and revitalize. The assembly of revolutionary artists
arises from the need to reject and transcend authoritarian forms of governance and institutional culture and societal structures which have been char-
acterized as discriminatory and dehumanizing for seeking to impose a single
version of reality and morality or simulacrum." —ASARO Manifesto

A 2007 exhibition in Oaxaca titled *Grafiteros al Paredón* (roughly "Graffiti Artists Up Against the Wall") demonstrates the second statement in ASARO's manifes-
to. This indoor replication of scenes (once visible, but since removed from Oaxaca's streets) asserts memory by remixing art and space. The exhibition serves as visual documentation of both artistic rebellion and state censorship. In it, a larger-than-life likeness of Oaxacan anarchist Ricardo Flores Magón overwhelms repeated profiles of Ruiz Ortiz with labels identifying the governor as many things, including thief, murderer, authoritarian, and innocent. Shown in the Oaxaca Graphic Arts Institute (IAGO), the installation is replete with added graffitied phrases like "Stop the information blockade," "Unite people," "The resistance continues," and "APPO lives." These regenerated works proclaim ASARO's continued employment of creative re-
vitalization to transcend discriminatory and dehumanizing authoritarian restraints.

"These icons are a way for young people to express their power. To say, 'Well, okay, let's
use these images that the State has appropriated but they can also be ours with symbolism that come from the youth.'" —Ita, ASARO

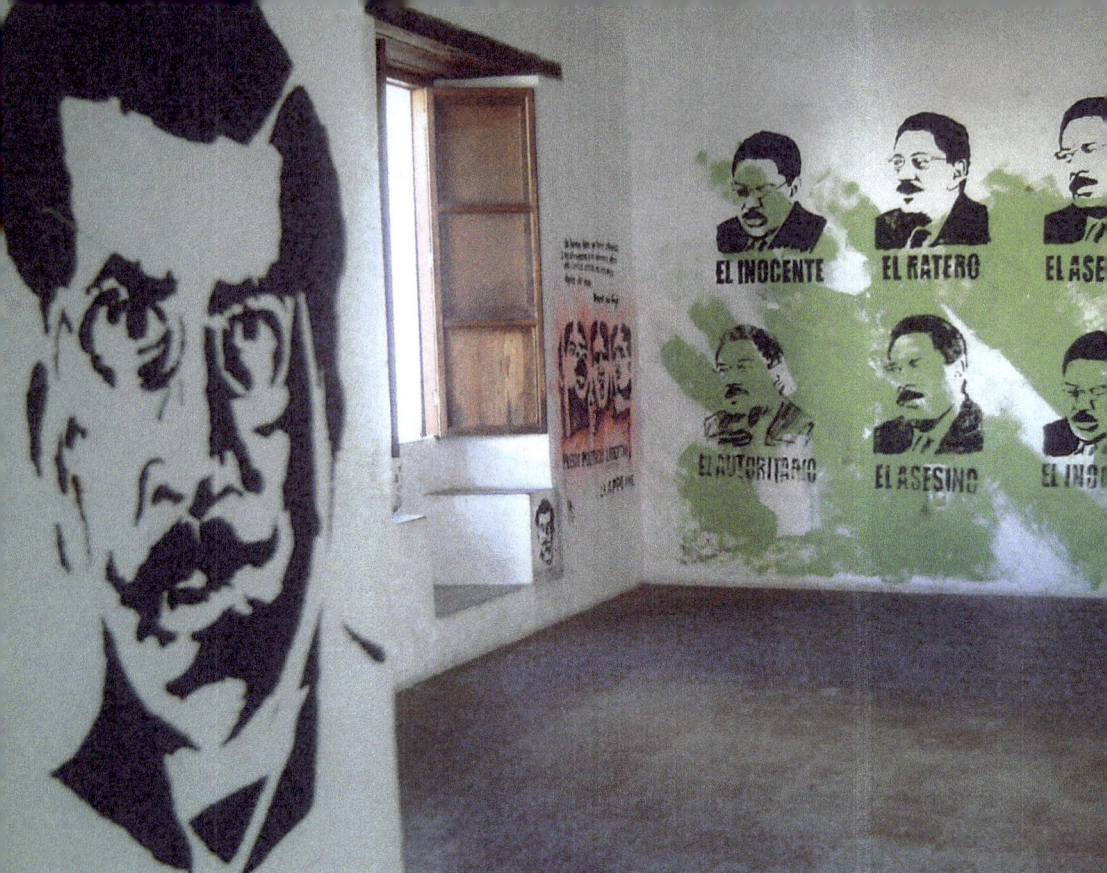

Grafiteros al Paredón, 2007, installation at Radio Plantón, Oaxaca.

Bringing retooled street images back together in a gallery provokes important debates about the consequences of Mexico's authoritarian history and Oaxaca's cultural patrimony. In 1920, Flores Magón wrote a letter to a Russian-American confidant denouncing the notion of "art for art's sake" by describing adherents as incapable of expressing feelings and ideas. His image encourages debate about art and space. Revered for equating public ownership with liberty, Flores Magón provokes questions about who is responsible for Oaxaca's patrimony. His image in this exhibit suggests that officials had it wrong a year earlier when they called ASARO's street installations "act(s) of aggression against the built heritage of Oaxaca." The exhibit asks: what is the "built" heritage of Oaxaca; who constructed it and for what purposes; and who determines its future?

"An intervention could start with a person reading a line in a magazine, or something written in the bathroom. Or it can be a vagabond every day in front of a pristine wall. The trick is changing the context and transforming it into something else. You don't change the natural state of the thing, but you change the context in which it's framed. . . . This place, the Espacio Zapata, intervenes with the dominant order. As you go to other galleries, you come to see other forms, other possibilities to intervene in the street." —Ita, ASARO

Posing questions like these inside a gallery rather than outside on the streets creatively repurposes physical space. It "gets back up," thus transcending institutionalized versions of events again, this time from the inside out. Participating in such a reciprocal dialogue with Flores Magón looking on is significant. The image of Flores Magón, who was exiled from Mexico for illustrating the absurdity of authoritarian "order," connects 2007 with the past and employs its memory for direction in the future. This creative remix harks back to indigenous Mexican beliefs in incarnate connections between the living and the dead celebrated throughout Mexico on the first days of November, and venerated in the artistic persistence of *calaveras* (skeletons) in Mexican art. The very belief in bridges between life and death rejects single versions of reality by encouraging empathy and communication across time and space. It suggests a cyclical rather than linear perspective further enhanced in artistic works that transform through participatory processes. For ASARO it is not so much "getting up" through public art as it is raising the people back up within it.

"Workshops help young people believe in themselves. For a struggling community, these workshops are power to grow and be stronger in their resistance to the problems they face." —César, ASARO

Creativity is not just distributing images for visibility; it is connecting—through those images and their circulation—with the past. The diptych print *Son Ellos o Somos Nosotros* (They Are or We Are) brings multiple historical events together in two artistic pieces. These works portray a general strike in which working people hold the line against fascism. Some of the characters depicted in the crowd hold signs favoring the socialist revolution or newspapers advocating anarchism. Some wave flags with hammers and sickles while others raise their rakes. These pieces are historical and contemporary, suggesting continuity and solidarity across time and space. The crowd in this image seems to be a throwback to early twentieth-century strikers, but the boy holding their banner wears a contemporary baseball cap cocked to the side with APPO's five-pointed red star.

Labels across the bottom of this diptych form a timeline connecting historical and contemporary Mexican rebellions. Guerrero identifies a prominent leader of Mexican Independence and Oaxaca's neighboring state, which served as a major theatre of the Mexican Revolution from 1910 to 1917. EZLN identifies the Zapatista National Liberation Army, which emerged as an internationally recognized rebellion in 1994. UNAM memorializes the student protestors who

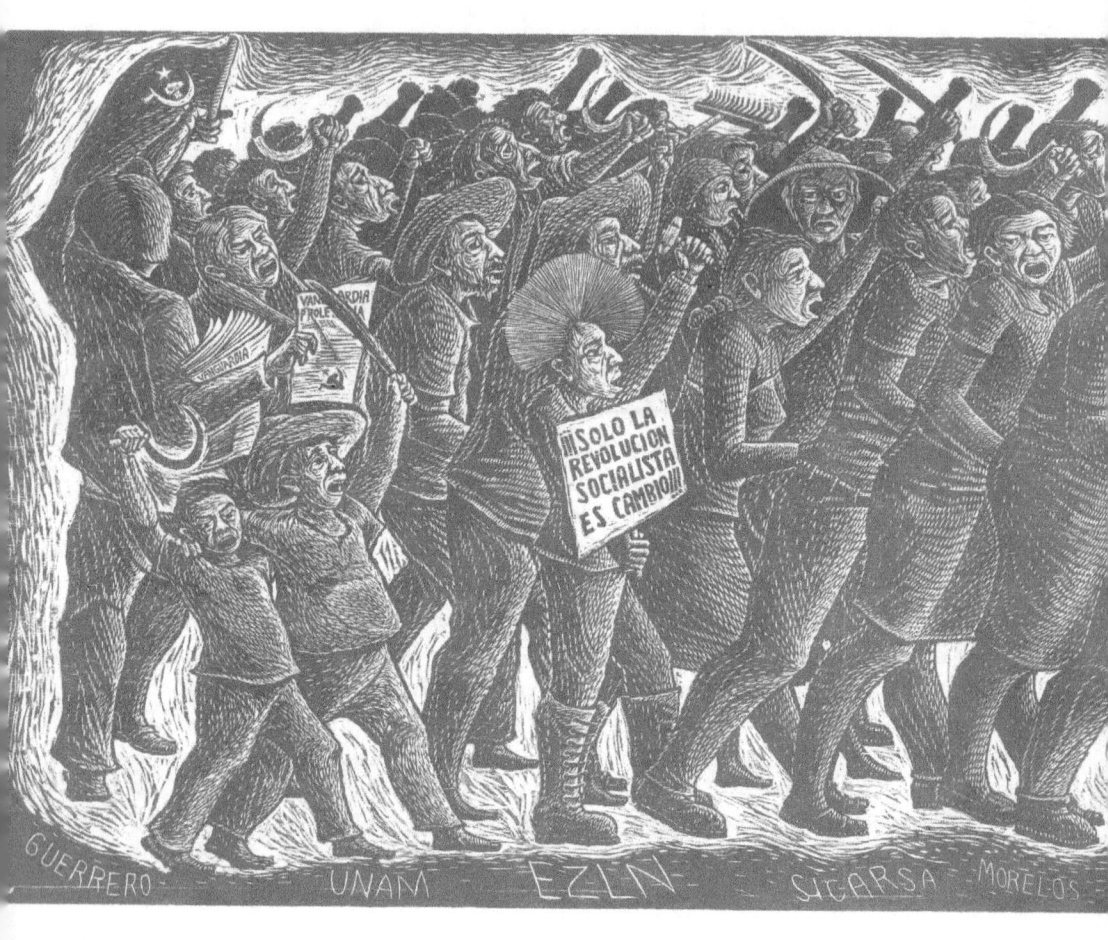

Son Ellos o Somos Nosotros (Parts I & II), 2010, block prints, 2 x 34" x 27 ½".

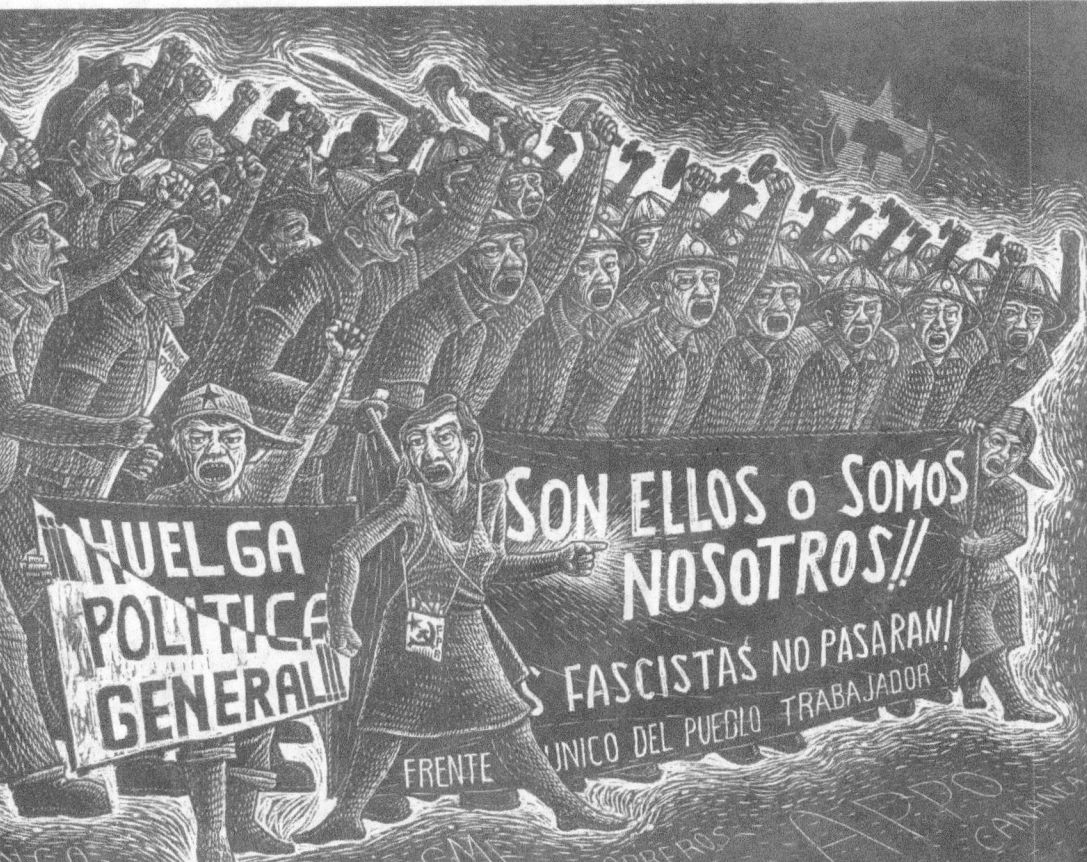

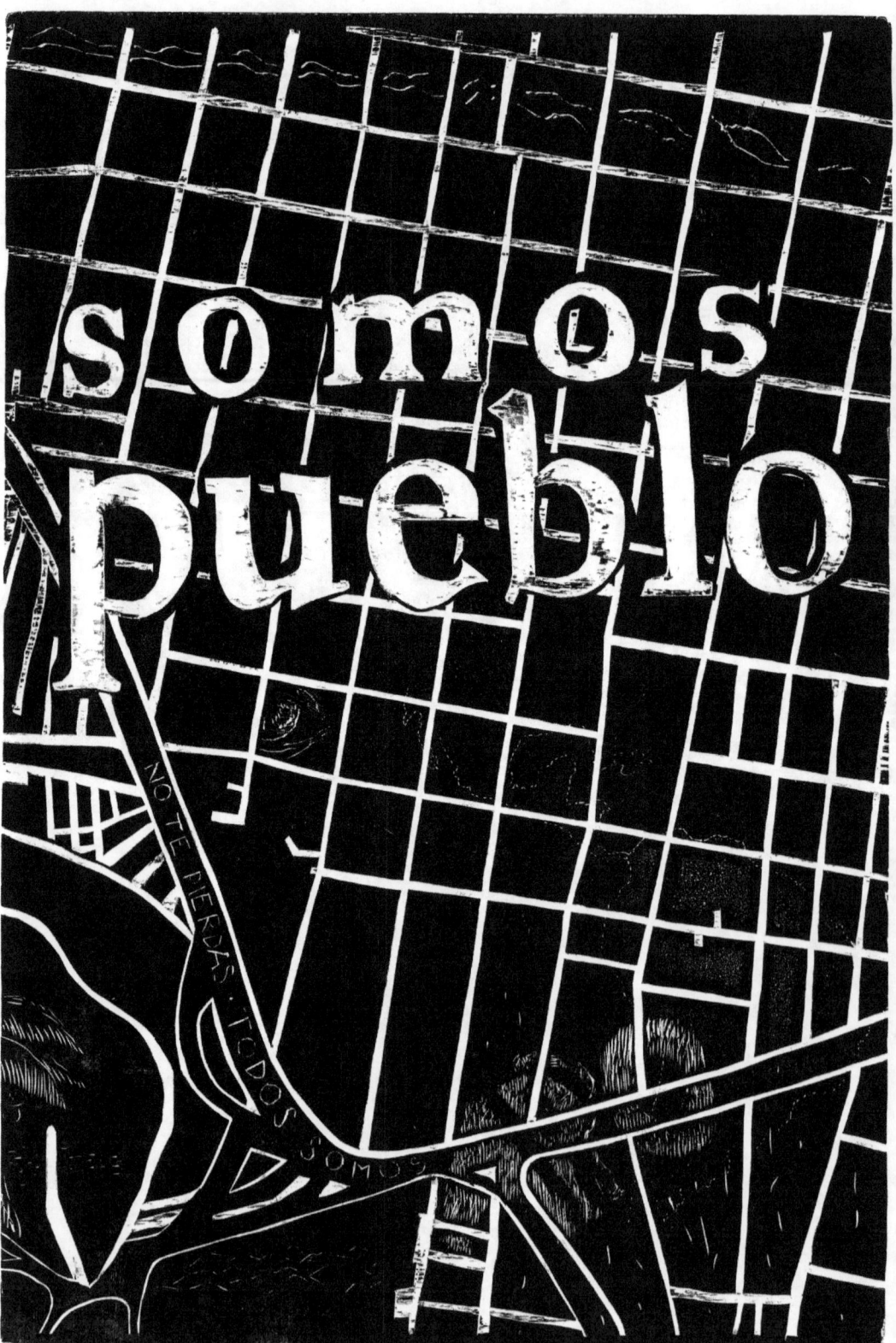

Somos Pueblo, 2010, block print, 27 ½" x 39".

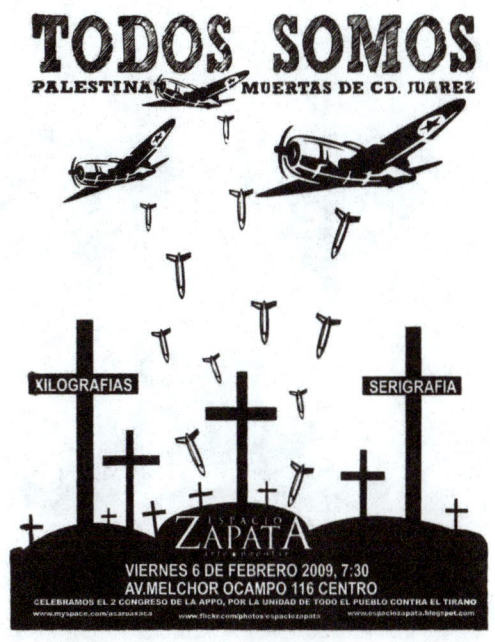

disappeared after a bloody conflict with police in Tlatelolco Square just days before Mexico hosted the Olympics in 1968. Atenco identifies a contemporary uprising against the displacement expected as a result of airport construction outside Mexico City in 2002. SME labels the Mexican electricians' union, past and present. Obreros recognizes workers everywhere at any time. ASARO adds APPO to this assembly of historic resistance, paying homage to the strides made throughout Mexico in collective organization and adding this contemporary network of social movements to the mix.

Todos Somos Palestina, Muertas de Ciudad Juárez, 2008, screenprint, 27 ½" x 38".

"During our struggles, our people have always used tools to make graphics reproducible. In Mexico we have a great tradition of graphic production used for utilitarian and social purposes. ASARO tries to further develop that tradition." —Mario, ASARO

Somos Pueblo (We Are the People) expresses this idea differently. It illustrates special interconnections in a stylized map of Oaxaca de Juárez. Against the black background, white lines form a cartographic depiction of Oaxaca's historic Zócalo. The words "Somos Pueblo" are superimposed in large letters on this rendering. They assert the central importance of a people united as one in this space, while rejecting the significance of its image as a tourist destination. Additional words placed on the "Periphery" highway that runs on the west side of the Zócalo read, "Don't forget that we are the people" as a means of underscoring who this map represents. Dotted lines on the bottom of the image form the Central and South American landmass below, extending the possibility for this network of streets and pueblos to reach into communities bordering Mexico's southern boundaries.

Todos Somos Palestina, Muertas de Ciudad Juárez (We Are All Palestine, Dead Women of Juárez) extends the same principal to other oppressed borderland peoples. This poster underscores a widely accepted notion that anyone could be identified as ethnically, politically, or socially different and therefore dangerous, then marked for death, especially within discriminatory and dehumanizing simulations of reality.

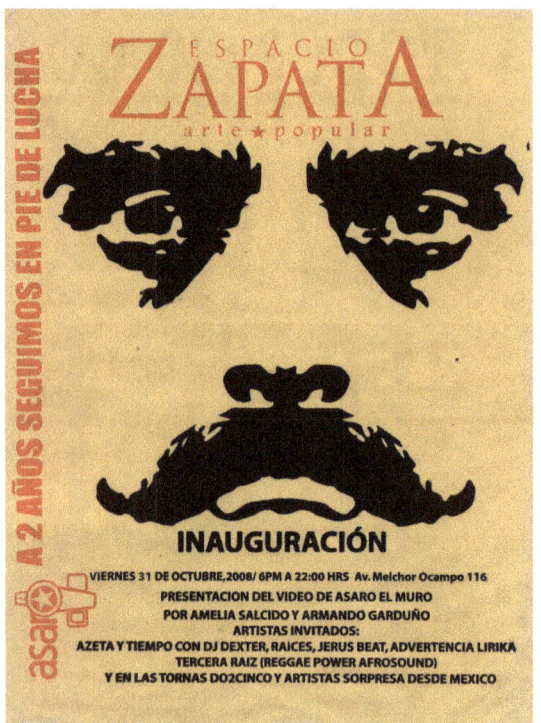

Espacio Zapata, 2008, screenprint, 27" x 40 ½".

"When I think of both Palestine and Juárez, I think about colonized bodies. I think of Palestine as a broken body due to the occupation of a foreign entity. Juárez also brings to mind bodies in a different way. The history of Ciudad Juárez assigns a different value to them. In both cases a foreign power imposed upon another has resulted in the death and impoverishment." —Anonymous

The message rejects autocratic governance and commercial monopoly and expresses international frustration with the chasm between governing powers, commercial industries, and people everywhere. The poster recognizes that this divide is at times created by troops and bombs, but also suggests that other insidious manifestations are to blame. It alludes to boundaries—some physical, others mental—separating people from one another. At the same time, this poster attributes blame to disingenuous representations designed to overlay ugly realities with contrived images. The stencil *Abre los Ojos* (Open Your Eyes) is a more direct challenge to blind compliance, integrated into the Espacio Zapata logo.

A more recent example challenges the idea that Mexican drug cartels are the culprits of violence in Mexico. The apostles in this *La Última Cena Mexicana* (The Mexican Last Supper) stand at the table not with Jesus, but a drug lord with a Texan hat grasping a semiautomatic rifle. The decapitated head of Benito Juárez lies on a plate in the center of the table surrounded by wine glasses, a plate of cocaine, and empty bottles. Some of the apostles at the table have identifiable faces, including the current president of Mexico, Enrique Peña Nieto; the second-wealthiest man in the world, Mexican Carlos Slim, shown with the Tel Mex insignia on his garment; former corrupt president of Mexico and supporter of Peña Nieto's campaign, Carlos Salinas de Gortari; former president of Mexico Felipe Calderón; the governor of Banco de México, Agustín Carstens; formerly the most powerful union leader of Latin America, Elba Esther Gordillo; and Uncle Sam. Gordillo was arrested soon after Peña Nieto's election.

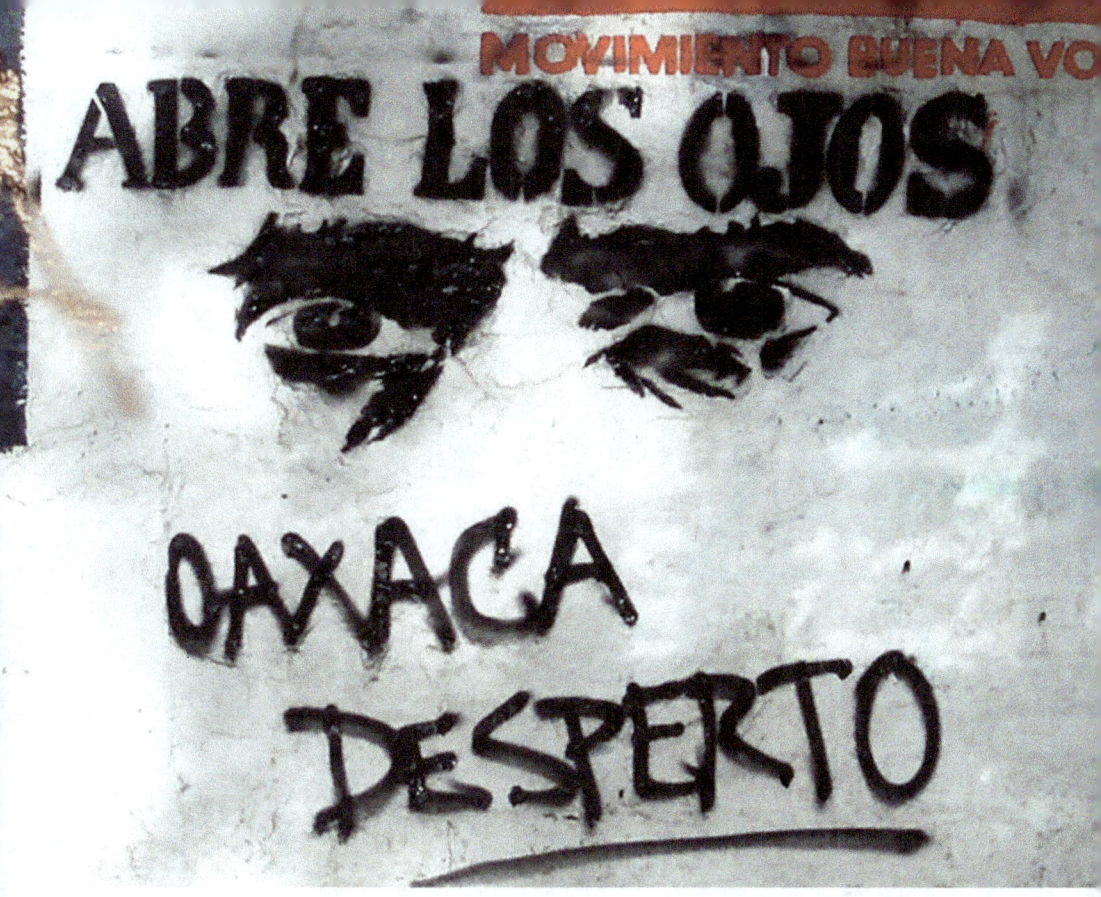

Abre los Ojos, 2006, graffiti.

"I want to make images that have become universal and play with them to change what they say. For instance, the image of the 'Last Supper,' it's an image everyone can recognize and the discourse on it here has been changed to criticize the powerful elite in Mexico. You could see the image from afar and know it's the last supper and as you look and start asking 'Who's this and that?' you start to learn what is happening." —Yescka, ASARO

Other nonspecific faces partake in the consumption of the feast as well, including a U.S. police officer in uniform and a topless prostitute. An obvious challenge to the morality of state, church, and corporate forces, this print also points to a collective responsibility for Mexico's violence. The liberal, nineteenth-century indigenous president is transposed by all of these participants into the drug lord's final meal, with all manner of church and government dignitaries celebrating at his side. The majority of Oaxacans who ASARO defends against discriminatory and dehumanizing labels are absent from this print; they simply do not have a place at this table. The use of an iconic image as the primary reference of communication requires all viewers to question their own blind faith and take a closer look.

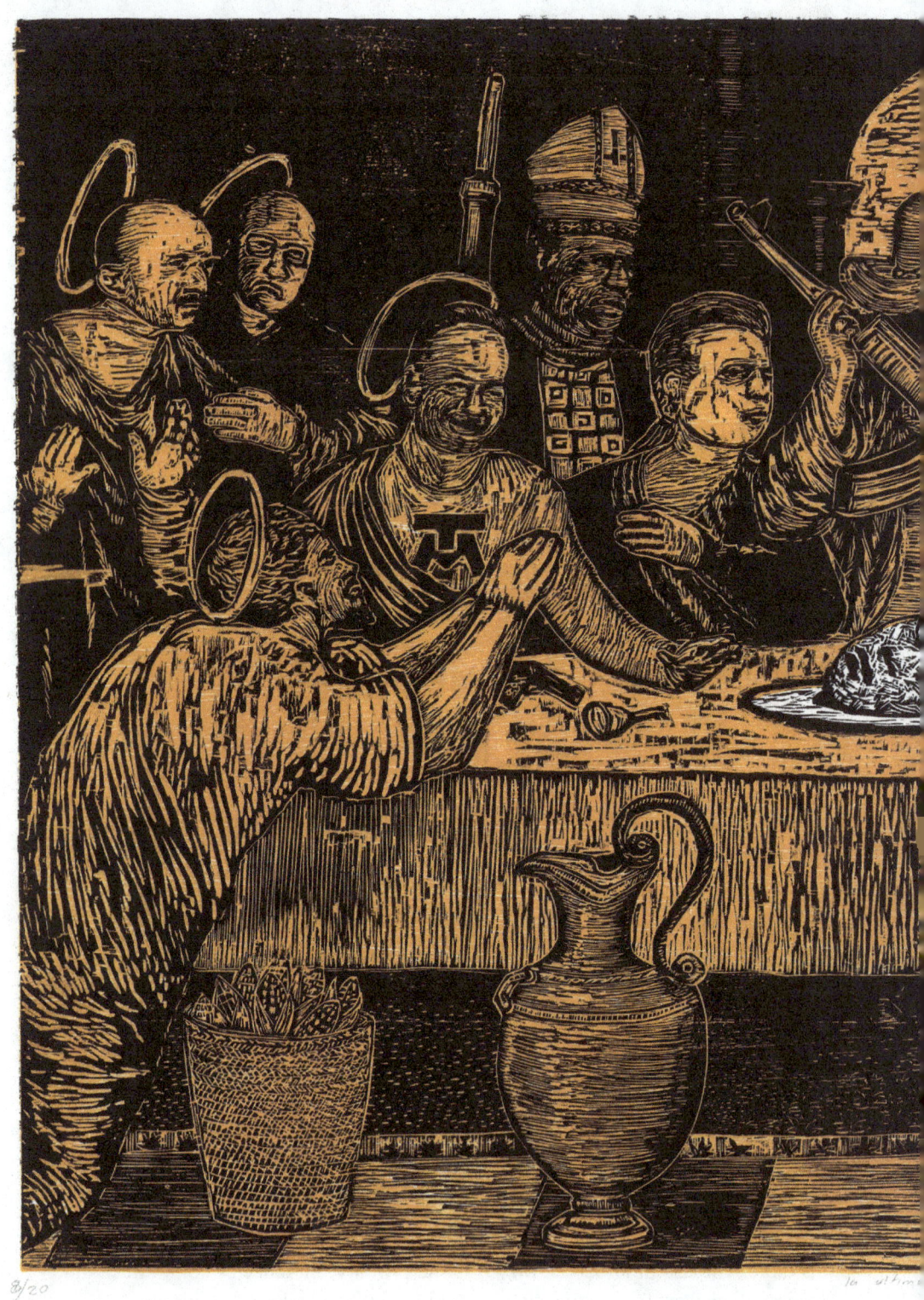

8/20

la última

La Última Cena Mexicana, 2012, block print, 27 ½" x 38".

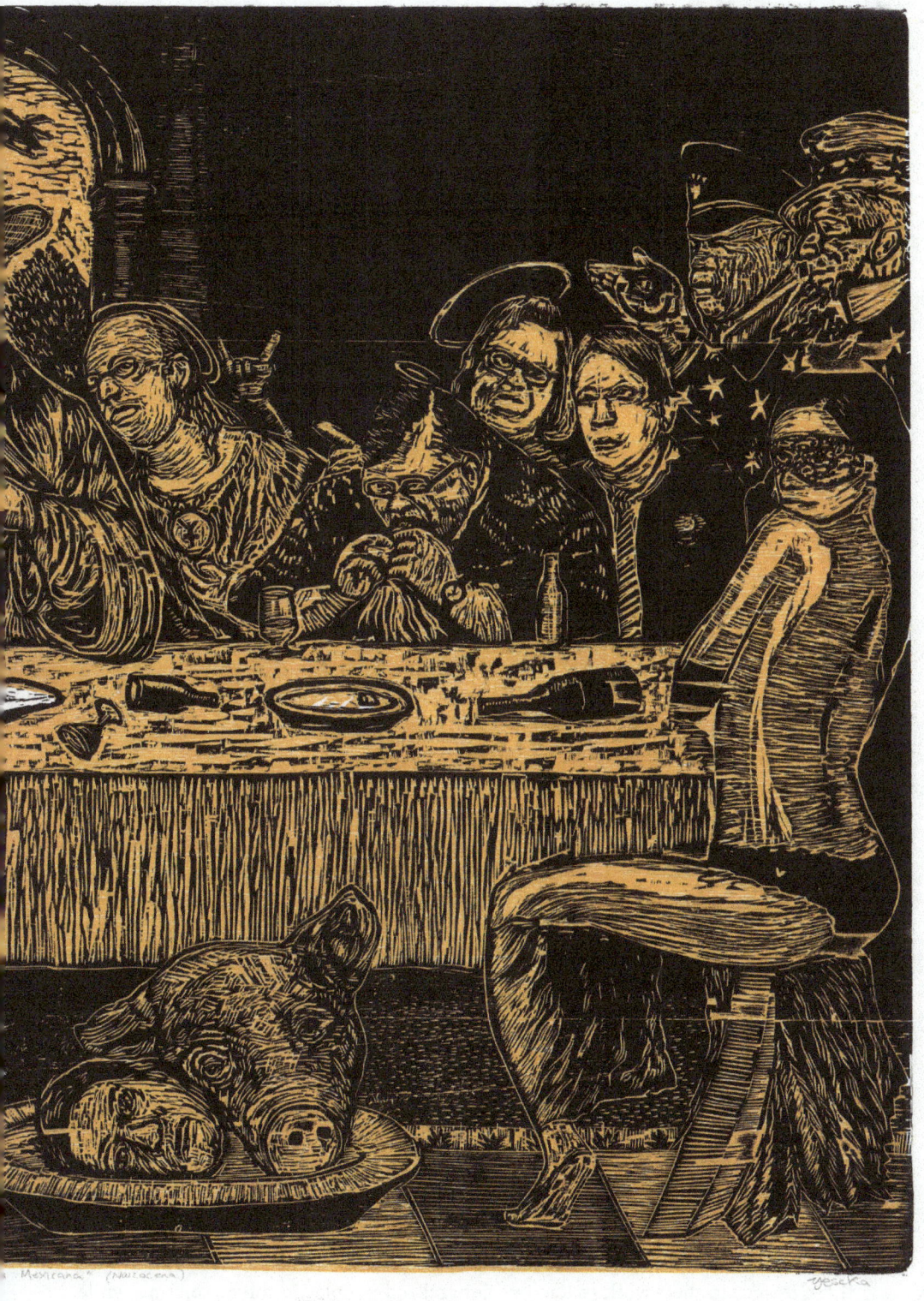

Mexicana" (Mexicana)   yeseka

PERIPHERAL GETTING IN

"ASARO seeks to create images that summarize the critical force that comes from the periphery, from the districts and villages." —ASARO Manifesto

Outside of Oaxaca's picturesque Zócalo, the urban expanse climbs up mountains and down rivers along its edges. The word *periferia* in Mexico generally identifies shantytowns located at the edges of cities. In more academic vernacular, the word means what is outside of the metropolis, as well. These peripheries are numerous in Oaxaca de Juárez. Every day, thousands of tourists take buses and taxis to gawk at the remnants of the ancient indigenous city, Monte Albán, located on top of a hill overlooking the valleys below. At the same time, people living in these peripheries move in toward the center, so that they might scrape together a living. Many who do not find work in the city must beg, play music, or perform to feed their families at home. For many who do find employment, transportation between the city center and the periphery means displacement in both spaces.

"Televised allegories of humble Mexicans in the big city don't actually reflect on the intelligence of indigenous characters, who are always bilingual from the start. Imagine a city person going to the fields and doing what farmers do. Let's see how they succeed." —Ita, ASARO

People tend to see this reciprocal marginalization as a natural part of the urban landscape; no one is ever exactly where they might be otherwise. ASARO exhibits this peculiarity in some of their work, asking viewers to question where they are and why. These works also ask what is natural about a destitute man on the city sidewalk or a migrant whose work chains him to a dizzying reality in which he is strapped to the exhausting processes of going out and coming back in. ASARO uses these images in their work to keep peripheralized peoples in the big picture while encouraging viewers to take notice and think about their own place vis-à-vis these individuals.

ASARO also challenges misconceptions about movement between centers and peripheries by reaching out to youth in the shantytowns outside the capital city. The collective offers workshops to teach young people drawing, painting, stencil-making, and printing techniques. These workshops bring youth into the city space and invite these citizens to leave their marks—tell their stories—on the walls and sidewalks. ASARO teaches these youths to act as integral parts of the cityscape.

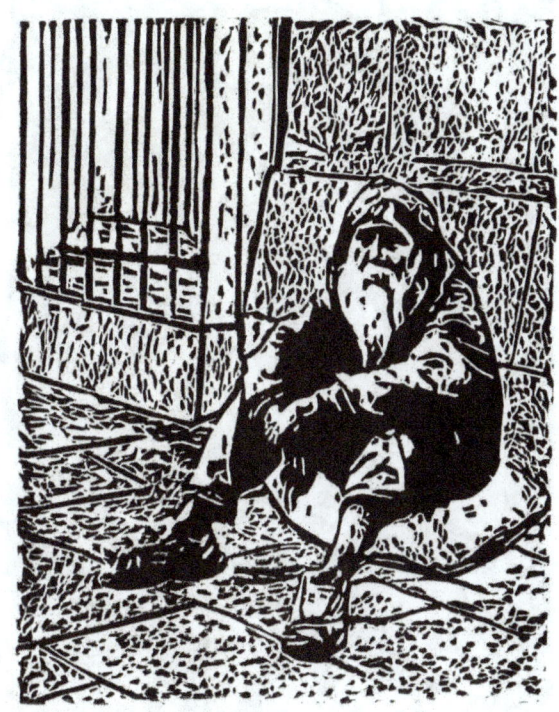

Old Man on Sidewalk, Desempleo Series, 2012, block print, 19 ½" x 27 ½".

"ASARO's intent is to turn the word art around; and it's something that's done from the ground up. Museums can be intimidating and people don't think they will understand or they see museums as churches where they are not permitted to touch anything. There is no option to interact with it. ASARO goes to the street, and puts something there. Sometimes it's something people don't want to see, but it's there, and not like other things in the street. It's an imprint. I've seen many graffiti stencils, which were really cool and complex, also communicate with people who didn't think they could understand art. I like that communication." —Ita, ASARO

Workshops held in San Juanito and Santa Rosa in 2013 included the making and use of stencils that reflected on Oaxacan indigenous dances, clothes, plants, and animals mixed with countercultural elements such as hip hop and punk rock.

That voice draws not only from the shantytowns at the edge of the city but from the surrounding countryside and rugged mountain passes where people live outside of the urban space. As result of their marginalization, their access to centralized power structures is tenuous. Beyond the outskirts of Oaxaca de Juárez, indigenous villagers and farmers work the land, generally for subsistence (though export to other parts of Mexico does occur). In this sense, agriculture is their lifeblood. The land may ultimately feed them, but unfulfilled, century-old promises of reform all too often result in landless farmers struggling to compete for sufficient yields. Even

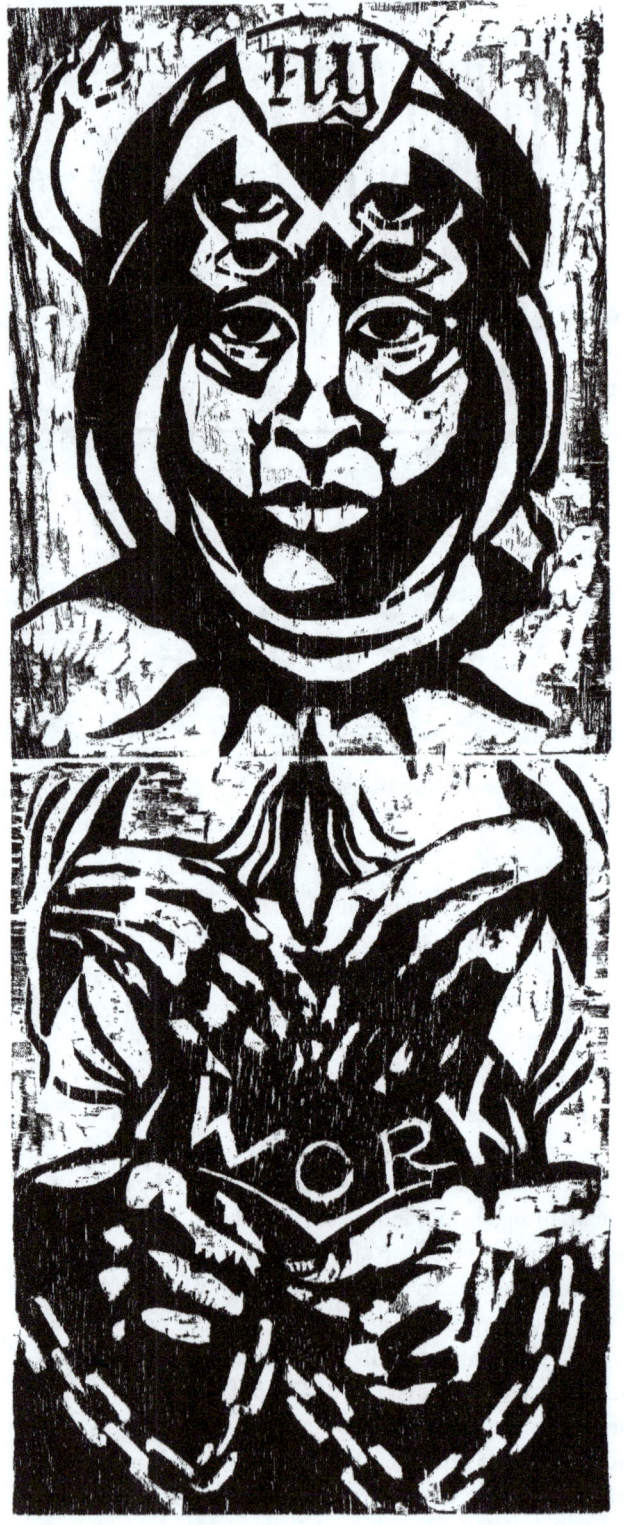

small landowners struggle to eke out an existence as outside markets set prices that are out of reach for most average Oaxacans. The introduction of toxic pesticides and GMO foods by exporters make it even more expensive for small farmers to grow and sell their supplies. It is little wonder that when Oaxacans spontaneously organized under APPO in 2006, rural state residents helped fill the capital with five hundred thousand mega-march participants. Much of ASARO's work brings these peripheral issues into the discussion as well.

"Oaxaca is a state that dedicates itself to agricultural growth. They use the image of the farm worker; and those who struggle most are farm workers and their children. In Oaxaca they are lots of 'megaprojects.' The state says they support development and job creation. But in our experience, the Mexican governing structure is corrupt. So, in this system, the organization that makes the decisions is the one that benefits from these projects."
—Mario, ASARO

NYC Chained, 2012, block print, 19 ½" x 27 ½".

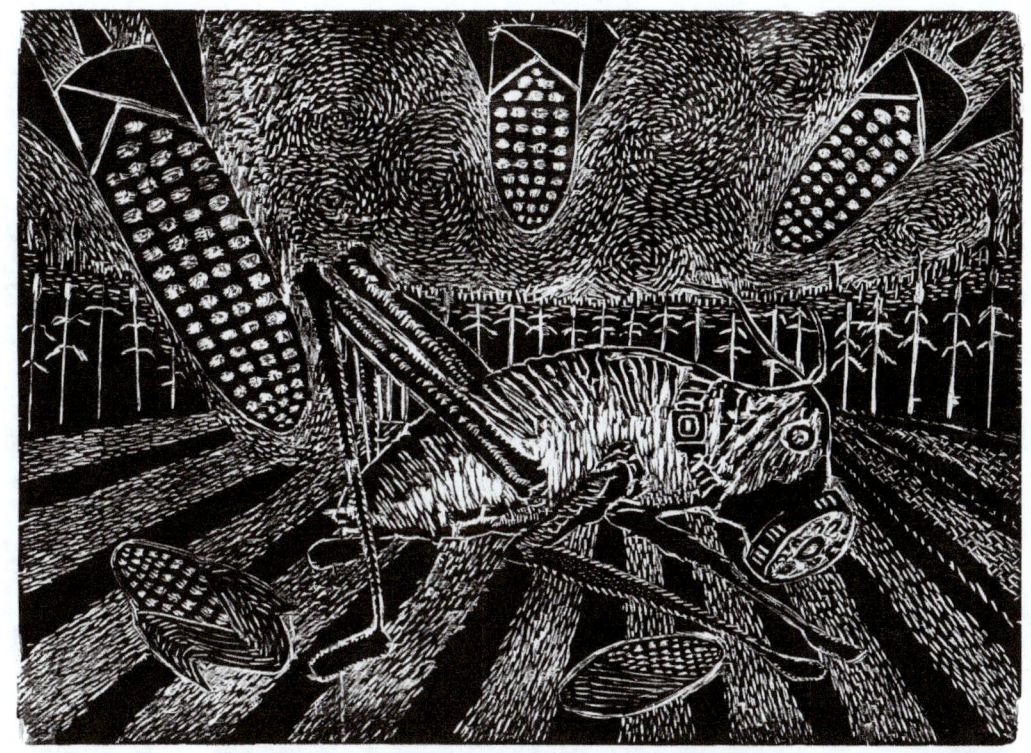

Transgénico, 2010, block print, 39 ¾" x 27 ½".

Economic prioritization of extractive industries such as oil further intensifies the plight of landless peoples and small landowners. Within the Wikiruta lands, a sacred pilgrimage site for the Huichol peoples since the beginning of time, destructive and constitutionally illegal mining continues while the Mexican government looks the other way. Other oil companies, such as state-owned Pemex (Petróleos Mexicanos), extract and refine oil in southern Mexico while delivering persistent ecological damage in return. Families whose homes are situated above underground pipes that funnel raw petroleum out of their communities find themselves at risk of dangerous accidents. Though the Mexican constitution reserves its natural resources for the national interests, its governance denies the majority of Mexico's citizens the economic benefits of this industry, sending them away instead.

"We did a series on petroleum. The rich and the powerful are the ones who ultimately suck up all the capital. The ones that hold the straw or the access keep the others wanting a piece." —César, ASARO

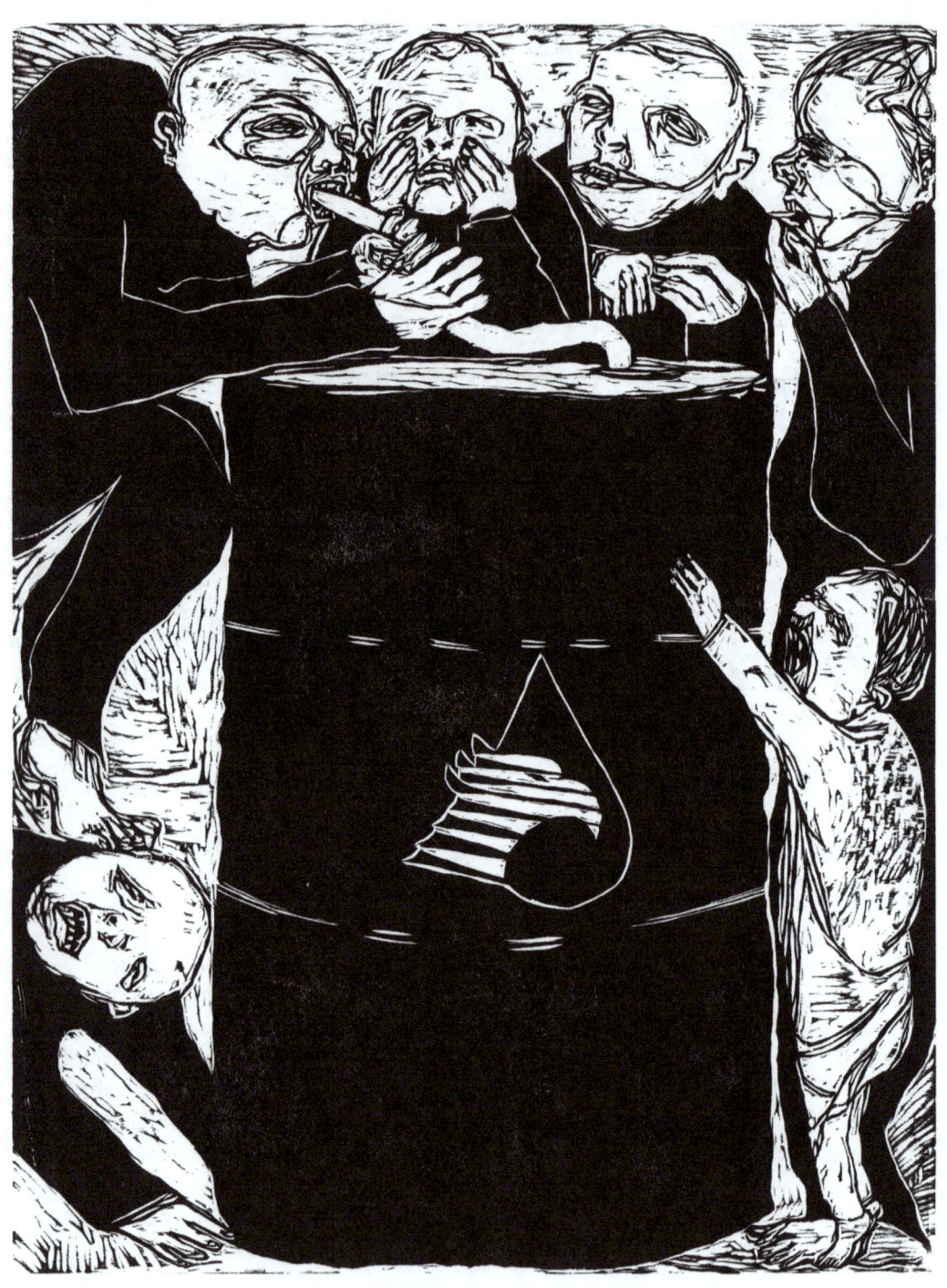

Petroleum Drinkers, 2011, block print, 27 ½" x 39".
¡Pueblo! ¡Defiende Tu Petróleo!, 2010, block print, 27 ½" x 39 ¼". »

¡PUEBLO!

¡DEFIENDE TU PETRÓLEO!

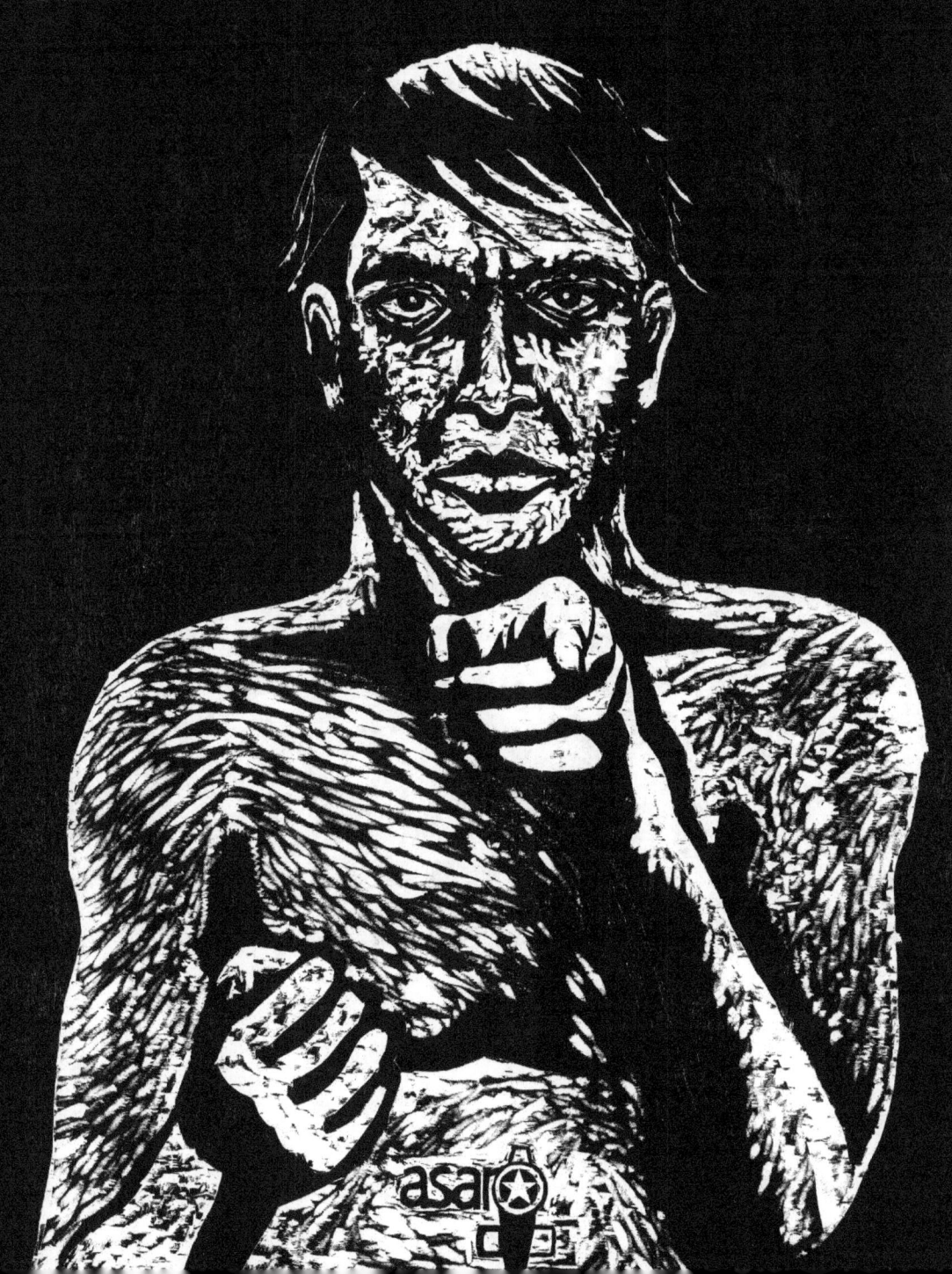

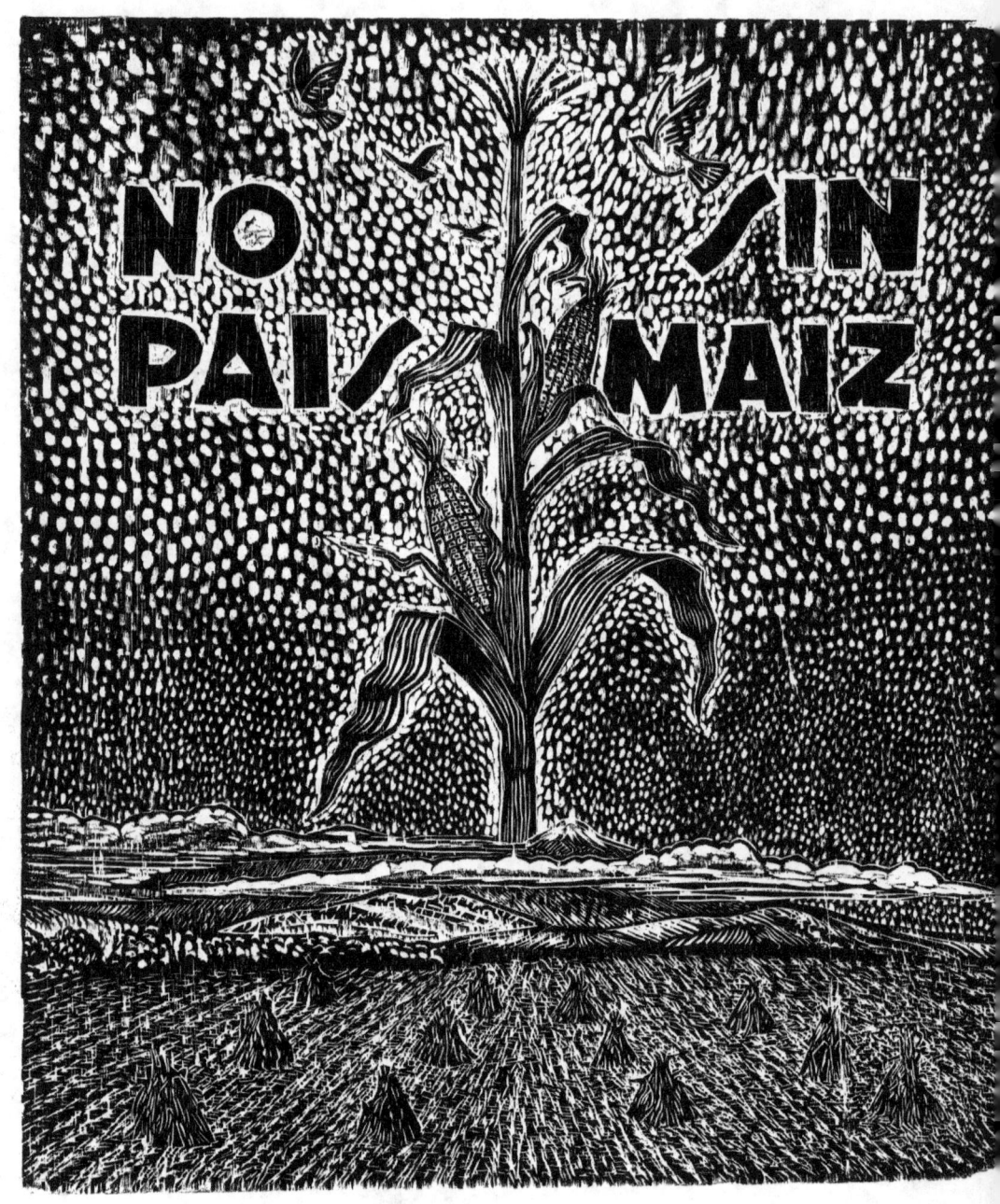

No País Sin Maíz, 2006, block print, 27 ½" x 39".

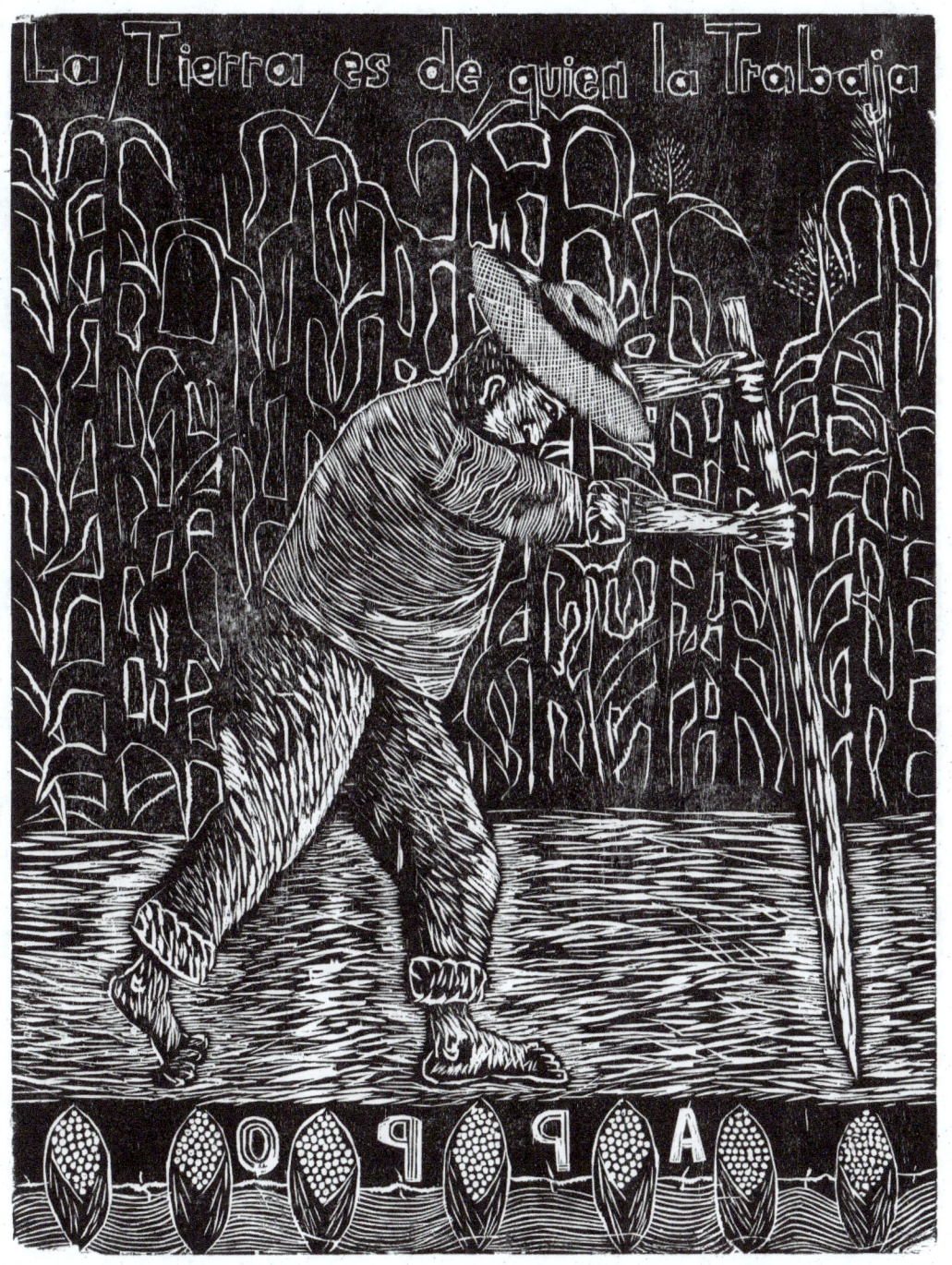

La Tierra Es de Quien la Trabaja, 2006, block print, 28" x 37 ½".

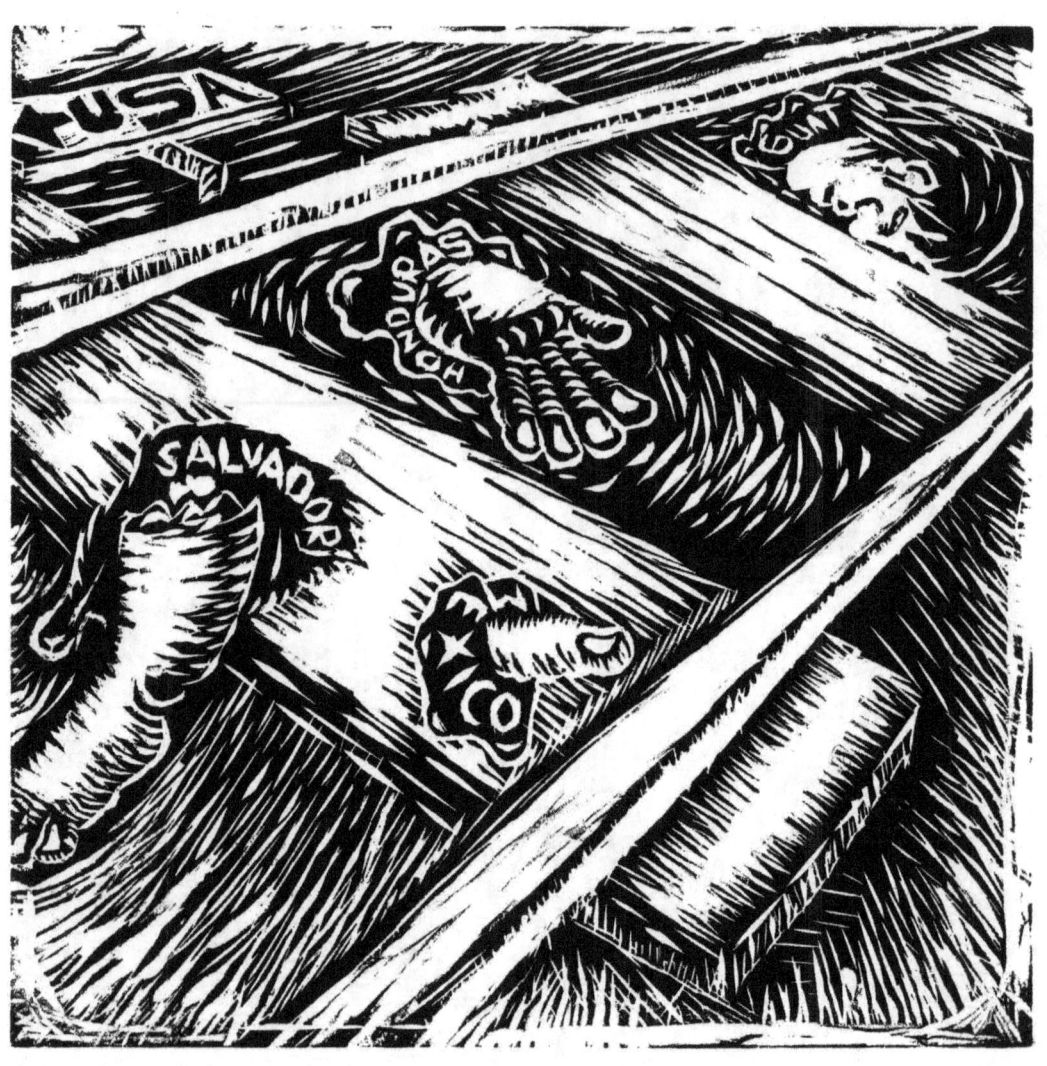

Body Parts on Railroad, 2010, block print, 16" x 16 ½".

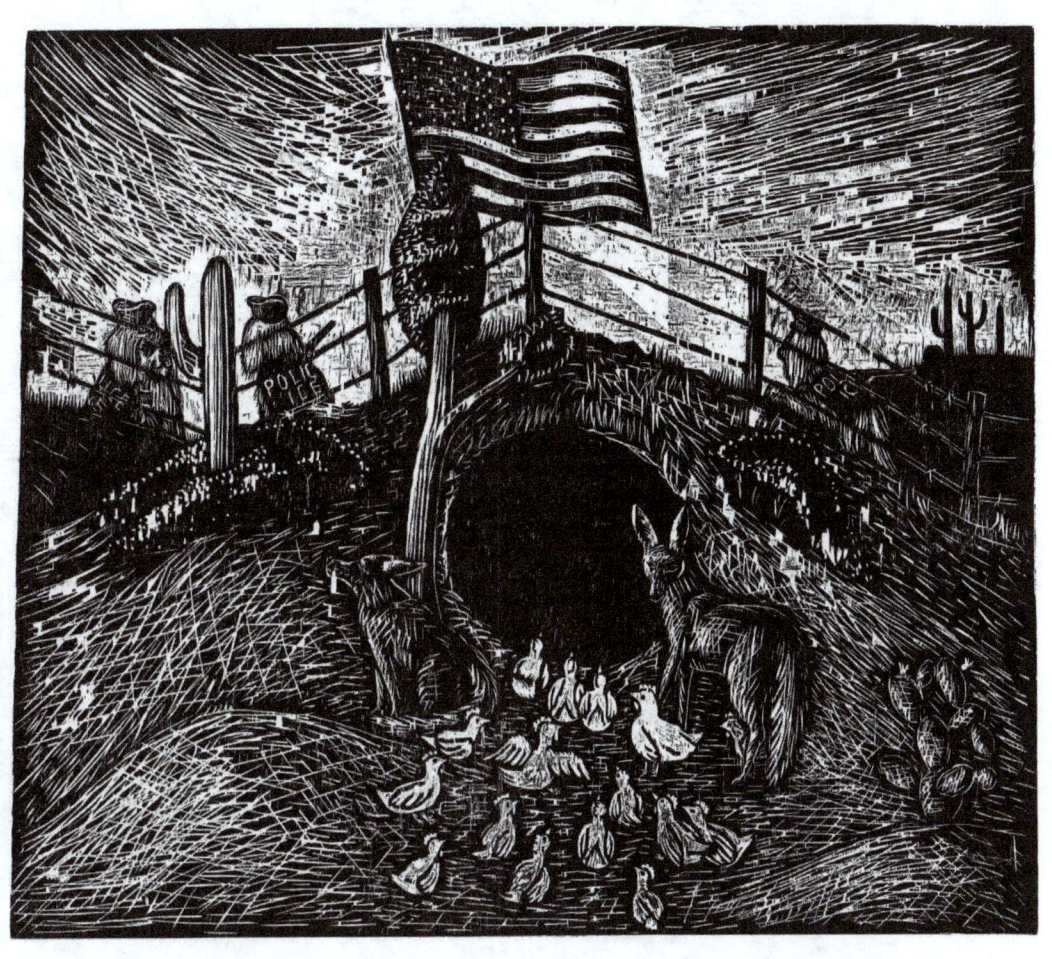

Coyotes and Chickens at Border Crossing, 2010, block print, 29" x 27 ½".

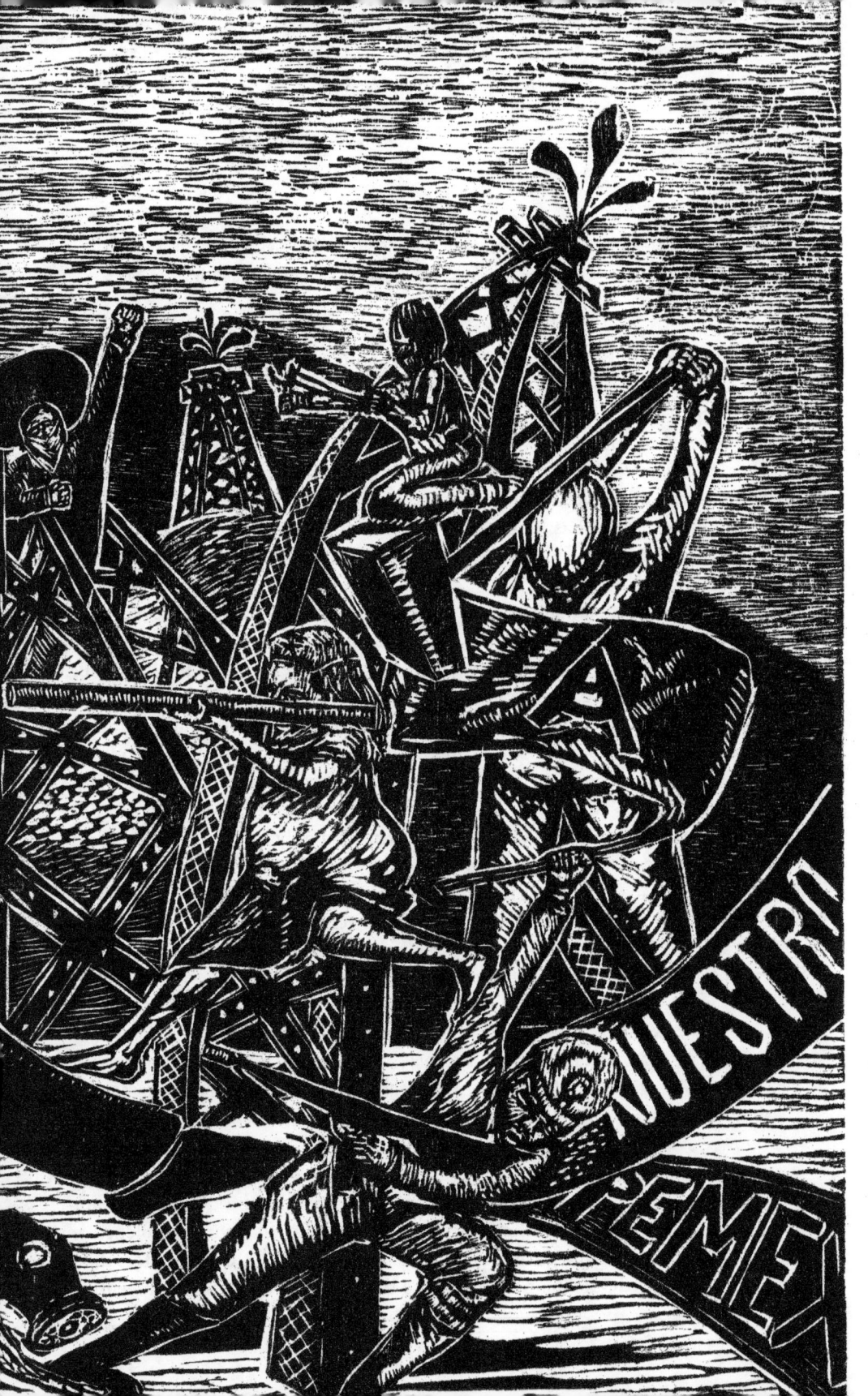

Petroleum Drinkers relays this message. A group of six greedy and decrepit in-human-looking figures surround a black Pemex oil drum. They run each other over in their haste to drink from this barrel, as others watch with agony and desire. A child cries as he reaches for his turn at the hose with these monsters. *¡Mi Patrimonio No Se Vende, Se Defiende!* (Don't Sell My Patrimony, Defend It), depicts the struggle to keep Mexican oil as well as Mexican citizens at home. The image of Chicago on top of the barrel, which has long been a destination for many Mexican emigrants, is certainly suggestive of a local frustration with disappearing human resources in Mexico too.

ASARO also documents socioeconomic difficulties at the northern edges of Mexico's national territory, where many different peoples cross the Mexican and U.S. borders, hoping to survive in what has long been considered to be the economic center of the hemisphere. Many people crossing this border have already traversed multiple national boundaries throughout the Americas, only to succumb to death in the end. *Body Parts on Railroad* expresses this paradox by depicting Honduran, Salvadoran, and Mexican body parts on the tracks bordering the United States. This disturbing image also comments critically on a tendency to treat people at this bor-der as expendable—bodies and hired hands identified only by their country of ori-gin. When they do make it across in one piece, they are decried as criminals, illegally entering into a place that is not theirs. This marginality makes them vulnerable to opportunists like the allegorical coyote or *pollero* (chicken-maker). This figure ap-pears in an ASARO woodblock leading chickens through a culvert into the United States, and then on to police forces, awaiting their arrival.

ASARO articulates the dangers faced by people crossing these borders in many works, perhaps out of concern for family and friends who do cross the bor-der. In Ciudad Juárez and other border cities, many people fall victim to violence or harsh elements. Here again, government turns its eyes away. ASARO disinters their hidden existence and puts them on display so they cannot be forgotten, preventing

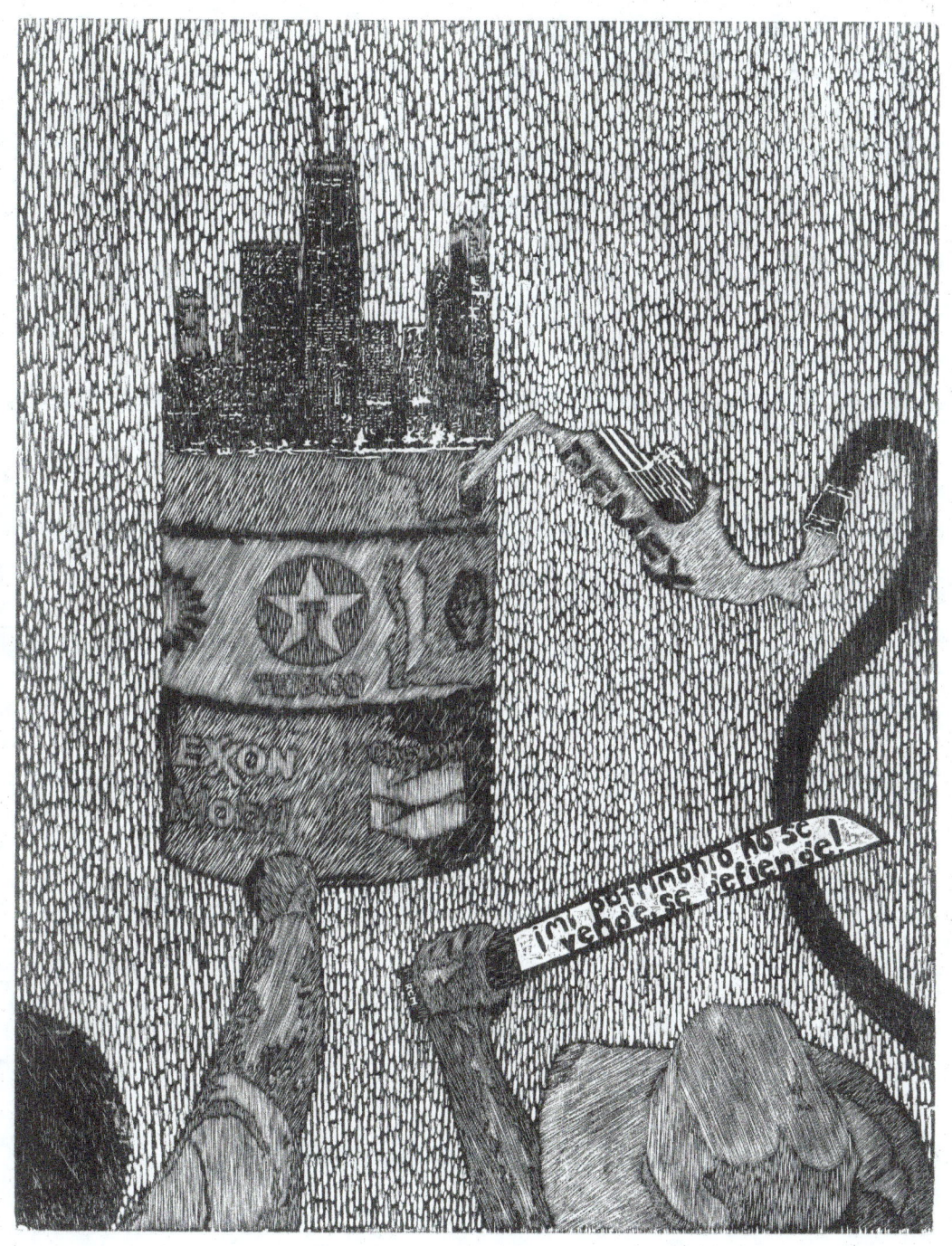

¡Mi Patrimonio No Se Vende, Se Defiende!, 2006, block print, 27 ½" x 37 ½".

"Pintando Mi Identidad," 2013, color photocopy, 8 ½" x 11".

those culpable from escaping blame altogether. Maybe the skeletal body in *Denunciar la Complicidad del Gobierno de Mexico* (Denounce the Complicity of the Mexican Government) is one of the seventeen people killed by police in Oaxaca during 2006. Perhaps this female corpse is one of many Mexicans, female and male, killed and buried in Mexico's borderlands without a gravesite or memorial. Regardless, her half-interred body, bones buried beneath the earth, is ripped from its grave by a scavenging canine, the bottom of the print identifying a culprit: complicity and inaction.

"Two Oaxaca's coexist: one is bottled and sold in *mercados* while the stories behind the person putting out their cup to beg go unnoticed. It's kind of like the way Artesanias are wrapped in newspapers that detail events, but no one pays attention to them." —Anonymous

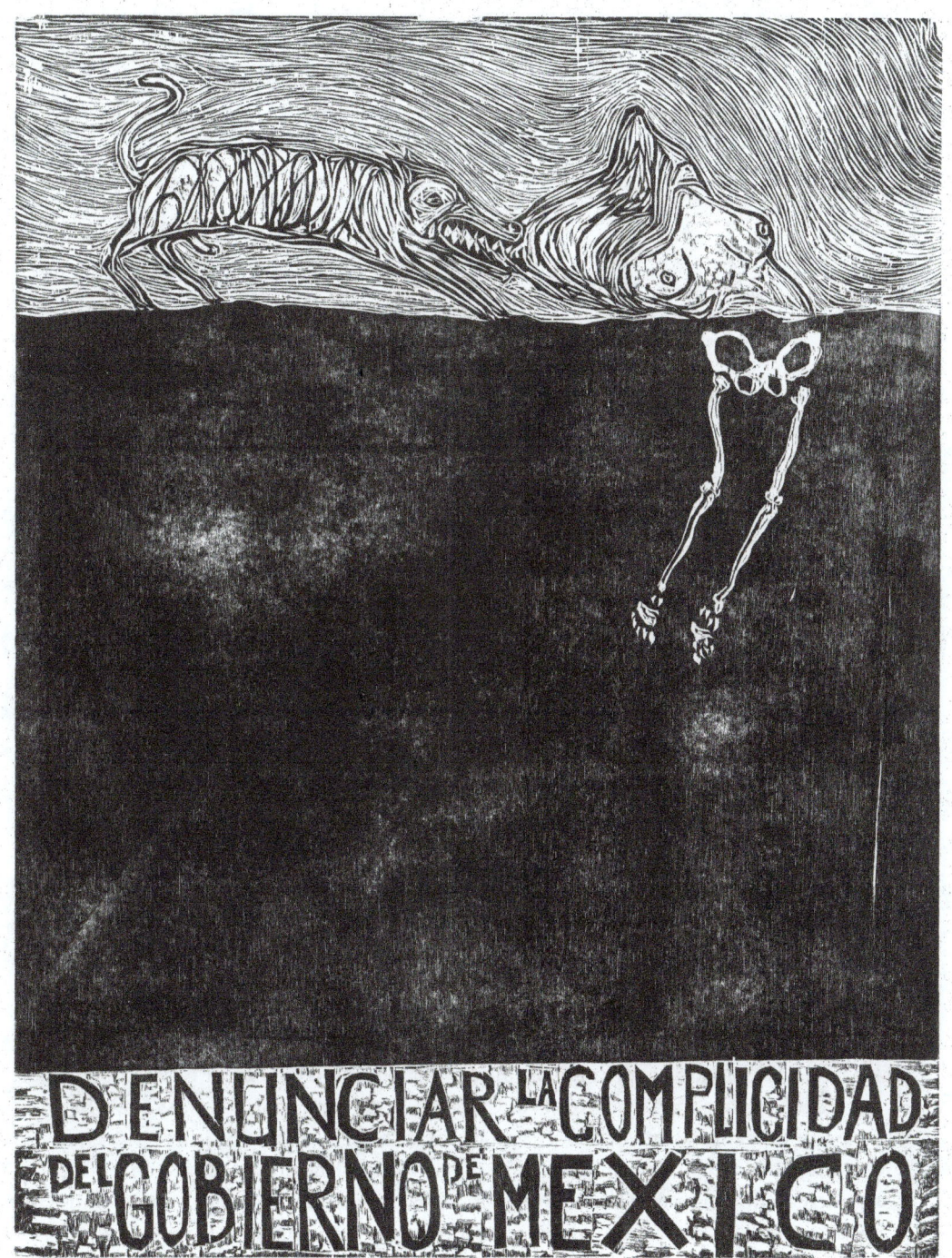

Denunciar la Complicidad del Gobierno de Mexico, 2006, block print, 28" x 37 ½".

MULTISPECTIVE
AND SOCIAL ACTION

"We resumed the form of the assembly because we believe in the possibility of recovery of force in the art community and because the assembly is the way we dialogue and make decisions based on the collective interests." —ASARO Manifesto

The poster *Espacio Zapata Presenta Revuelta Cultural* (Zapata Space Presents Cultural Revolt) inaugurates the opening of ASARO's Taller, or printer's workshop, and advertises a cultural event bringing ASARO together with other artists' collectives from Oaxaca and Chiapas. These additional organizations included Arte Jaguar, Coatlique, and Revolver. The MySpace description of this "disturbance," as the term *revuelta* translates literally in English, presents the occasion as a renewed opportunity to dialogue about a mutual engagement with community problems. Most prominent in the graphic is the dancing boxer at the center, dressed in a formal suit, face transformed into the sprayer on a paint canister, gloves raised and readied for the fight. This clever reference to the arts slam scheduled in the Espacio Zapata also reflects ASARO's belief in the promise of dialogue and the power of assembly.

Collectivism has strong roots in Oaxacan social organization, most likely because the state's isolation spared it capitalist investments in private property. As a result, *comunalidad* (communality) rejects individualist motivations, privatization, and mercantilism in favor of reciprocal responsibilities that respect diversity and replicate plurality. In this kind of system, each individual, supported from within by a network of others, contributes his or her unique talents for the good of the whole. The existence of a common purpose helps sustain this practice across communities so that historical mobilization against economic and cultural repression facilitates continued commitment to the form of assembly. It is difficult to find that common purpose, however, because domination and resistance have laid intricate patterns of oppression. Untangling them requires complex, but very practical, points of convergence, not to mention meaningful symbols of unity that reject individualism.

In Chiapas and beyond, the contemporary remix of the Zapatista Army or EZLN found this symbolism in the mask they wear. It serves multiple functions while also relaying an important message. On one hand, the mask confronts prejudicial equations of indigenous peoples as nobodies without voices, showing others what they might look like in an overt and assertive way. On the other hand, it pragmatically pro-

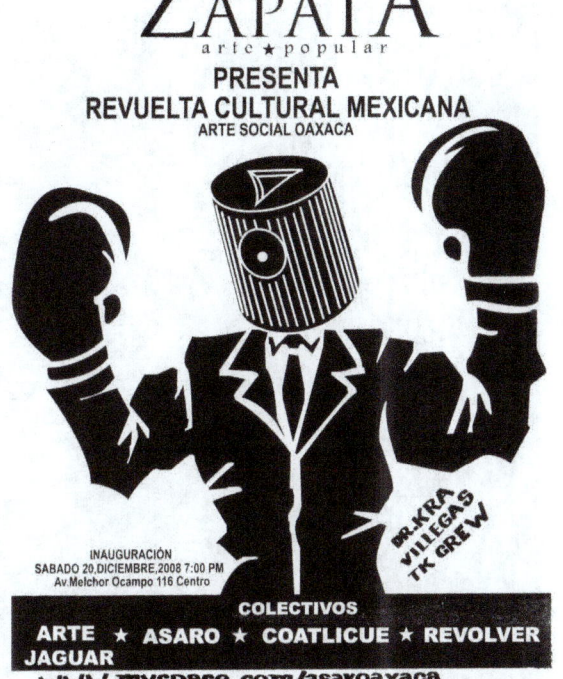

Espacio Zapata Presenta Revuelta Cultural Mexicana RCM, 2008, screenprint, 27 ½" x 38".

tects individuals within the EZLN from identification and subsequent punishment. In more philosophical terms, the mask covers individual faces and mouths and projects a group image. As one EZLN soldier puts it, when he wears the mask he is a Zapatista rather than just another Indian. Unified active resistance generates a power that individual articulations cannot. Several ASARO pieces pay homage to this idea and to the EZLN leader Subcomandante Marcos, who since 1994 has been a spokesperson for the recovery of force through dialogue and collective action.

Not unlike the EZLN mask, ASARO's collective signature protects individual anonymity while enhancing the reach of their artistic voice through collectivity. Just like the EZLN mask, their group-conscious collected corpus is a symbolic weapon, uniting the creator of art with other artists and with viewers as well. ASARO's logo includes stylistic letters that spell out "ASAR" and "O" as a gun pointed at the viewer with a revolutionary red star in the middle. The star is like a stencil marking the viewer with this symbol of solidarity, just as a sprayer on the paint canister marks their shared space. Cultural events like the disturbance advertised in the Espacio Zapata poster create opportunities for ASARO artists to network with others to develop pragmatic, bottom-up installations that do not speak for the people so much as they dialogue with them.

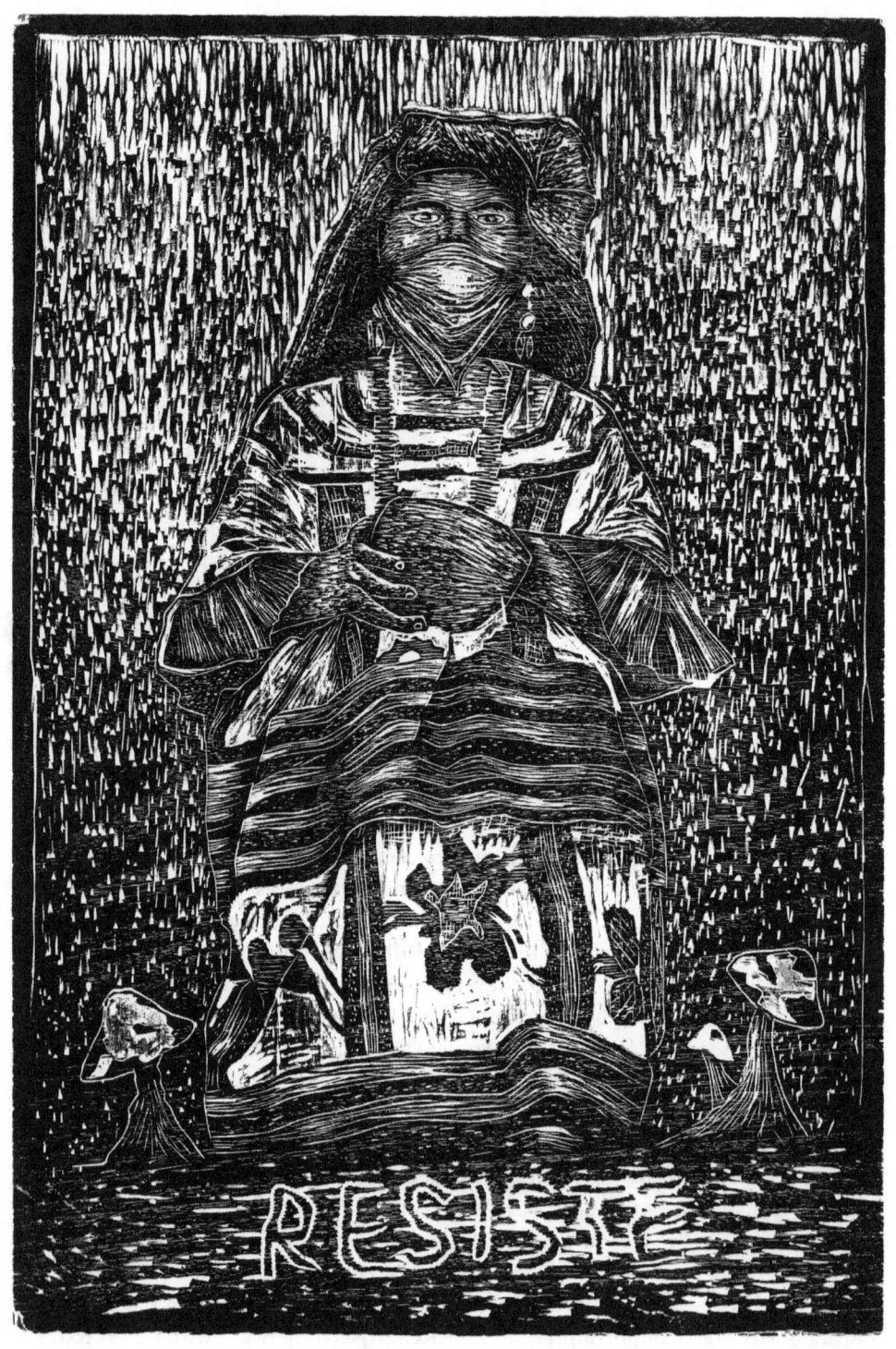

Resiste, 2010, block print, 22 ½" x 30 ¼".

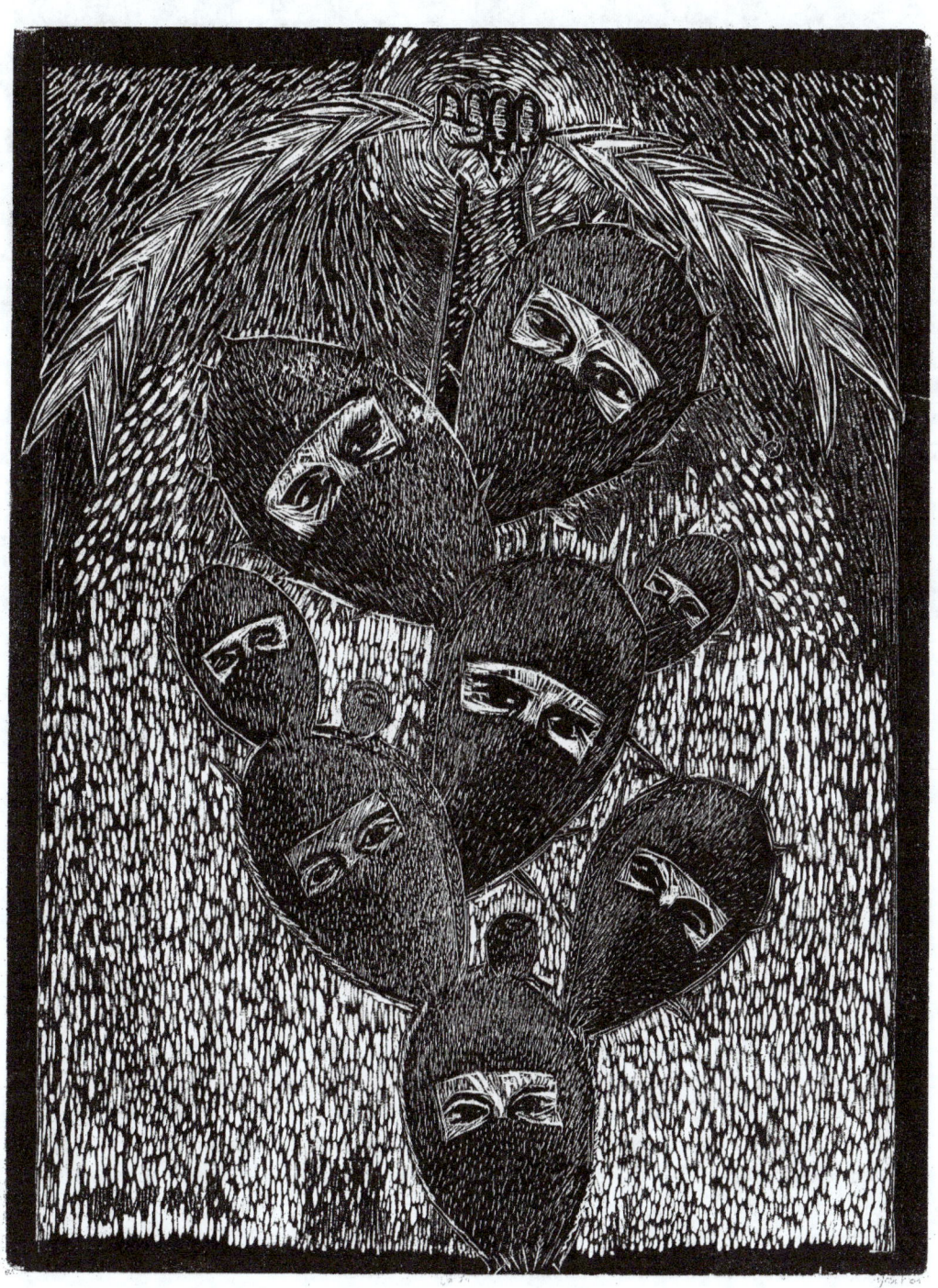

Zapatista Nopal, 2011, block print, 27 ½" x 37".

Presos Políticos Libertad, 2006, stencil, 12' 1" x 4'.

"Over several years the group continued and had diverse goals, especially to share what we know. Not only broadcasting images but working with the people, in towns and small villages, to experience the power of sharing our technical and other knowledge for mutual enrichment, rather than vertically, communally with long-term projects, where people organize within their various neighborhoods and communities and have the tools to translate into art their contexts, thoughts, complaints, problems, etc." —Mario, ASARO

Historically, community-based protest has proven powerful in Oaxaca, so it was no surprise that Oaxacans organized in assembly after being attacked by the governor in 2006. Similar kinds of mobilizations had deposed three other state governors in 1946, 1952, and 1977. The umbrella organization of different popular assemblies in Oaxaca, APPO hoped to accomplish the same in 2006 but failed when the federal government assisted the governor in violent repression instead of negotiating on behalf of the citizenry. Both Ruiz Ortiz and Vicente Fox rationalized their aggression against Mexican citizens as "restoring order."

"It was awesome. It would have been one thing if we were the only ones writing *'Fuera URO'* (Get out Ruiz Ortiz) but you could see the same phrase tagged everywhere." —Anonymous

One of ASARO's first collective installations was building sand sculptures in the Zócalo in 2006 for the Day of the Dead. On this occasion, they collaborated with performers so that song, dance, and theatre could transform the square from the war zone it had become. As riot police stood watching them, the artists pushed back by physically extending the sculptures to the edges of police "defenses." These actions brought a traditional festival, and the activities commonly associated with it to bear on exposing the culprits for the losses Oaxaca had experienced in recent months. It also provided an occasion for artists to actively mock the notion of restoring order through police control of peaceful cultural events.

"For me there is no 'art for the people,' rather I think there is art that you make with the people. The people in this case participate with a type of visual language that will help to communicate what is happening. It is an art where everybody can participate." —Irving, ASARO

After this event, ASARO agreed to meet formally in assembly and debate ideas for addressing other incongruities. Most members suggest that integrating artists with different points of view enhanced their work and their understandings of complex social issues. The assembly provided a means to empathize and work from

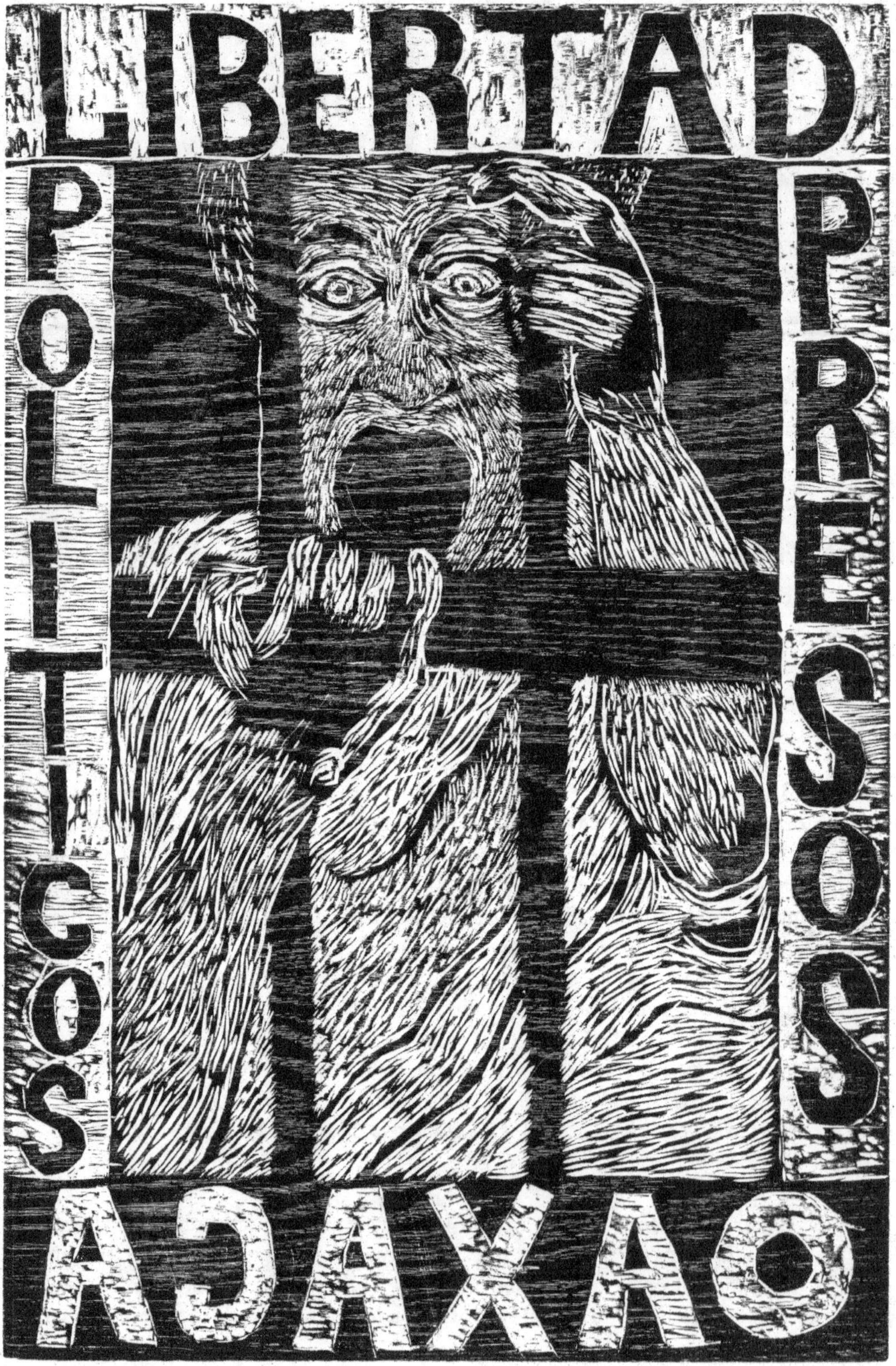

LIBERTAD
POLITICOS
PRESOS
OAXACA

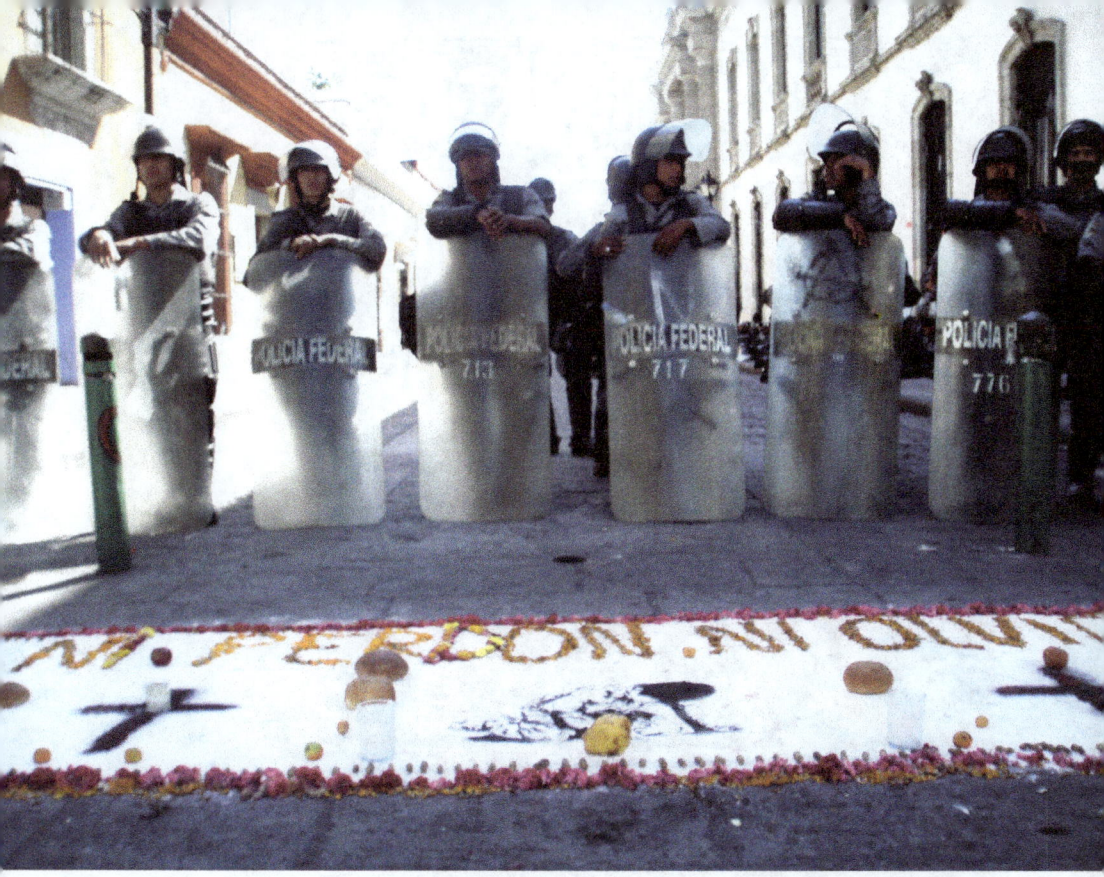

Ni Perdón Ni Olviden Sand Sculpture and Police, 2007, documentation of public installation.
« *Libertad Políticos Presos*, 2006, block print, 24" x 17 ¾".

an understanding of diverse perspectives. One ASARO member describes assembly as the most equitable—albeit imperfect—format for making community decisions. Another, more recently joined member credits ASARO's commitment to assembly as the reason for their work's tremendous presence of community.

ASARO's corpus embraces all manner of artistic expression as well as varying techniques and talents. Whether the topic is political (addressing, for instance, disputes over disappearances); social (confronting questions regarding violence against women); economic (disputing the benefits of capitalist expansion); or a combination of these three, and regardless of whether the primary subject is a historical figure, a contemporary event, a popular sentiment, or the centerpiece debate, multiple artists address the topic in varying formats from individual and group perspectives.

The pieces in this chapter address missing peoples and political prisoners. They also reflect ASARO's different styles and their incorporation of specific symbols. ASARO images scream to free political prisoners in both stencils and block prints.

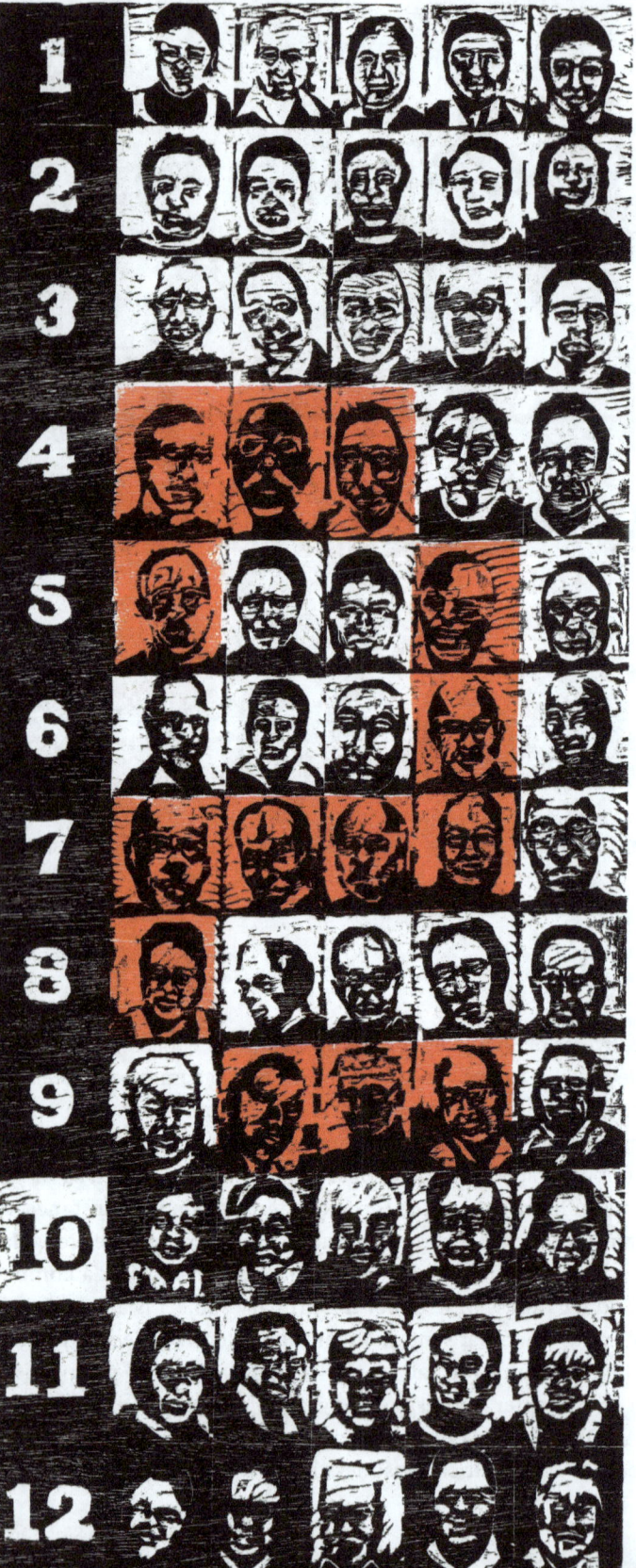

Each of these formats present faces as memorials, suggestive of the posters families made demanding to know their loved ones' whereabouts after the October 2, 1968, massacre of students in Tlatelolco Square. An ASARO painting with skulls staked atop one another in a large grid is suggestive of the same processes. Other prints address alienation and displacement in the contexts of economic traps, as in *Todo Lo Que Tiene que Pasar un Mexicano Para Obtener el Sueño Americano* (Everything a Mexican Must Pass to Obtain the American Dream).

"The walls of Oaxaca are never quiet. They are always talking, with comrades throwing up stencils and communicating something. What I found interesting was that someone would come and put up a stencil and then someone from the government would come and paint over it. After that the same determined person would put up another stencil. This whole game involved people that would come to intervene, people that knew about art and those that might not have agreed with it, but the ensemble of forms became so interesting, so vital that you were interacting without even know that you were communicating." —Irving, ASARO

« *2/10 Tlatelolco*, 2011, block print, 19 ¼" x 39".

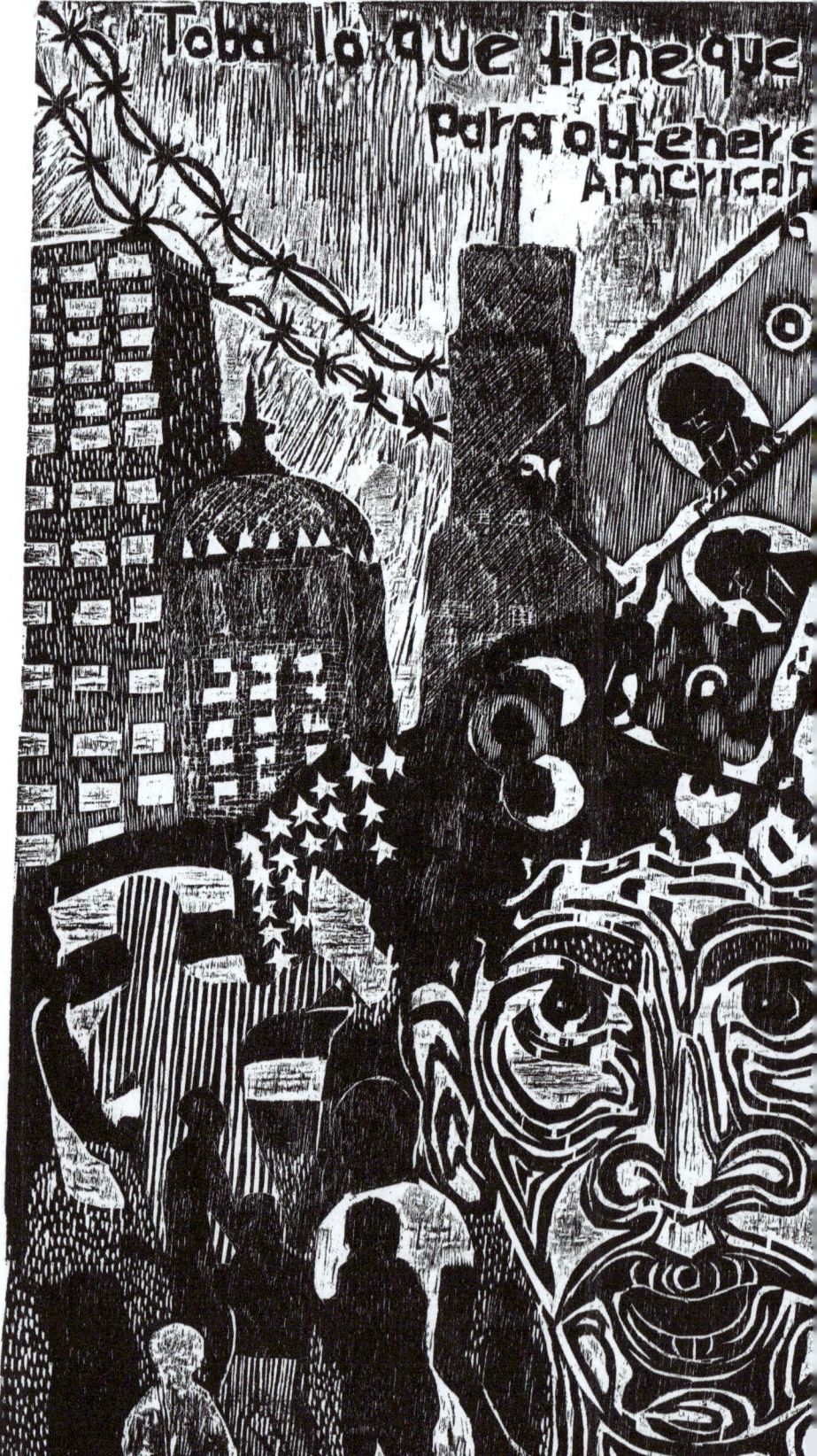

Todo Lo Que Tiene que Pasar un Mexicano Para Obtener el Sueño Americano, 2010, block print, 30 ¼" x 27 ½".

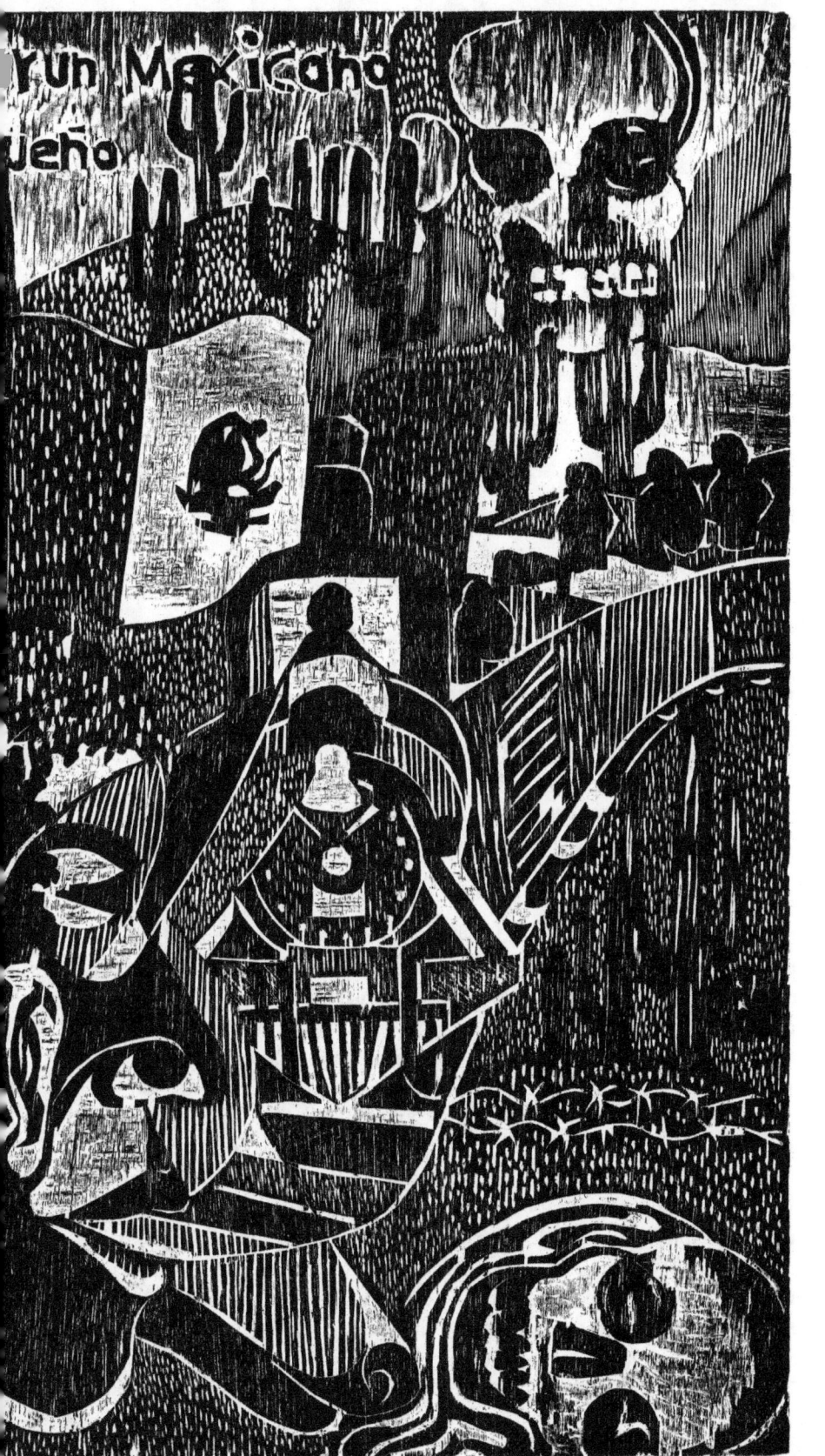

COUNTERCULTURE
AND CONSCIOUSNESS

"ASARO is in favor of inclusion and the fight to create new rules of social participation and of a profound change in the consciousness of the Oaxacan. We
are a counterculture movement of artistic creation." —ASARO Manifesto

"ASARO seeks to create awareness and generate ideas to help build a new
contemporary ideological current, which has at its center humanist values
that break the mold set by the system and create a society free of alienation
as well as a revolutionary art—that transforms, while advocating for change
and innovation." —ASARO Manifesto

In a glance, invisibility is shattered and a woman is captured in a shout. She wears
a traditional *rebozo* covering her head. Her Oaxacan *huipil* or blouse and the pan
raised in the air employ a contradictory visual vocabulary. Together they challenge
this figure's socially inscribed categorization as passive, silent, and victimized. This
woman's opened mouth and raised arm suggest she is none of those things. By raising an implement signifying her "place" in the kitchen in an act of protest, she breaks
the cultural mold that inherently dissociates the kitchen with activism and challenges the fictive symbol of a woman at home in the kitchen. While Oaxacan women can
certainly be found in the kitchen at times, they are also in the streets, often working
away from the home out of necessity.

Rays of red and white explode from the woman's image transforming the two-
dimensional physicality of the piece into a three-dimensional exchange that reaches
beyond the edges of the image. Also distributed in the streets as a stencil, this work
illustrates how ASARO creates awareness by challenging viewers with tangible examples that question socially accepted stereotypes. The cues in this image provoke

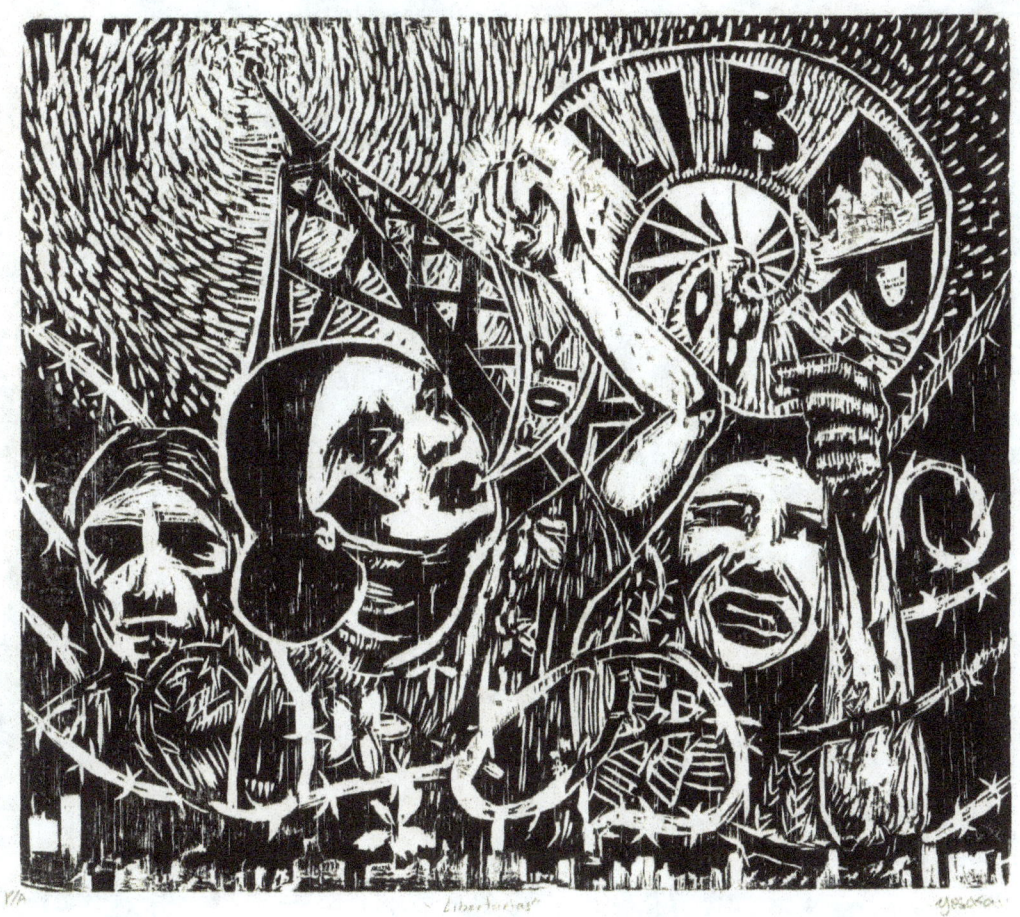

Libertarias, 2010, block print, 18 ¾" x 19".

myriad discussions in different communities, but in Oaxaca the image is read first as a memorialization of an actual event in 2006. On that occasion, women used the implements available to them in their homes, such as pans, to defend against aggressive police if necessary.

"In 2006, many of us were employed by the people to do dirty work. We were young anarcho-punks and they gave us spray-paint cans while others were given Molotov cocktails." —Anonymous

Another ASARO print references this event more overtly, paying homage to the women who took back the local television and radio stations for Oaxacans. Frustrated by the media's silence on the clashes between protesters and police, they

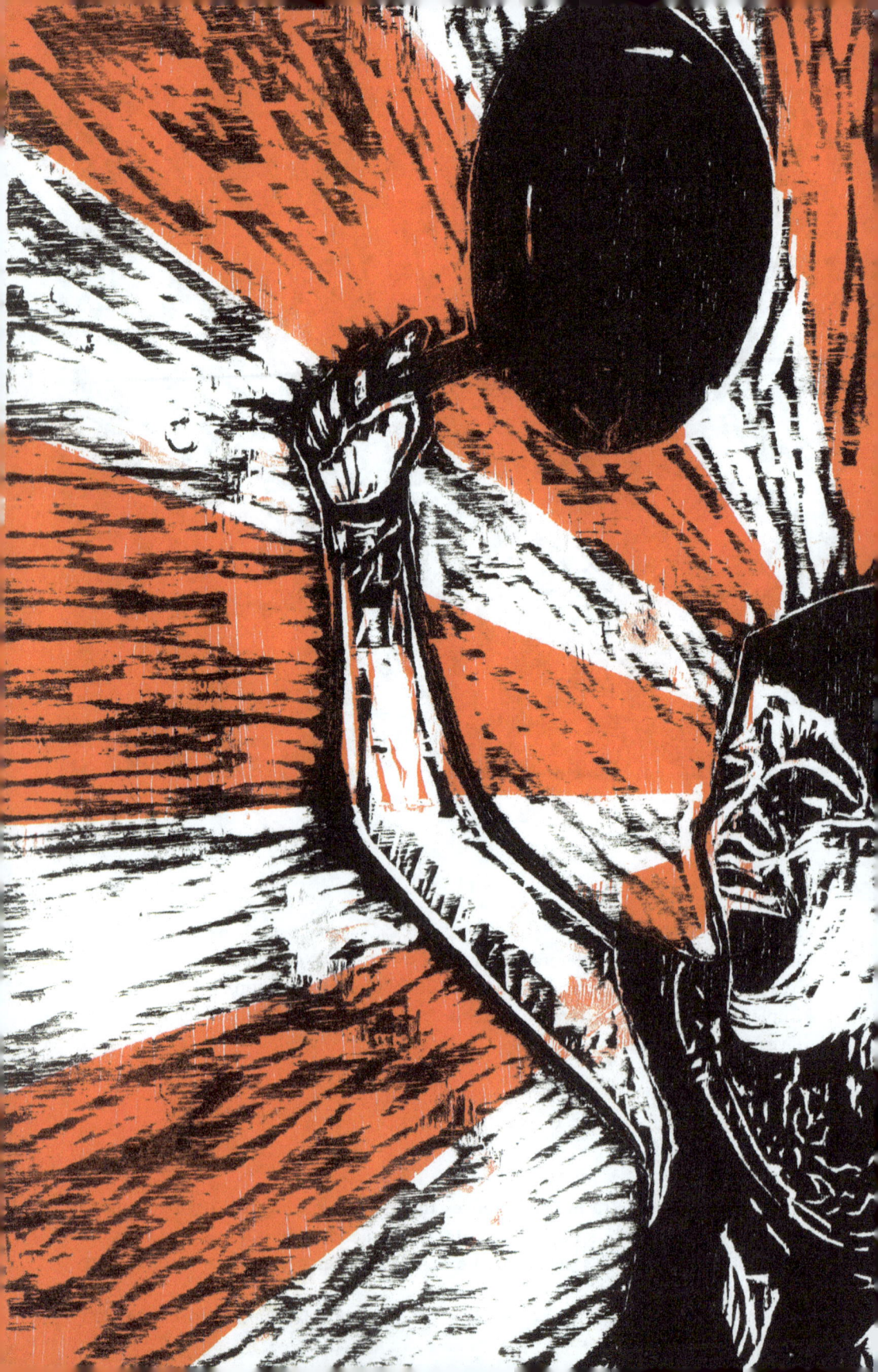

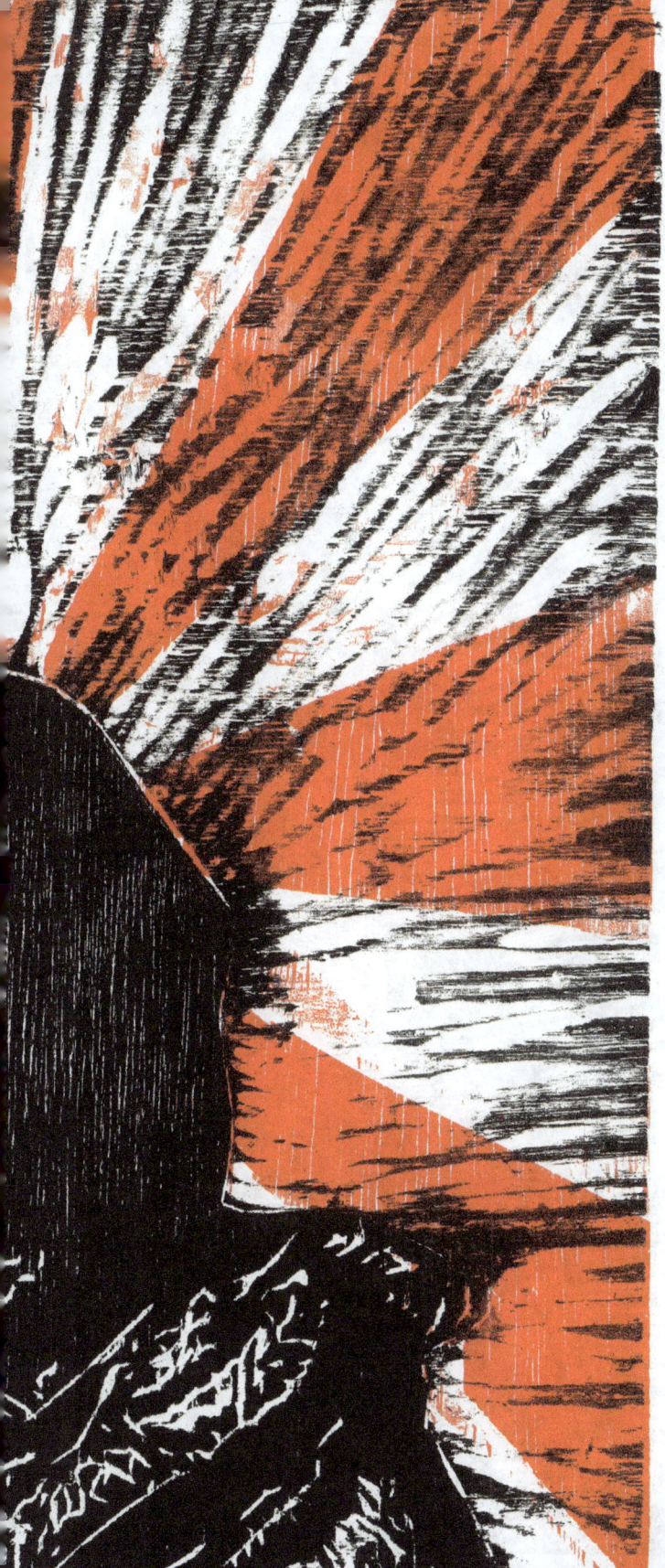

Woman Screaming with Pan, 2010, block print, 19 ¾" x 15 ½".

Following page spread: *Cuando una Mujer Avanza . . . no hay Hombre que la Detenga*, 2006, block print, 39" x 27 ½".

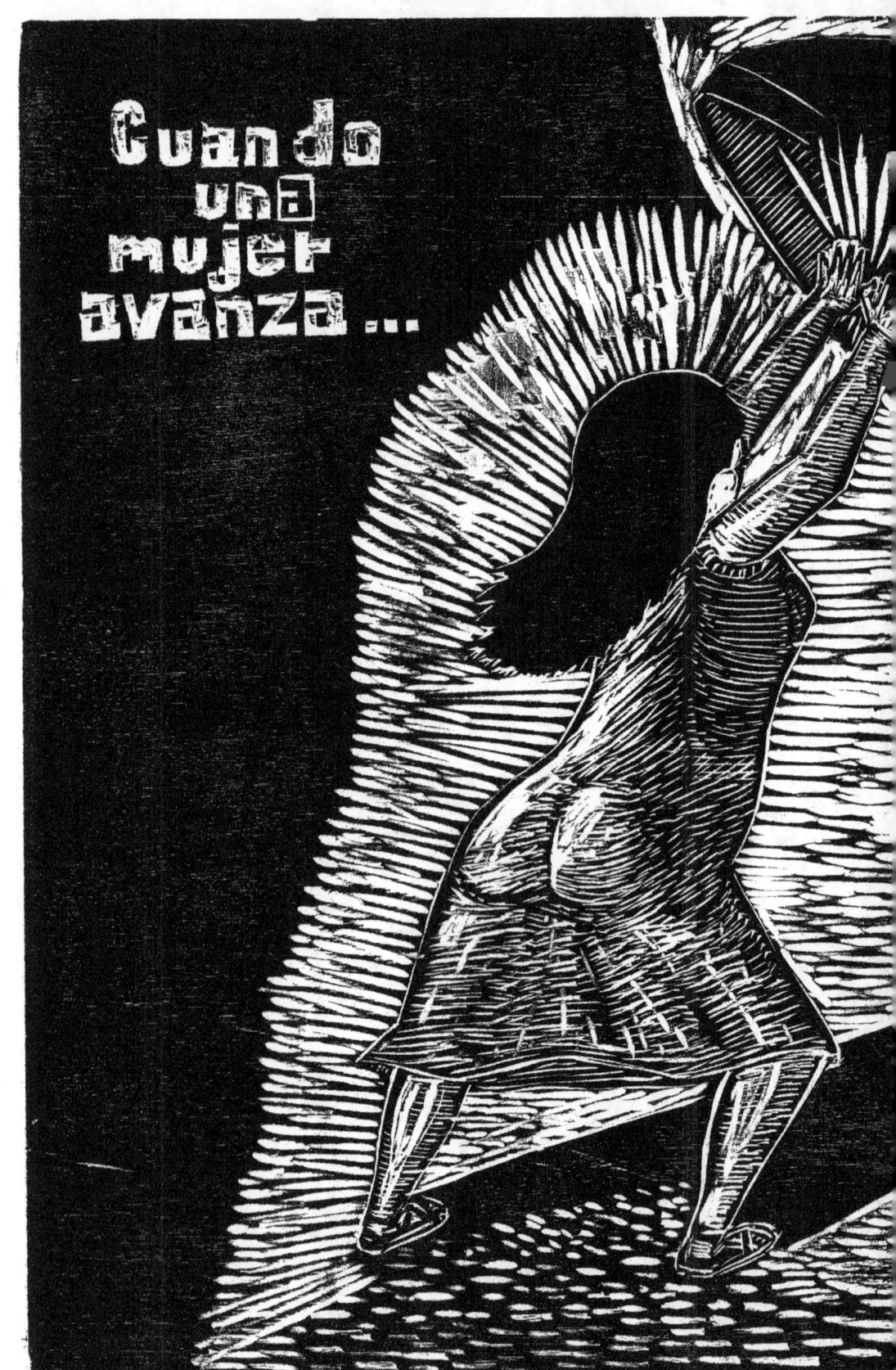

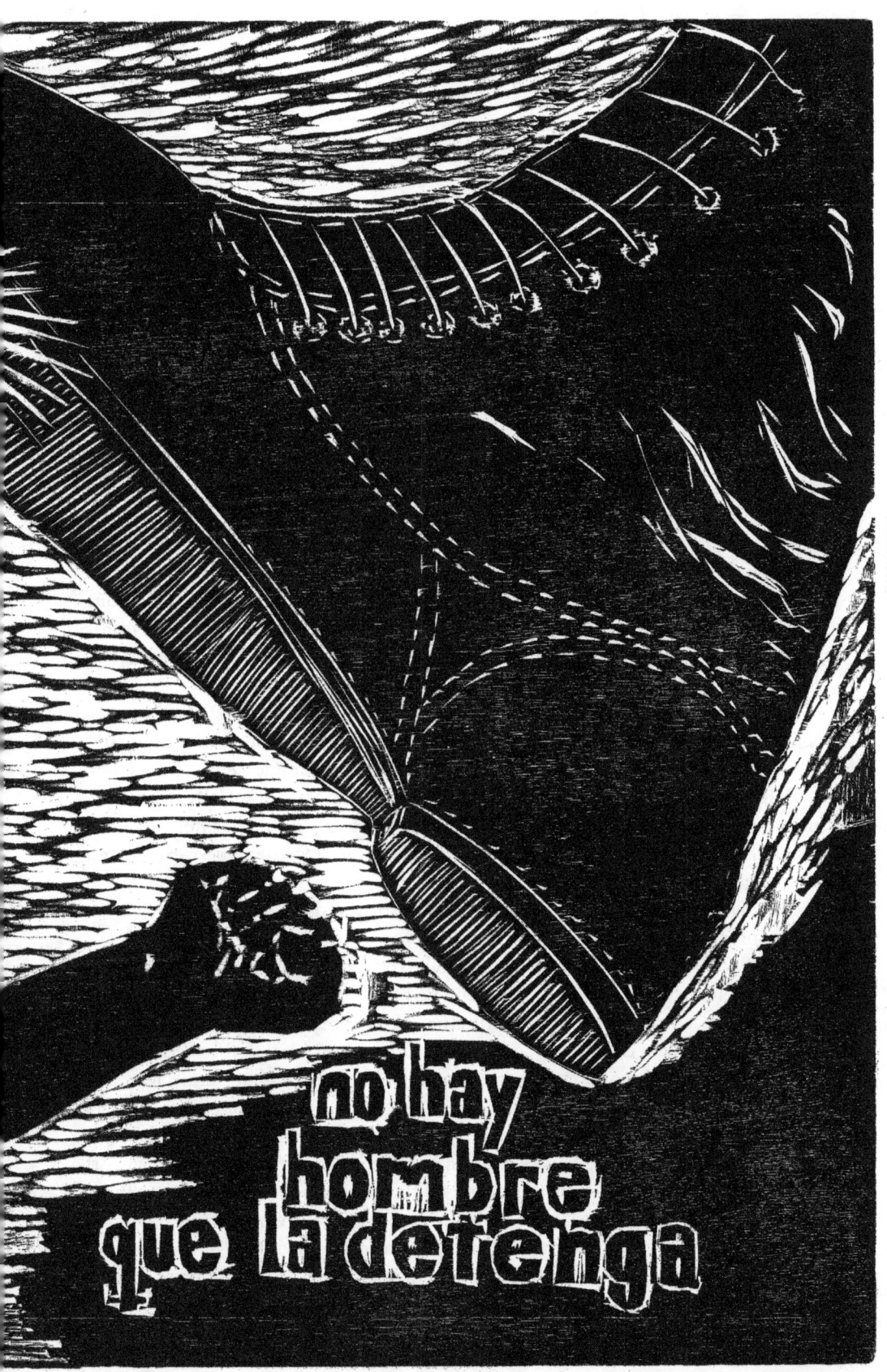

could hear plainly outside their homes and see on their streets, nearly 350 Oaxacan women armed themselves with pots and pans and marched on the state-owned television station. They demanded a spot on the air and, when refused, seized control of the tower. Later that evening they broadcasted live on television and on two local radio stations, one of which they renamed Radio Cacerola or "Pots and Pans Radio." Their programming enabled the dissemination of information regarding police whereabouts as well as the announcement of tragic fatalities and arrests. These broadcasts also provided a space for el pueblo to address their concerns collectively and watch documentaries about other grassroots movements in Mexico and abroad.

In *Libertarias* (Freedom Fighters), a radio tower leaning against the background emits visual airwaves while women dressed in flowery *huipils* occupy the foreground, defiantly throwing their fists into the air. Barbed wire unwinds across the print to reveal a speech scroll reminiscent of ancient Mesoamerican depictions of a king or *tlatoani*, a Nahuatl term which literally means "great speaker." This phrase emerges from the mouth of the central figure who takes to the air "for freedom." The act broke the state-imposed silence, even if only briefly. Government forces reclaimed these stations after twenty days, but the women's voices reverberated as loudly through Oaxaca as they do in this illustration.

Depictions memorializing assertive women in public protest document female participation in social movements while also challenging normative discursive structures equating traditional indigenous dress, cooking implements, and women with limited visibility and power. Representing prominent and socially effective female subjects implicitly situates women front and center in the rebellion, ensuring that if their contributions are lost in official publications regarding these events they do not go unrecognized by the public. "Bombing" the city streets as well as the internet challenges complicit stereotypes about female and indigenous docility. It is a means of "raising a social art."

This social art creates the new collective consciousness and countercultural movement addressed in the fifth and eight statements of ASARO's manifesto. ASARO's process for making and distributing these prints and stencils embody their commitment to "get up" for the people. *Libertad* is a memorial to the sacrifices that some artists made to counter the government in 2006. More importantly, it reveals how far they will go to challenge the information divide. Stacks of books on the right side of this print serve with a dark figure up against the wall on the left side as a frame for the image of a bleeding hand holding a paintbrush. This image memorializes artists who painted in blood from their hands at the barricades in 2006 as well as those who lost their lives during that time. As prints these images are highly repeatable and ubiquitously distributed, not only in stencils that make them part of the Oaxacan cultural landscape but in multiple copies circulated far and wide. Moreover, anyone

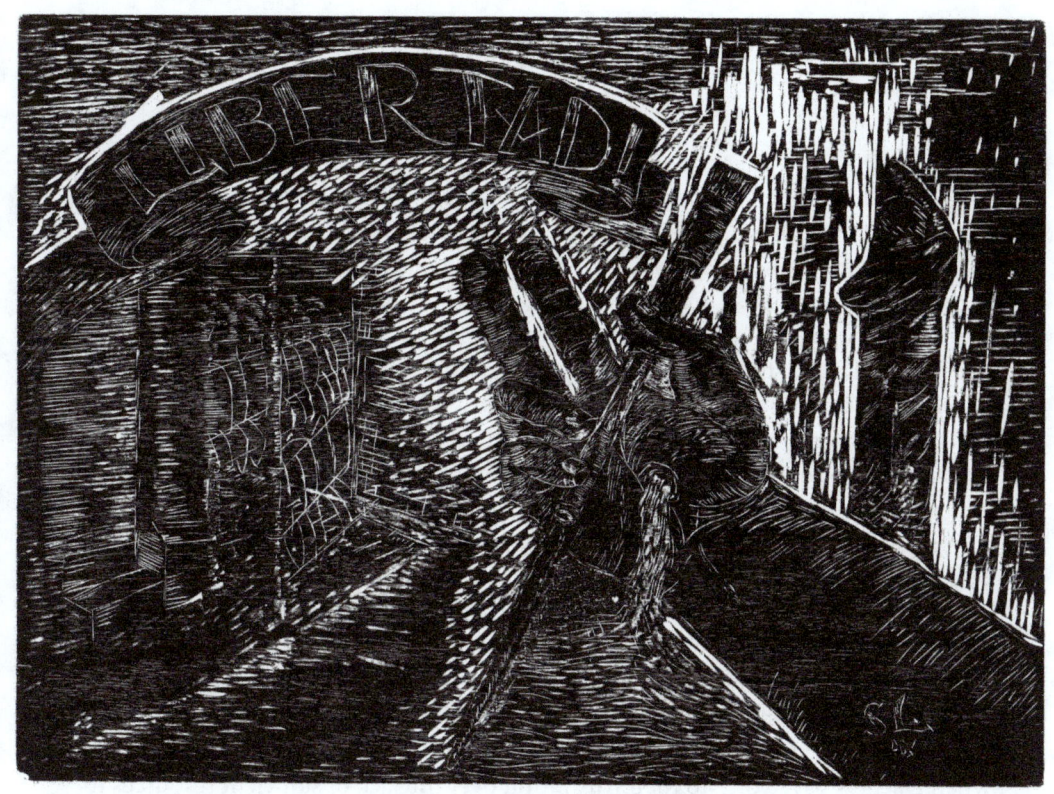

can put paint to these stencils and participate in leaving a collective mark.

It is interesting to note that this revised Oaxacan cultural landscape is woven from images referencing events, ideas, and feelings recognizable to Oaxacans and not to the casual tourist. Filling Oaxaca de Juárez's historic city center with images designed by and for Oaxacans is a direct challenge to old rules of social participation in that space.

"We live in a society where space is not socialized, it is owned privately, so we say that since the walls encircle the people, we need to take them—the walls, intervene for/with the people." —Mario, ASARO

It is also a profound means of changing the local consciousness through a countercultural movement. ASARO's disruptions in the quaint veneer of the city center unsettle the image of the destination promoted through tourism. They reintroduce Oaxacan diversity to this place, revealing social problems alongside the colorful customs favored by tourists.

Inviting other Oaxacans to add their own perspectives further enhances the social quality of this work while including additional Oaxacans. ASARO's ongoing work with children speaks to the importance of inclusion in their public art, creating a new consciousness. In one of these workshops, ASARO artists help children create and modify a stencil depicting a traditional Oaxacan woman dancing. The children remix the stencil's traditional portrayal of their local indigenous culture by covering the bottom half of the figure's face with a bandana. As with the EZLN mask, this symbolic implement openly signals rebellion and belonging. It also reflects on a pragmatic lesson learned during 2006: a bandana soaked in vinegar dispels the effects of tear gas. In addition to offering a space for children to learn about their recent history and to recreate it in the public space as a group, this workshop builds community between ASARO artists, children, and their shared space. They post pictures of these workshops online to further extend their reach. Even as ASARO works with young people in the city center, they reach out to the municipalities. This centripetal and centrifugal movement challenges the structures that have inhibited such communication, bringing the Oaxacan population that has been cut out of its capital city back into the public view. The 2006 uprising in Oaxaca essentially began when teachers gave voice to their frustration over the lack of sufficient resources to instruct their students. It is fitting that ASARO artists have summoned their dedication to present youth with an opportunity to learn about art while publicly expressing and exhibiting their unique perspectives in the local visual landscape. In so doing, ASARO "gets up" pa'l pueblo from within a celebrated tradition of collective printmaking workshops, pictorial storytelling, and rebellion.

"Our workshops are a form of giving back to the people who don't have creative spaces and supplies." —Chapo, ASARO

Fuera URO, 2013, stenciling in progress. »
Following page spread: *Mercado Sanchez Murals*, 2013, mural.

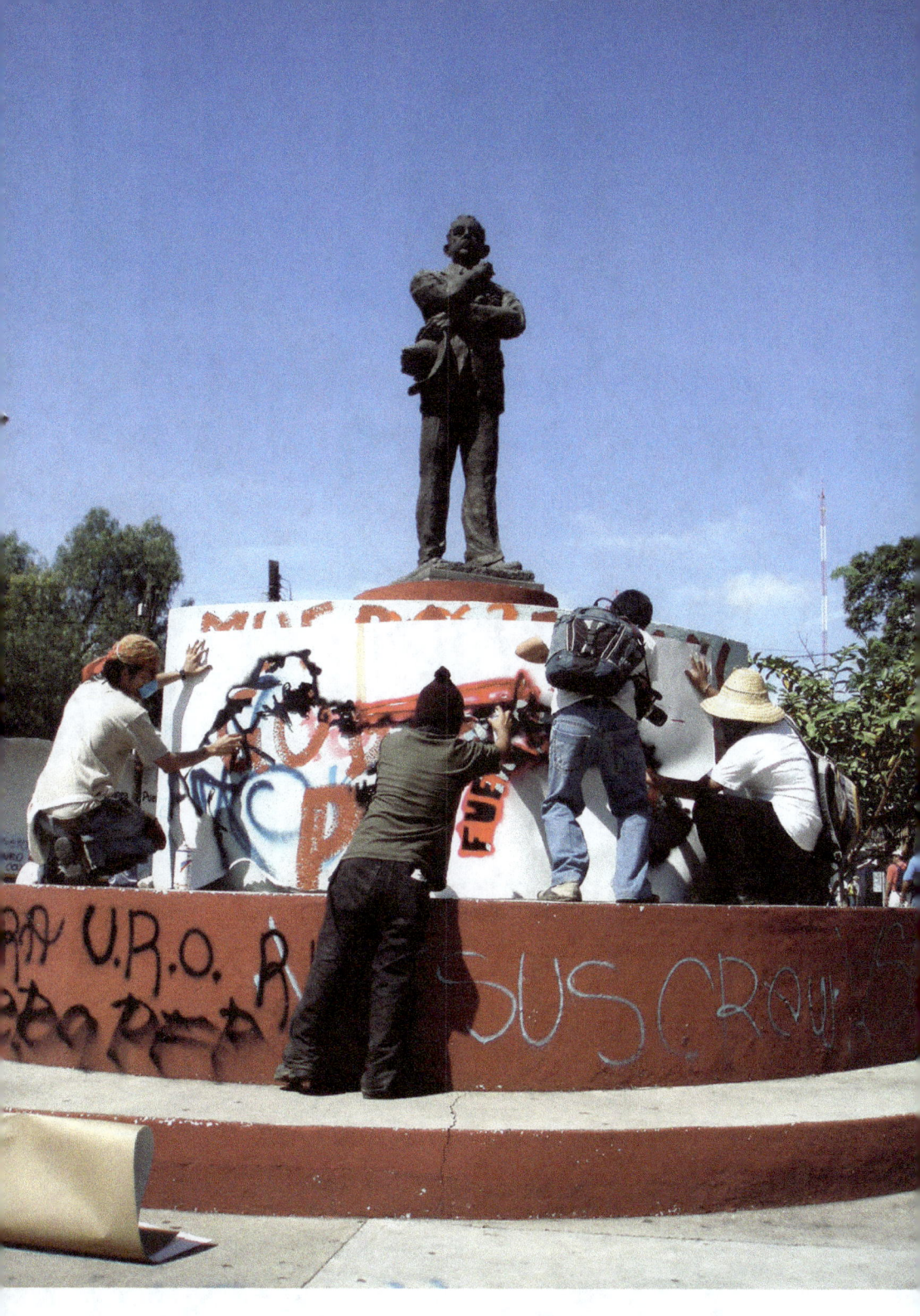

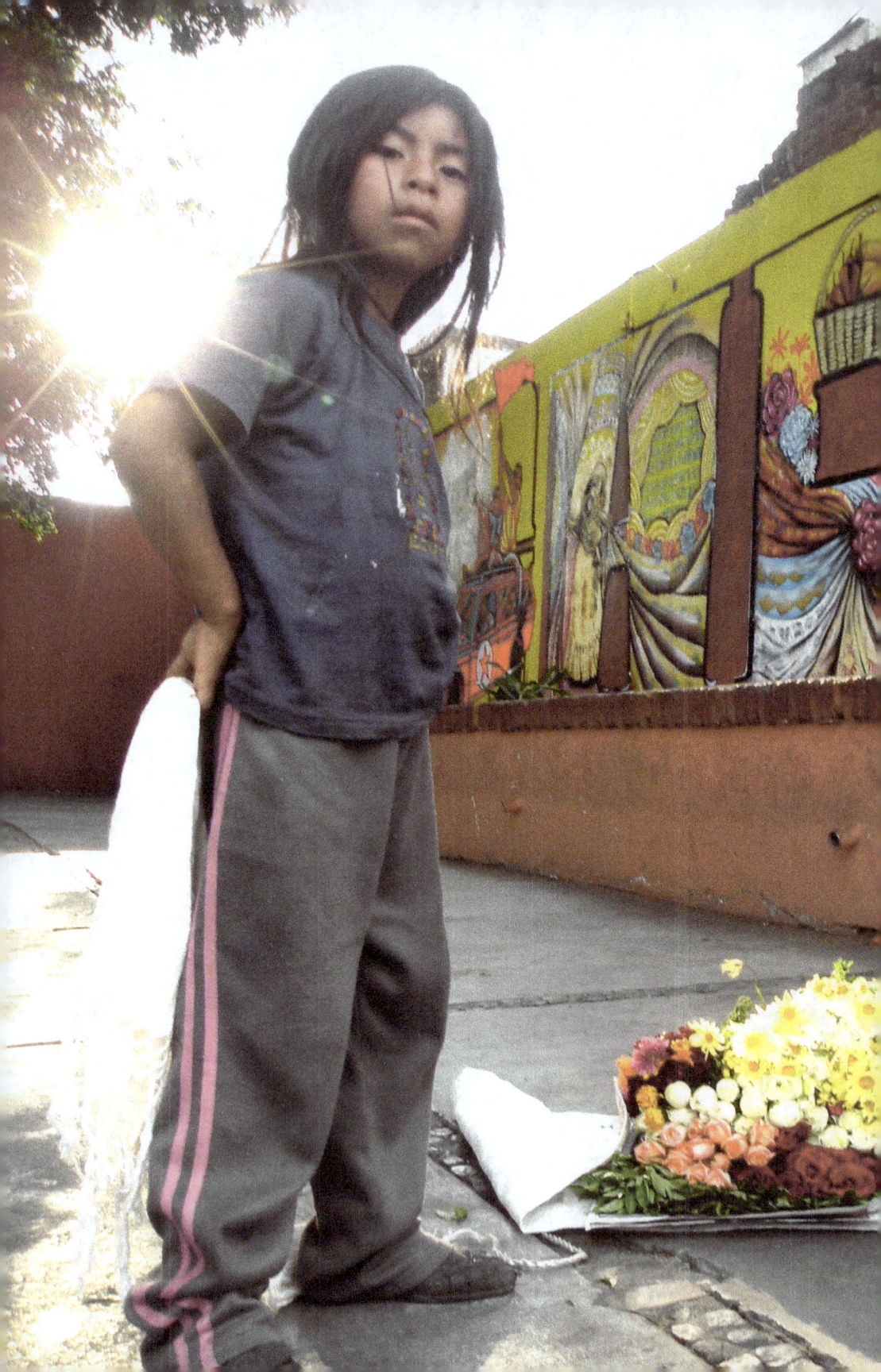

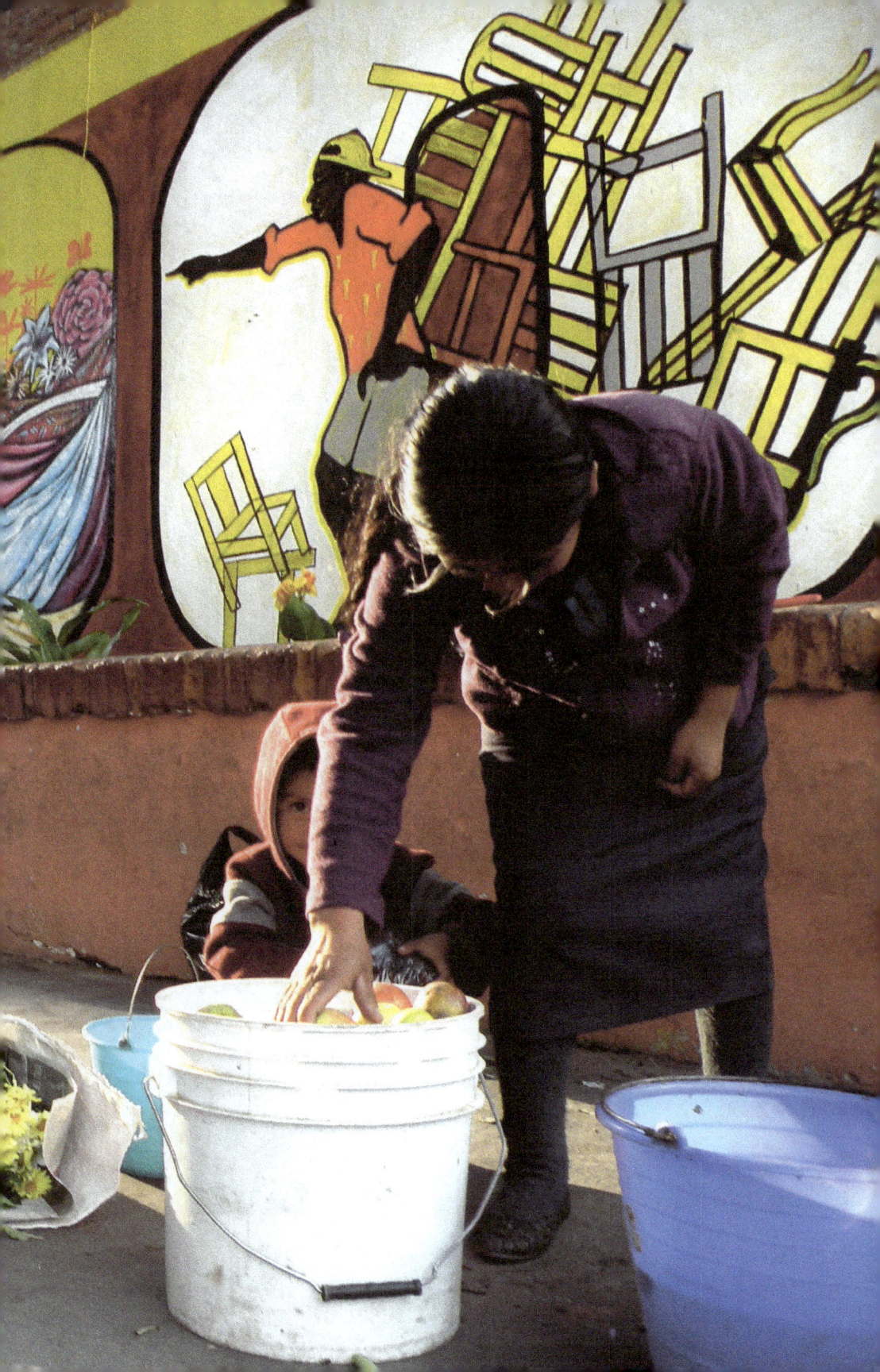

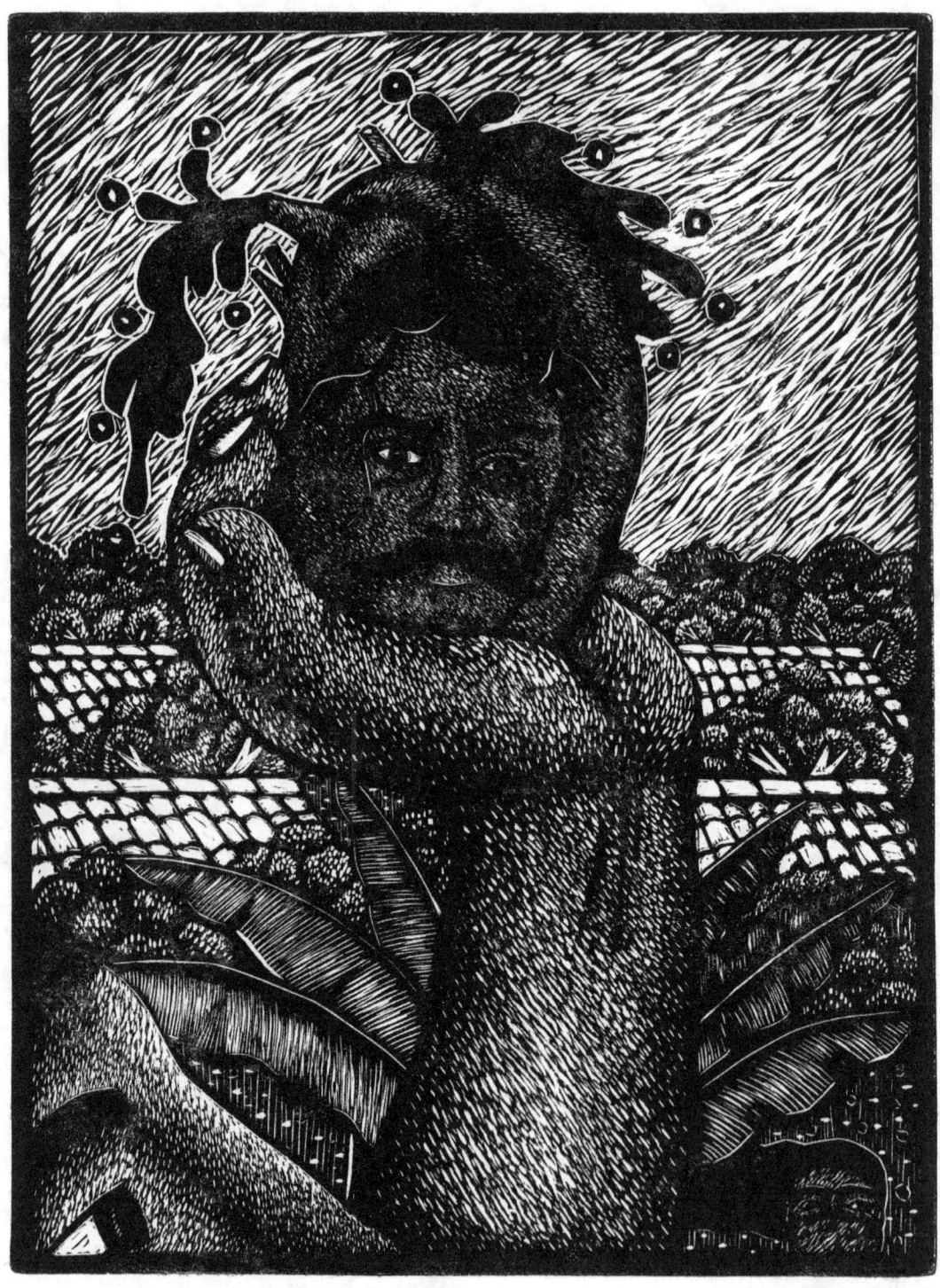

Hand and Zapata Heart, 2010, block print, 19 ½" x 24".

PA'L PUEBLO/FOR THE PEOPLE

"We propose to start an art movement in order to be in direct contact with people in the streets and public spaces." —ASARO Manifesto

"We believe that artistic expression needs to be a form of communication that allows dialogue with all sectors of society and enables the display of real existing conditions, rules, and contradictions of the society we inhabit." —ASARO Manifesto

"Represent" is a loaded term and the act of representing is equally charged. On the one hand, the verb means to speak for or, alternatively, to stand on behalf of another. On the other hand, it signifies presenting something anew. Art for the people necessitates both of these practices acting together as reflected in the sixth and seventh statements of ASARO's manifesto. Public art also embodies another relevant definition of this verb: to portray or set forth in words or symbols. The Spanish language extends this last notion into the dramatic arts where a performance is "represented" rather than acted.

ASARO employs performance in planning and implementing their interventions, thus depending upon audience response. Their street projects are comprised of multiple connecting pieces drawn from complimentary fragments, each with their own signification. Spectators who see the resulting work as a big picture read it differently from those who see the details within it as separate, isolated statements. This process modifies the originally intended message while at the same time revealing the problem inherent in speaking on behalf of others. The audience has a voice, too, and more often than not their participation adds to or subtracts from the representation, creating something new. While some audience members may represent the work as important cultural patrimony, others might portray it as unnecessary vandalism. In either case, they assign the performance a value that is intrinsically social.

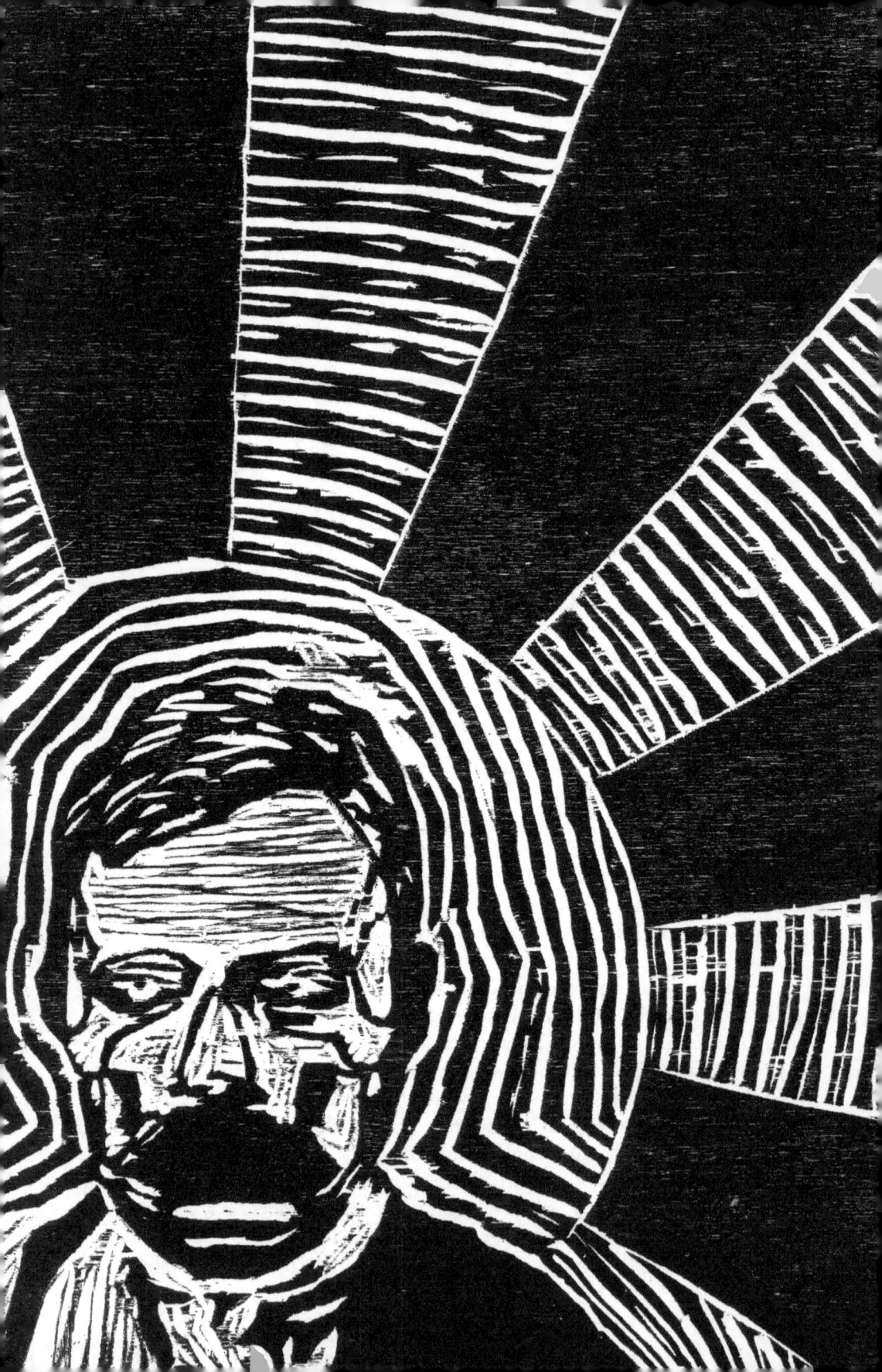

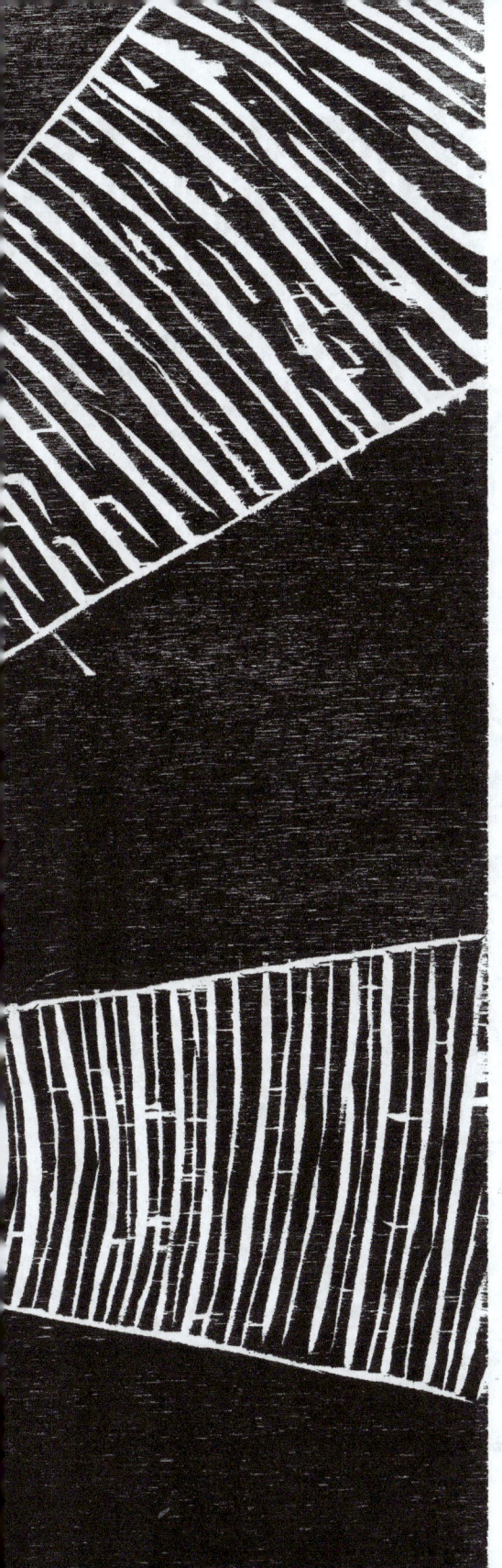

« *Zapata in Sunlight*, 2010, block print, 14 ¼" X 13 ½".

As an urban countercultural youth movement in a peripheralized state, ASARO creates pieces that blend urban hip hop ideas with the indigenous concepts of communality. For this reason it is important to recognize that opposing hip hop definitions for the term "represent" fit well within a culture that embraces the hip hop notion of setting a good example while standing in as representative of a community, as well as its opposite meaning of annoying others with your presence. The ranks of the EZLN in their masks embody this notion of simultaneously standing for a community and serving as a taxing reminder of indigenous perseverance. By nature of its place among the people, street art also accomplishes both of these objectives; its ability to do so is likely why some ASARO artists see it as the preferable medium for representing the pueblo.

"The strongest and most important art is in the streets." —Yescka, ASARO

Print work is also provocative of audience participation and transformation as well as communal persistence; consequently, it has occupied an important place in Mexican history and art. Prints are the result of putting an engraved block to ink and paper so their images can be repeated in different inks and papers. They are thus represented in wheat pastes glued to exterior walls, fliers, and pamphlets generated through

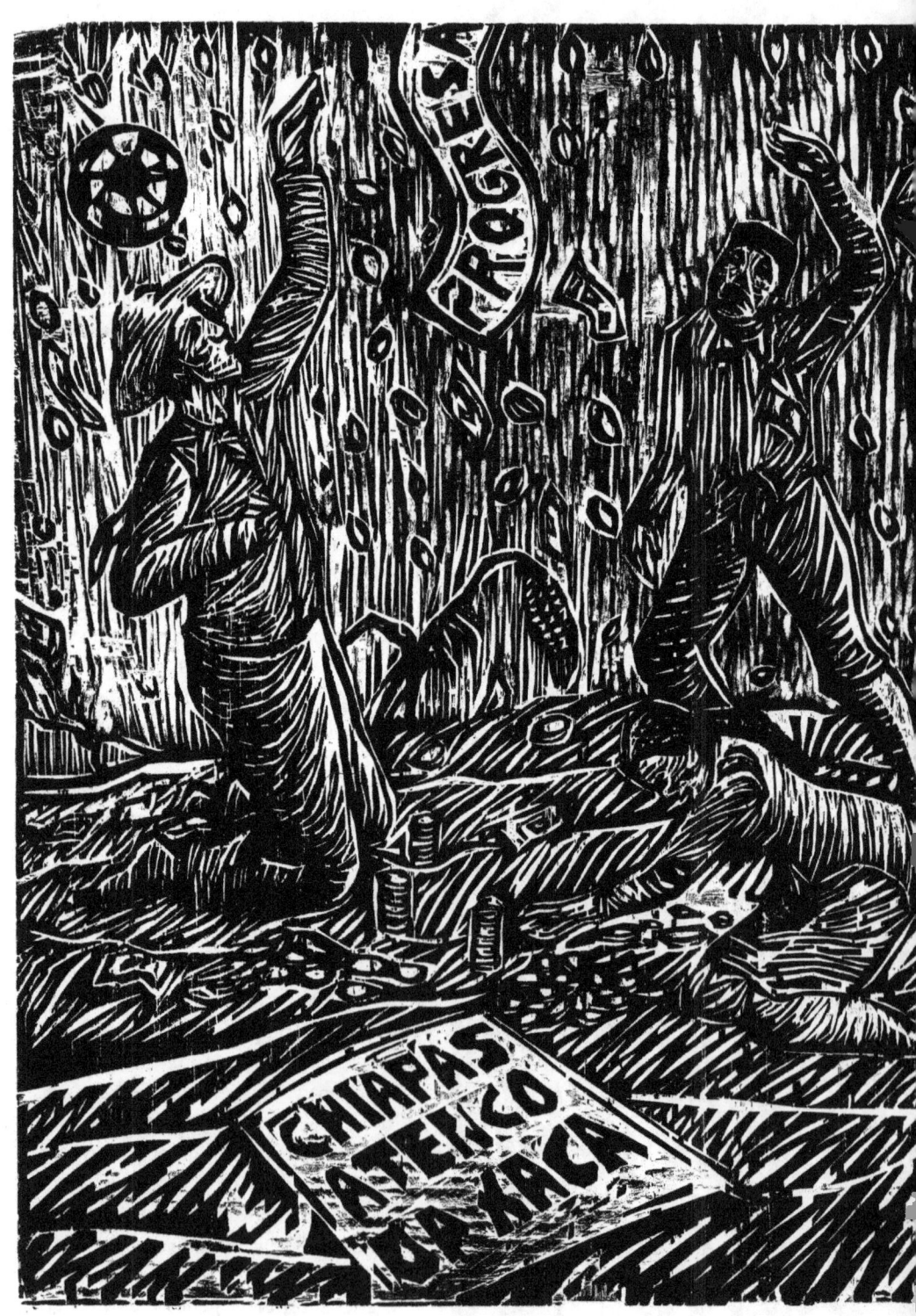

Chiapas, Atenco, Oaxaca, 2011, block print, 27 ½" x 19 ½".

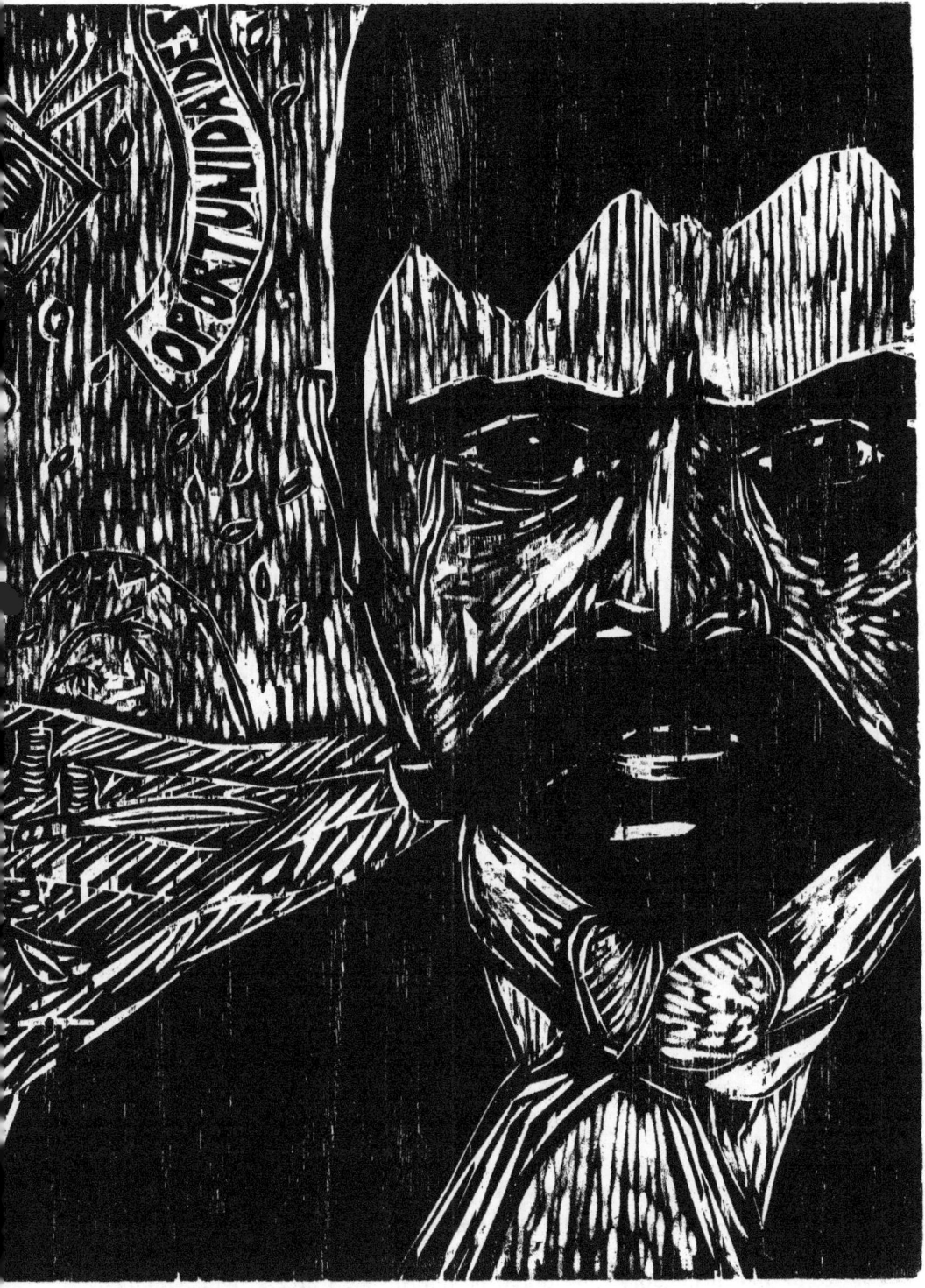

street networks, electronic media, and collectable prints exhibited in either public or private galleries.

> "Initially we sold our pieces to support infrastructure, to pay for a workshop space and supplies. Once we made a little more, we sought to create spaces for exhibiting and disseminating our works and those of other collectives. We want this material to reach more people." —Mario, ASARO

The print extends ASARO's audience beyond people physically present in the streets of Oaxaca, inviting a wider audience to value the images by interpreting and representing them.

Zapata

Speaking for and representing something significant enough to be meaningful for a community requires an engagement with deeply embedded symbols in that community as well as a dependency on already agreed-upon visual cues. Throughout Mexico and in much of the Mexican-American or Hispanic Southwestern United States, the image of Emiliano Zapata equals revolutionary. A smaller grouping within in a disperse community sees him more familiarly as a man of the rural people, representing their rights to land. In this sense, Zapata's image is the periphery fighting back for possession of their land. His representation is invoked for these purposes even outside of Mexico by those marginalized as a result of colonialist and imperialist land-grabbing. This sentiment is well reflected in the northern New Mexican slogan "Tierra o Muerte," meaning Land or Death and used repeatedly with Zapata's image in the late 1960s by *La Alianza*, led by Reies López Tijerina.

In Oaxaca the revolution that Zapata led lives on as its population fights to resist authoritarian political structures and capitalist economic priorities that persist today, more than a century after the beginning of the Mexican Revolution. Zapata may stand even stronger now as the iconic symbol of an unfinished movement.

> "Today we have more access to images; and sometimes, while mixing what you learned in fine arts, you come across some other icon, a new visual space through graffiti. These icons and personages are mediums for young people to express power." —César, ASARO

It is his heart that beats from the grave representing contemporary movements in Atenco, Chiapas, and Oaxaca. Despite the groundbreaking constitutional reforms of Mexico's 1917 constitution which established provisions throughout Mexico for free, mandatory education, land reform, and workers' rights, too many

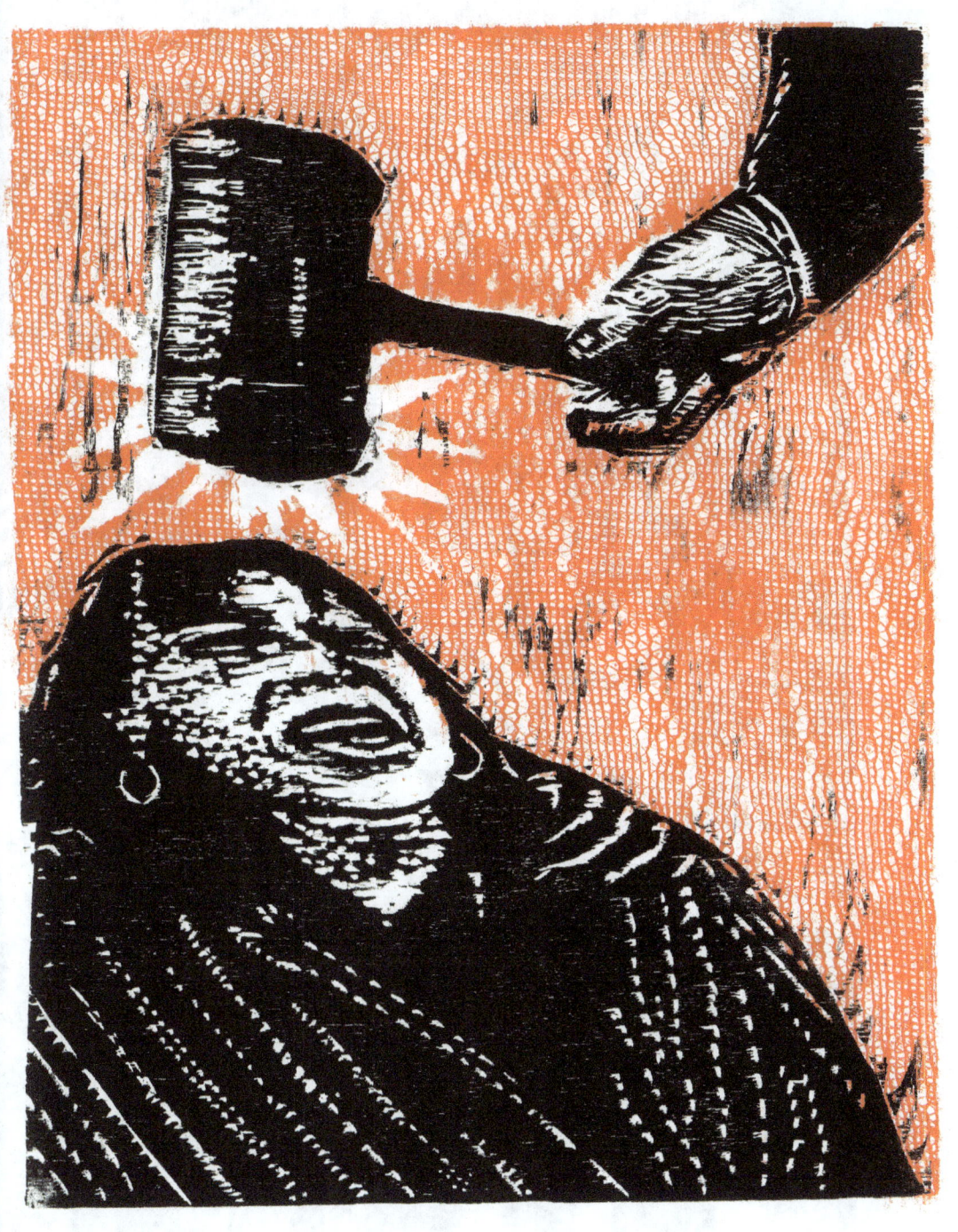

Woman Being Hammered, 2010, block print, 14" x 19 ½".
Following page spread: *Pun*, 2010, block print, 13 ½" x 12 ½".

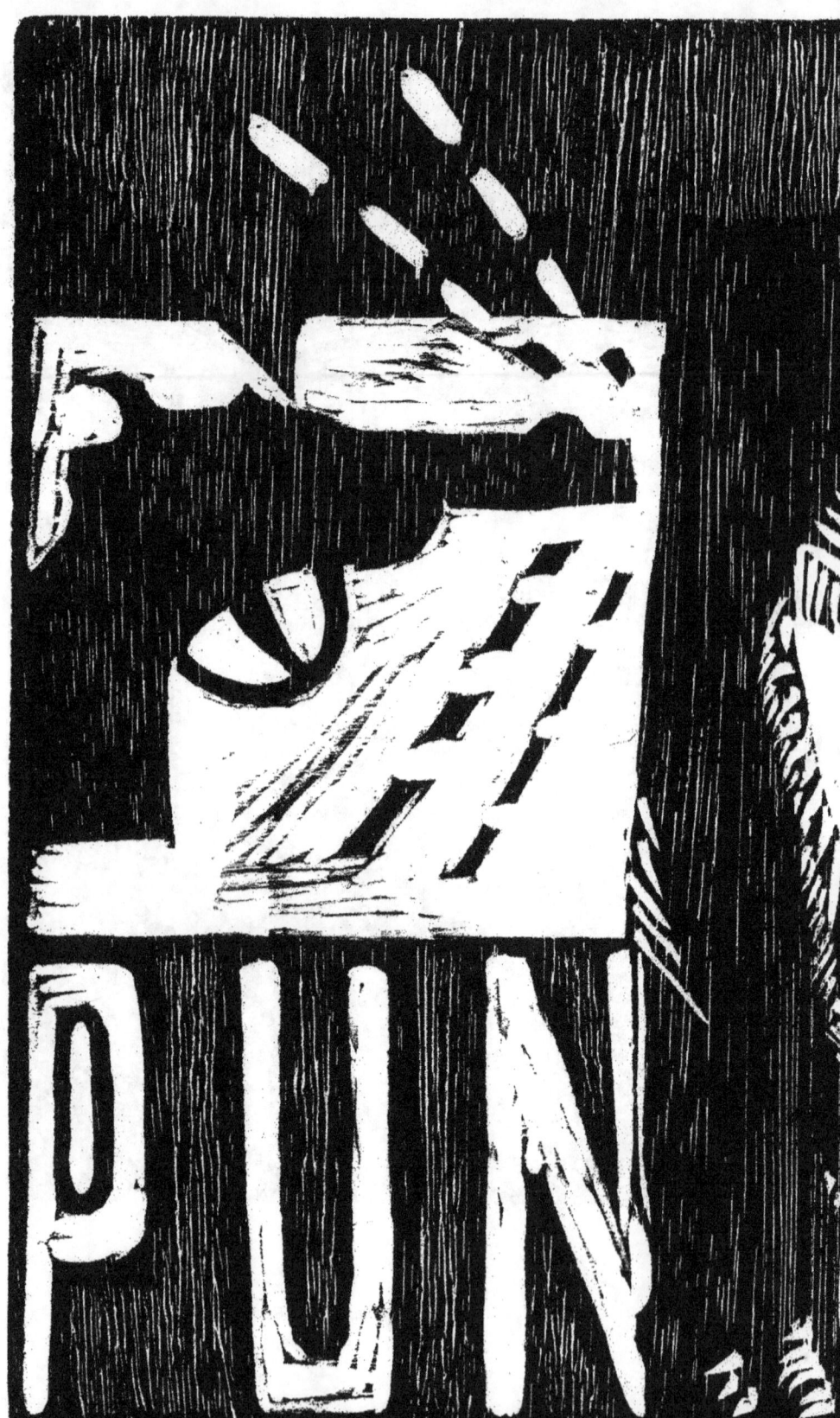

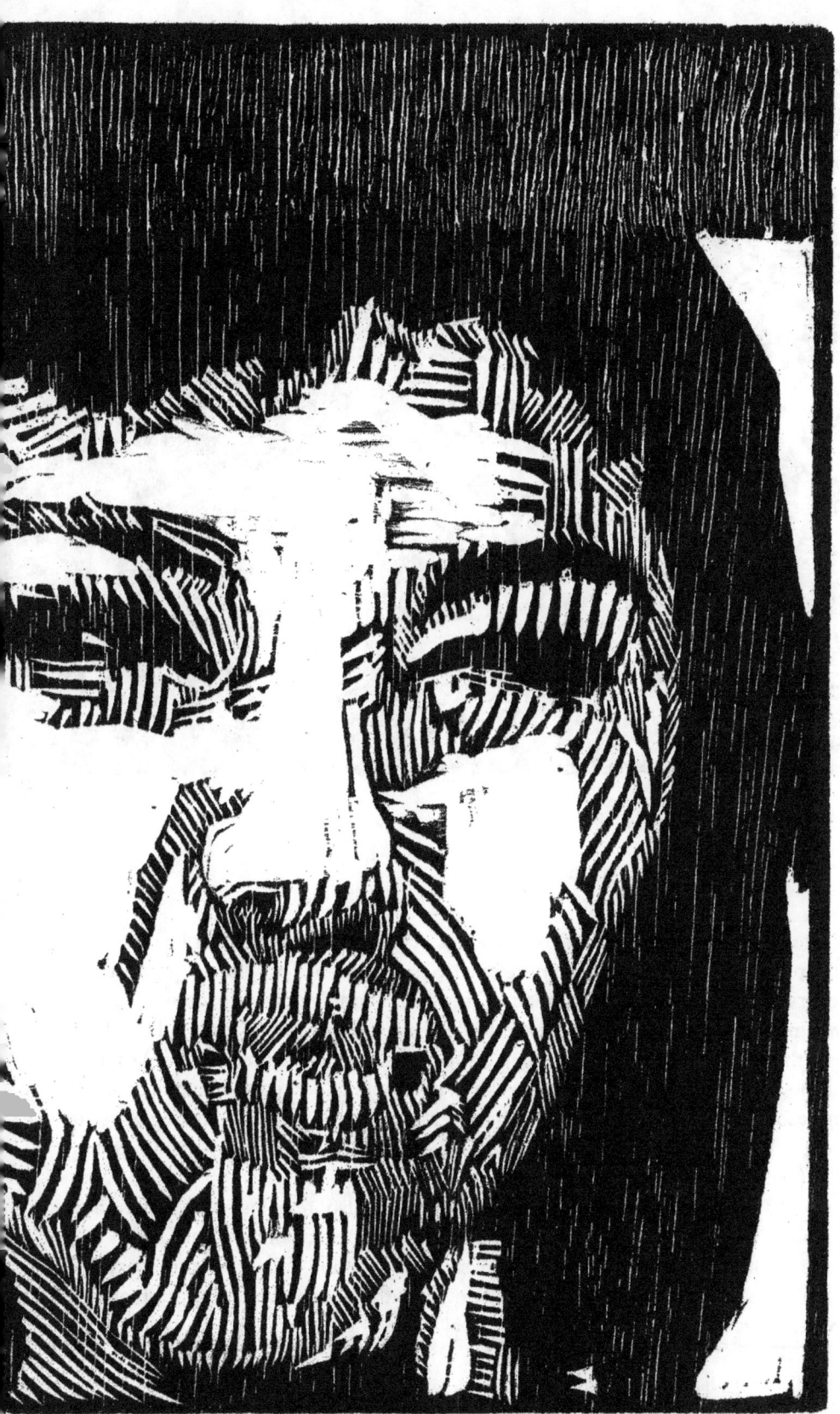

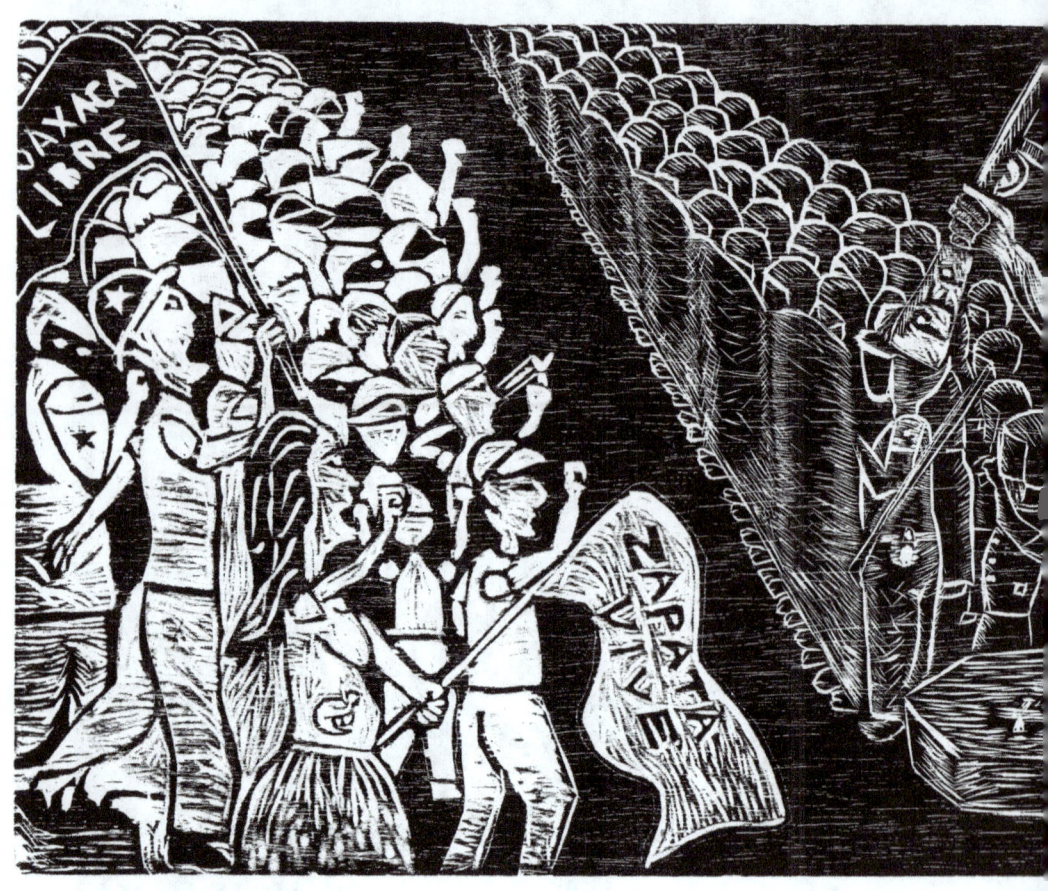

Oaxaca Libre, Zapata Vive, 2006, block print, 27 ½" x 19 ¾".

Mexicans suffer without access to education or property while a select few prosper beyond anyone's wildest imagination. Even as more than half of Mexico's population hovers near poverty, multi-billionaire Carlos Slim and drug lord Joaquín Guzmán are among the richest men in the world. Despite statistics suggesting middle-class growth in Mexico, most people struggle. Opening Mexican markets to international businesses has resulted, generally speaking, in crippling local entrepreneurs or abusing resources in short supply. Deals between top players and high-ranking government officials have effectively excluded the Mexican majority. Opportunities are slim (pun intended).

To add to these grievances, state control also remains with the ruling Revolutionary Institutional Party (PRI). This clientelist political party has controlled political opposition in Mexico since the period following the Mexican Revolution. It has generally maintained power with the occasional exception of the conservative National Action Party's (PAN) gain of the presidency under Vicente

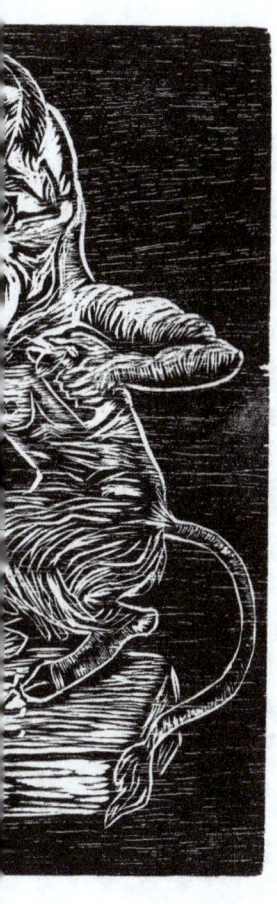

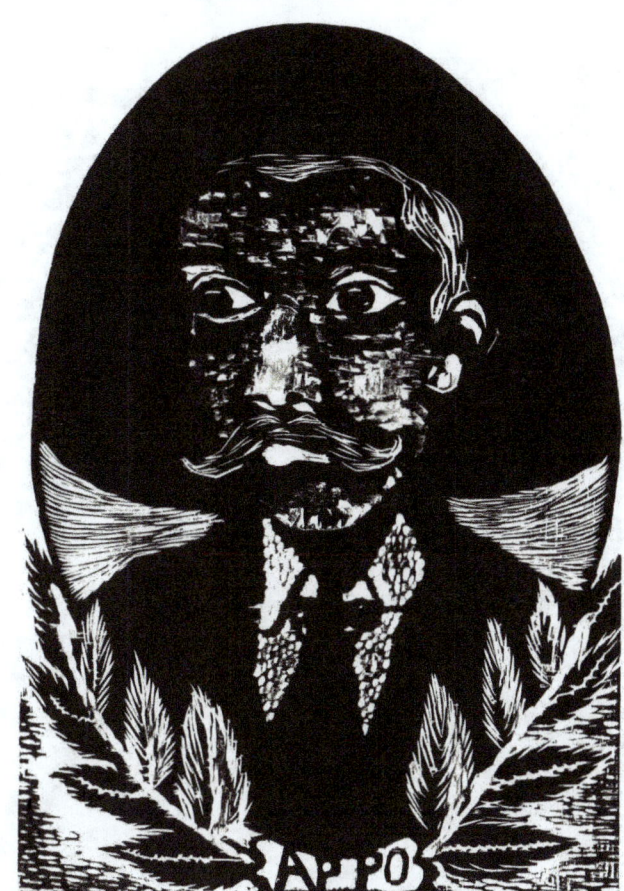

Fox (2000–2006) and Felipe Calderón (2006–2012). It recently lost the governorship in Oaxaca to a new, more liberal coalition comprised of Workers Party (PT) and Democratic Revolutionary Party (PRD) members who unseated Ruiz Ortiz in 2010. It is difficult to separate these anomalies from PRI ranks, however, because so many of the PRD candidates, including current Oaxacan governor Gabino Cué Monteagudo and some PAN membership, were once PRI functionaries. Since pragmatism rather than ideology generally underlay these changes of heart, it is difficult not to wonder when they might revert back. Regardless of party affiliations, the Mexican national government maintains the guise of stability through repression, caring little for the social cost of injustice.

In this environment, Zapata represents social expectations for systematic change. ASARO reappropriates his iconic image to speak for other Oaxacans and Mexicans in a symbolic act of taking their country back from the PRI as in *Oaxaca Libre, Zapata Vive* (Free Oaxaca, Zapata Lives). In this print, a rat-like figure leads

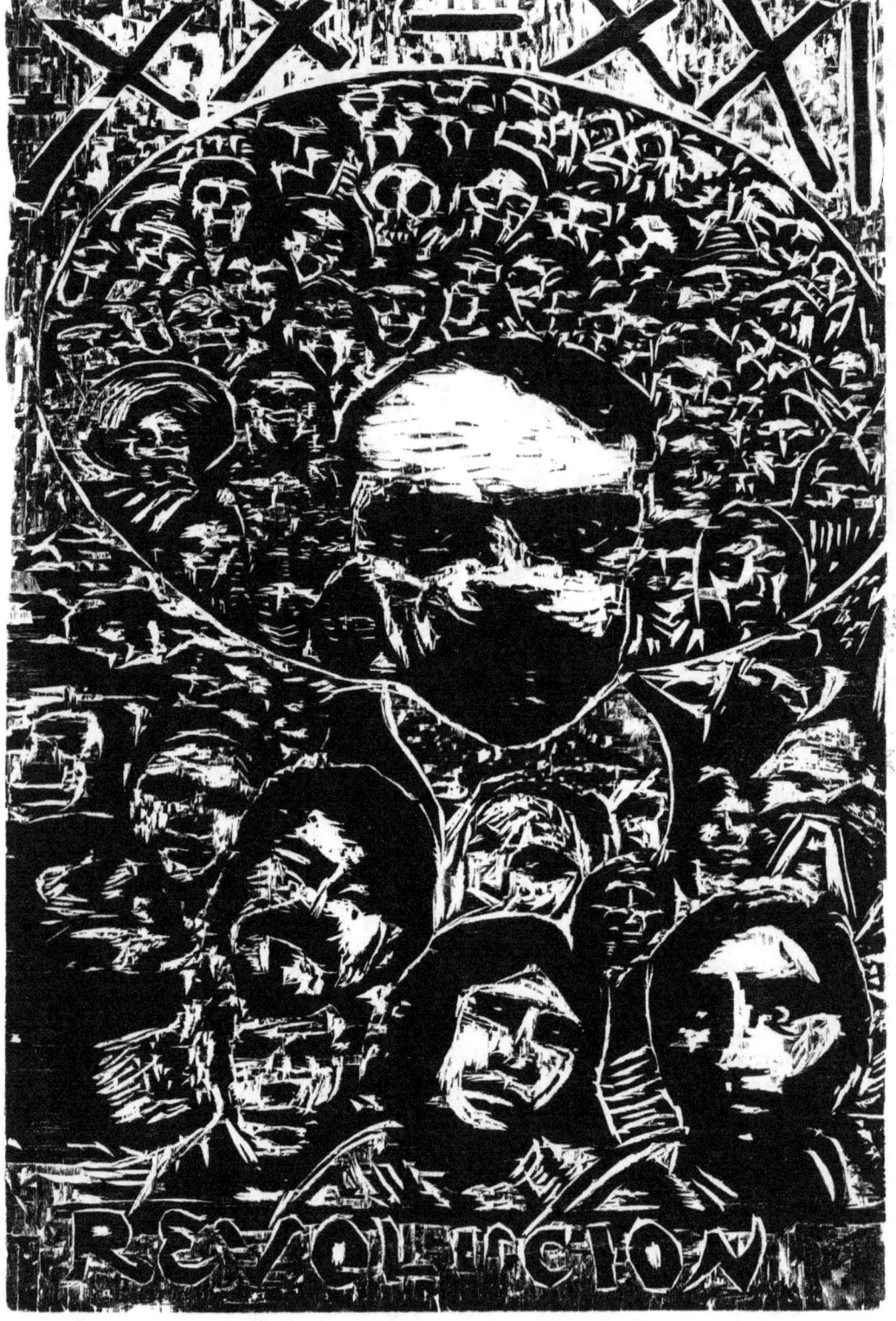

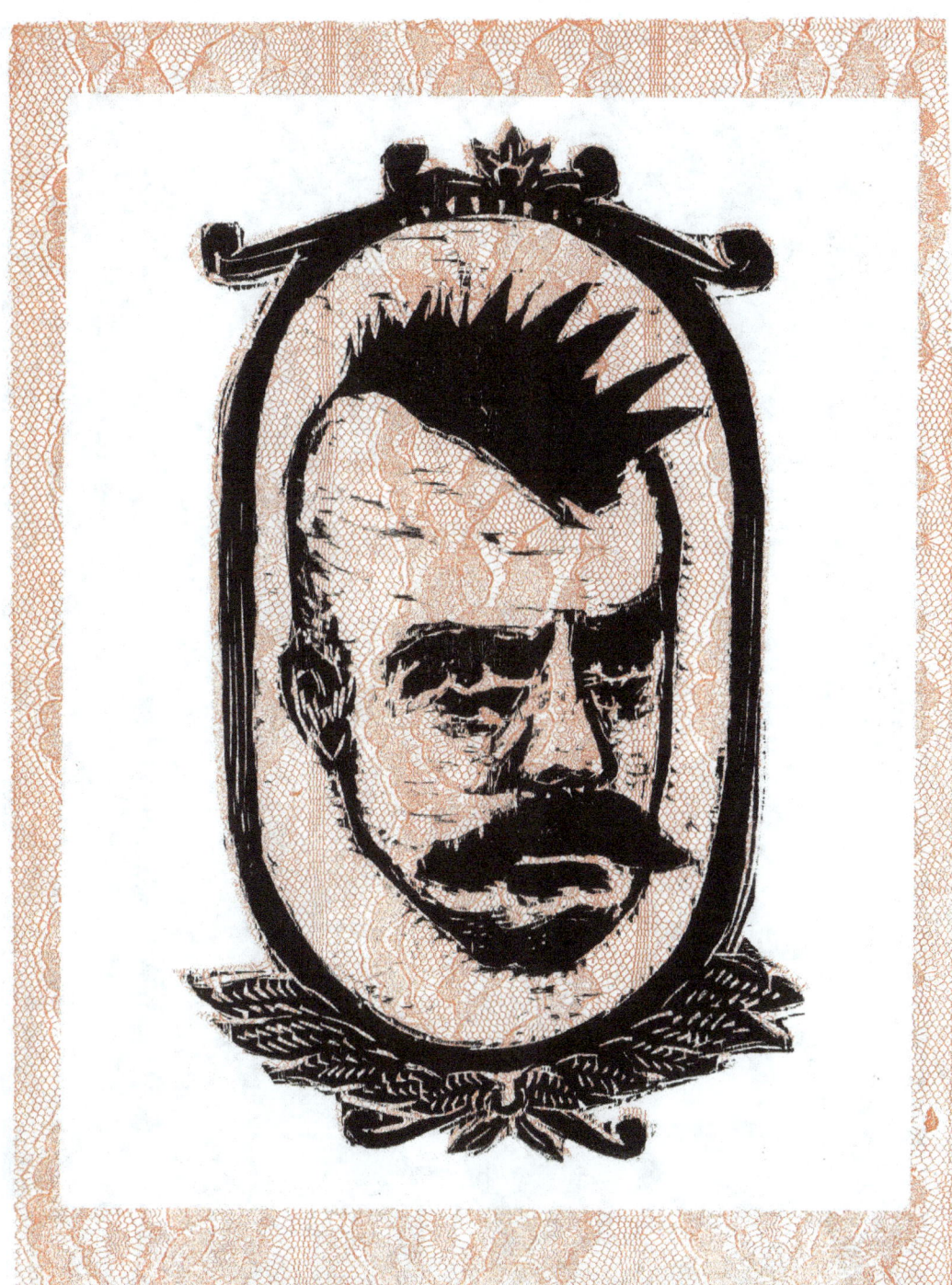

ASARO, *Punk Zapata*, 2010, screenprint, 13" x 18".
« *XX—XXI Revolución*, 2008, block print, 19 ½" x 27 ½".

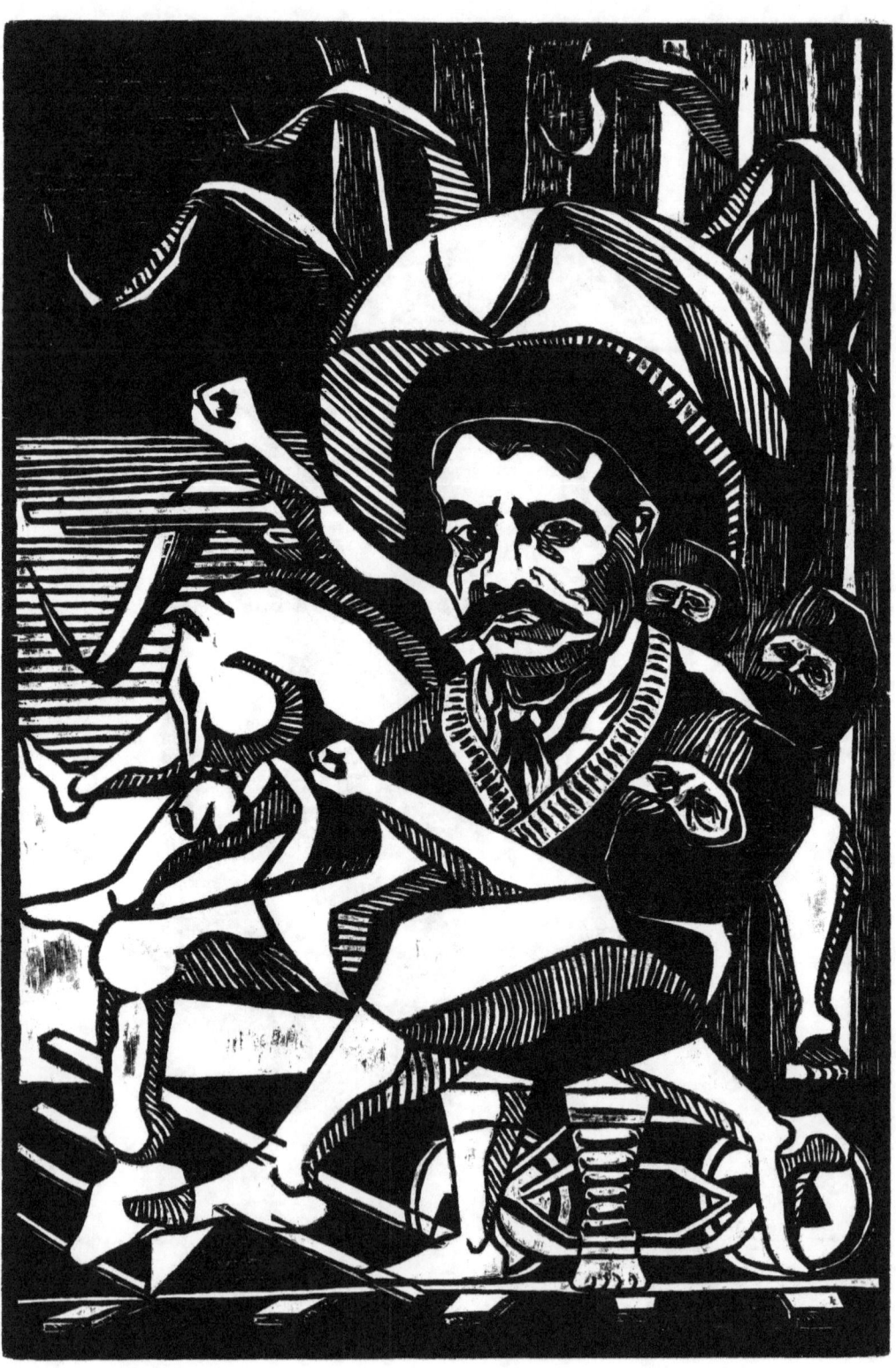

a military stand against people advancing Zapata's revolutionary ideal of communal ownership and workers' solidarity. The crowd carries his banner and embodies his perseverance with flags stating: "Zapata Lives" and "Oaxaca is free." In other words, the print says "Oaxaca is getting back up and it understands Mexico's revolutionary struggles and losses as part of its own history." They are readied to take it back from the repressive ranks and the monstrosity that the PRI became. It is tempting to present ASARO's depictions of Zapata as reiterative or opportunist because of the immediate recognition afforded his mustached face inside and outside of Mexico. While there is certainly some element of replication and opportunism in ASARO's use of his effigy, the act of repurposing his representation for contemporary contexts is deliberately performative.

The print *XX–XXI Revolución* reenacts Mexican revolutionary history while also representing a historical Mexican print titled *Homenaje a E. Zapata*, which the TPG supplied for a newspaper in 1947. More importantly, this work restates the power of community action and the connections between the living and the dead in Mexican history. In addition to the obvious textual references framing the print, XX–XXI on the top and Revolution on the bottom, this composition pays homage to Mexican revolutionaries, living and dead. The *calaveras* in Zapata's sombrero are a tribute to those who have died, while the crowd under the *sombra* or shadow of Zapata's hat, honors those still fighting. The rebellion literally lives on in Zapata's image. ASARO expresses this same idea quite differently in *Punk Zapata*.

"Until Zapata's last day he kept fighting, demanding better conditions. Zapata is associated with the revolutionary. In Morelos he established a government of the people; and with them armed you didn't need a specialized police force. It was the people that made sure there wasn't delinquency. He gives us a model our communities can identify with."
—Mario, ASARO

Cubist Zapata is a bit less obvious to those unfamiliar with the historical remix reflected within. In this print Zapata rides atop a Trojan horse, crossing railroad tracks. The tentacles of what seem to be transgenic corn stalks shade him and the masked EZLN soldiers ride in on his vest. The piece is a direct reference to the strategy the EZLN used to successfully enter San Cristóbal de las Casas as the ink dried on the North American Free Trade Agreement on New Year's Day 1994. Several months before this planned attack on governing forces in Mexico's southernmost principal city, EZLN soldiers began infiltrating the Mexican Army and security police in town, enabling them to slow the military response when their comrades attacked. They seized several towns and cities throughout Chiapas and set fire to police stations and military barracks in the city. The federal government responded

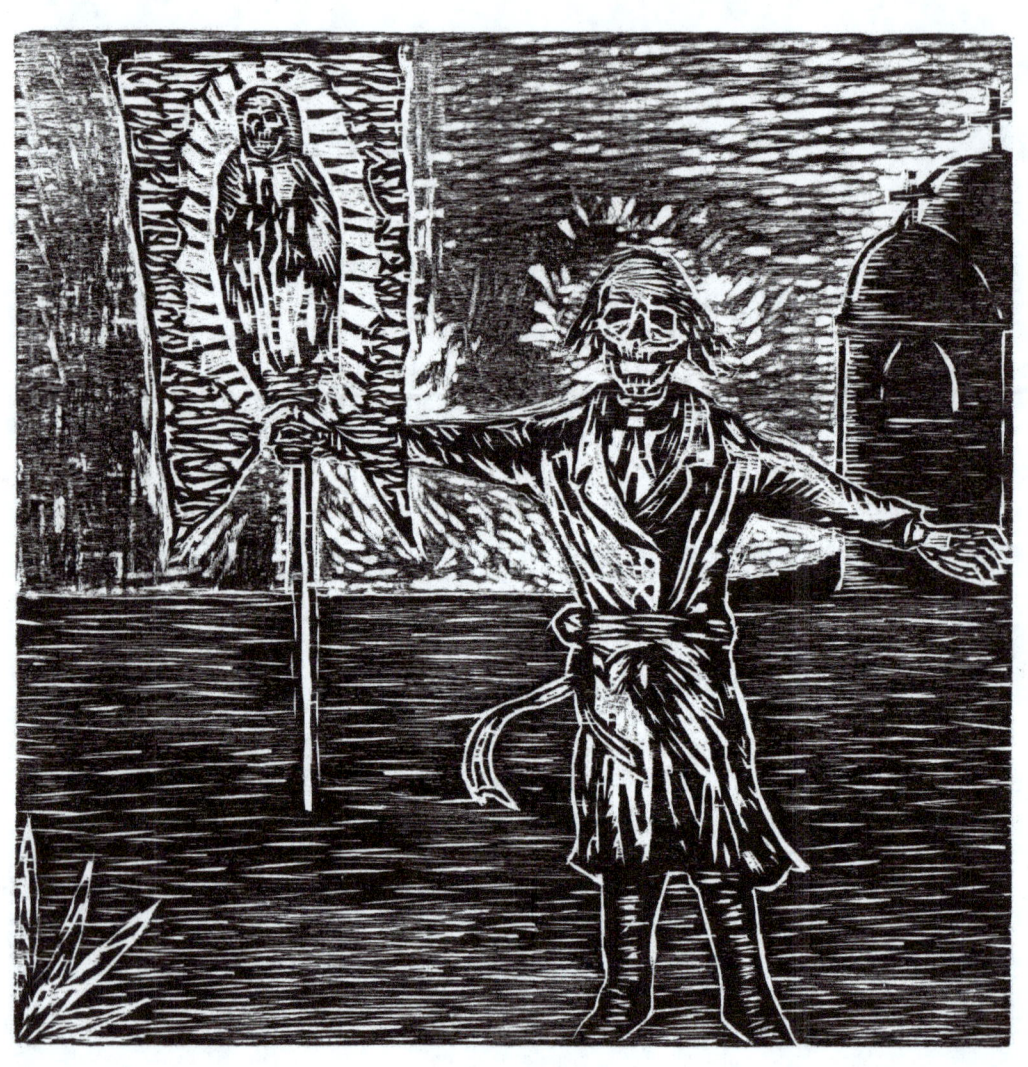

Hidalgo with Guadalupana Flag, 2010, block print, 13 ¾" x 17".
Agradesco la Virgencita de Guadalupe, 2006, block print, 39 ¼" x 27 ½".

swiftly and violently. Fighting continued for twelve days. Even though the EZLN lost the battle, international news reports from the scene carried their story and their grievances far beyond Mexico. This important event embodies the act of "getting up" and representing for the people.

Guadalupe

Zapata is not the only icon speaking for and representing struggling Mexican communities. His female counterpart, the Virgin of Guadalupe, is also significant, albeit not as easy to define. Zapata's armies carried flags with her image, but that was not enough to equate her likeness with revolutionary. This use of her likeness represented Guadalupe as a patroness of resistance, however, recalling other histori-cal moments of struggle. One century earlier, Father Miguel Hidalgo had rallied his troops behind Guadalupana flags in the battle for Mexican Independence. Even the EZLN named the mobile city from which they organized their movement in her indigenous honor, calling it Guadalupe de Teyapac for Tonantzin's home. As the syncretized image of Tonantzin and the Virgin Mary, Guadalupe is symbolic of re-sistance in Mexico.

Her story is part and parcel of colonization and Catholic hegemony. According to tradition, she appeared miraculously in 1531 to an indigenous man, Juan Diego, asking him in his native Nahuatl to build a temple for her at this site, which he had visited because of its significance in his native culture as the home of the indigenous mother-goddess, Tonantzin. The Spanish had previously de-stroyed the temple there. Despite multiple inquiries into the veracity of this story, Guadalupe stands as representative of unification, the apparition of a patroness who is both Aztec and Spanish. ASARO also evokes her image in the service of community. In their work, she is a guardian deity, mass-produced in stencils, T-shirts, prints, and key chains. She protects the spaces in which she is represented, be they in the fields protecting peasants' corn from genetic modifications or on the streets as a modern young woman on the cross.

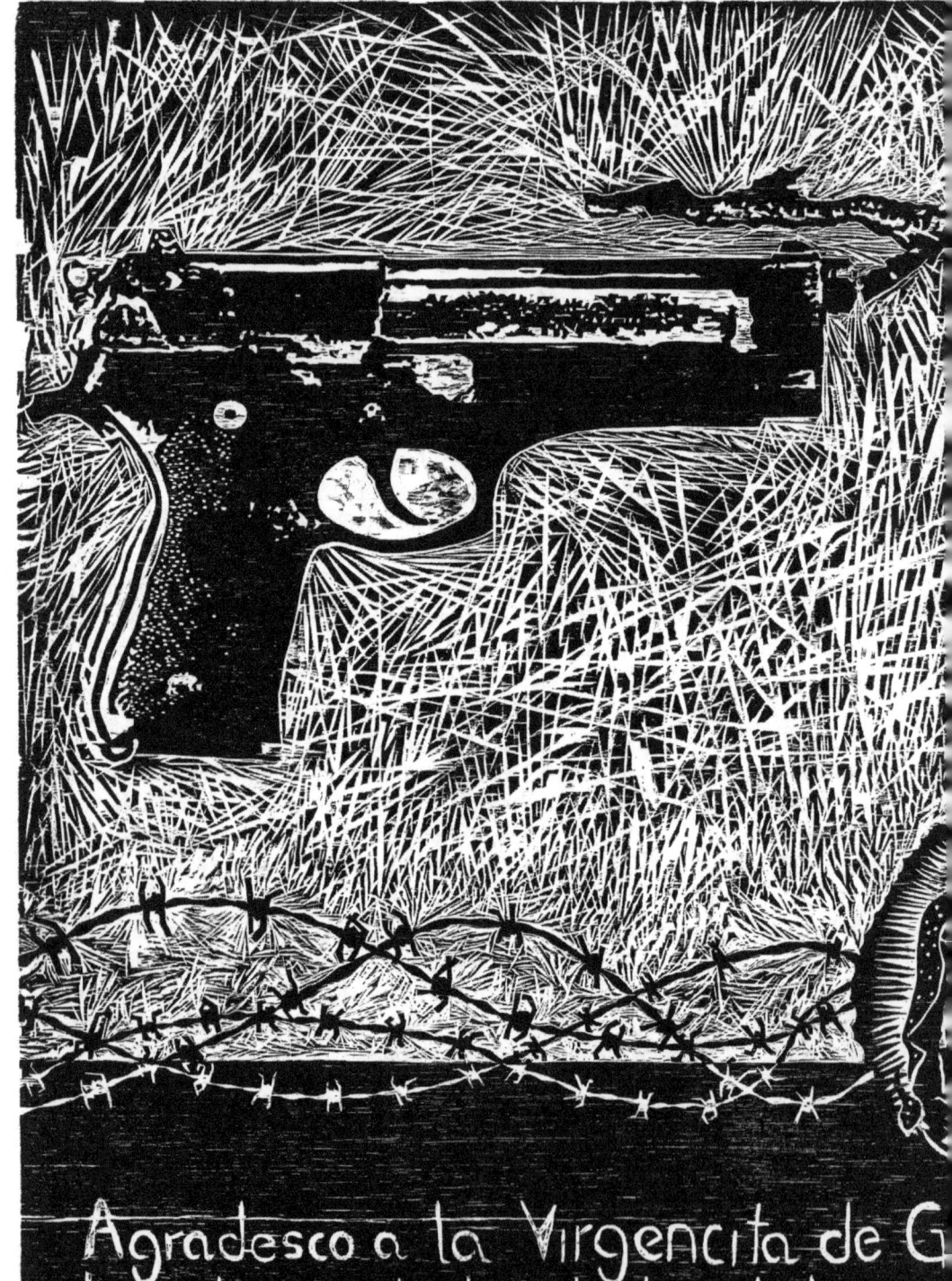

Agradesco a la Virgencita de G
he sobrevivido las balas del gob
R

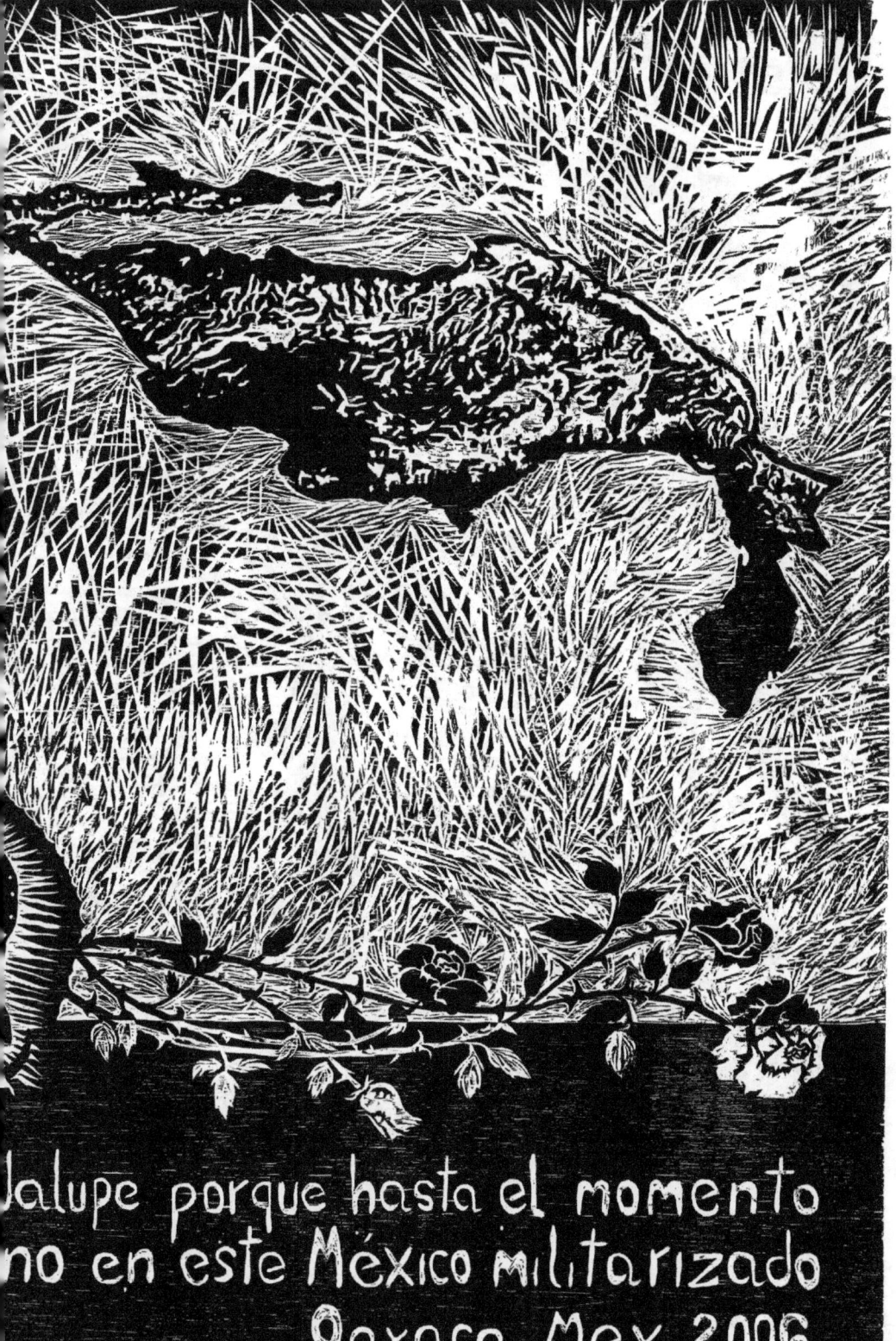

Jalupe porque hasta el momento
no en este México militarizado
Oaxaca, Mex. 2006

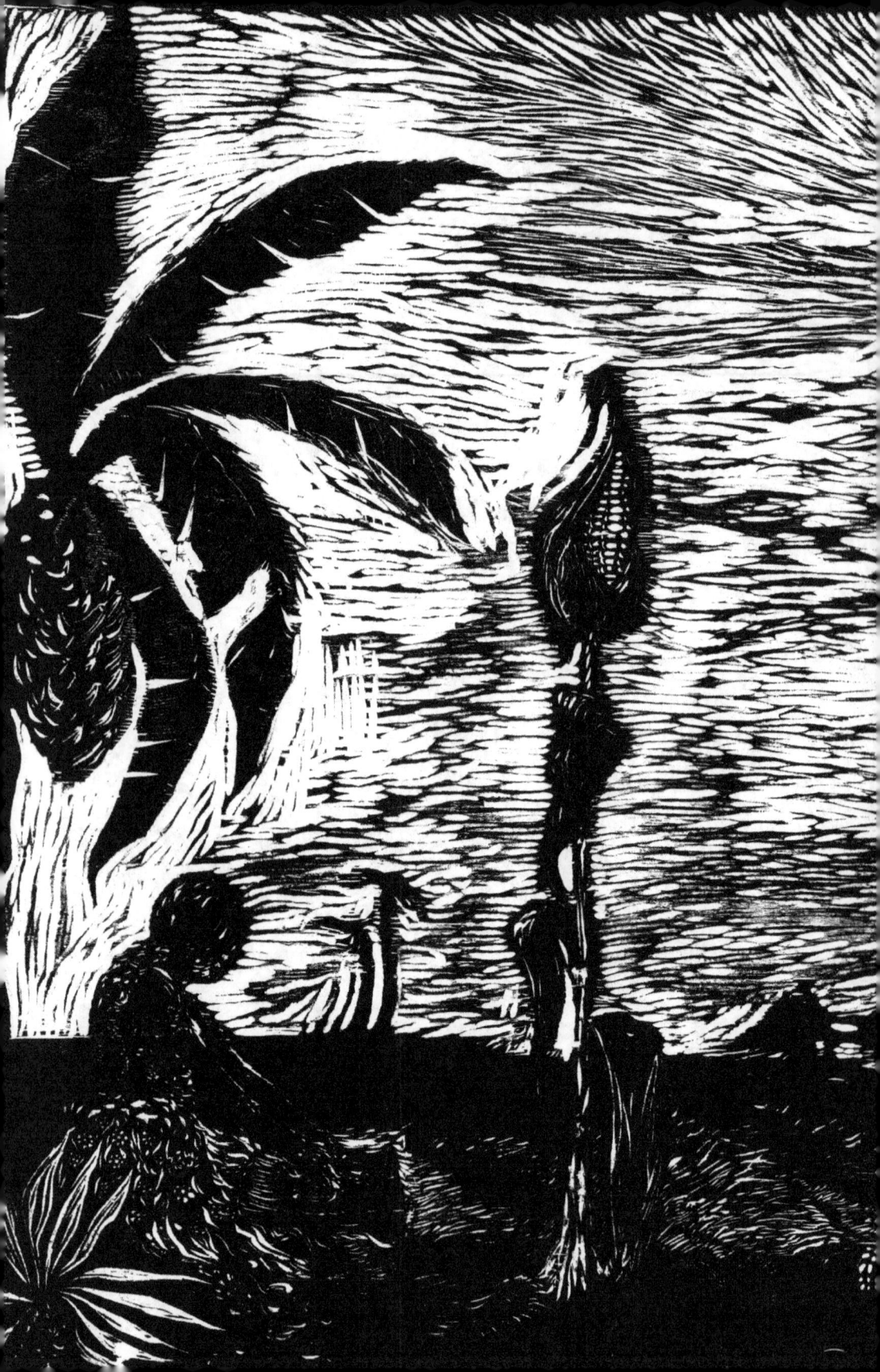

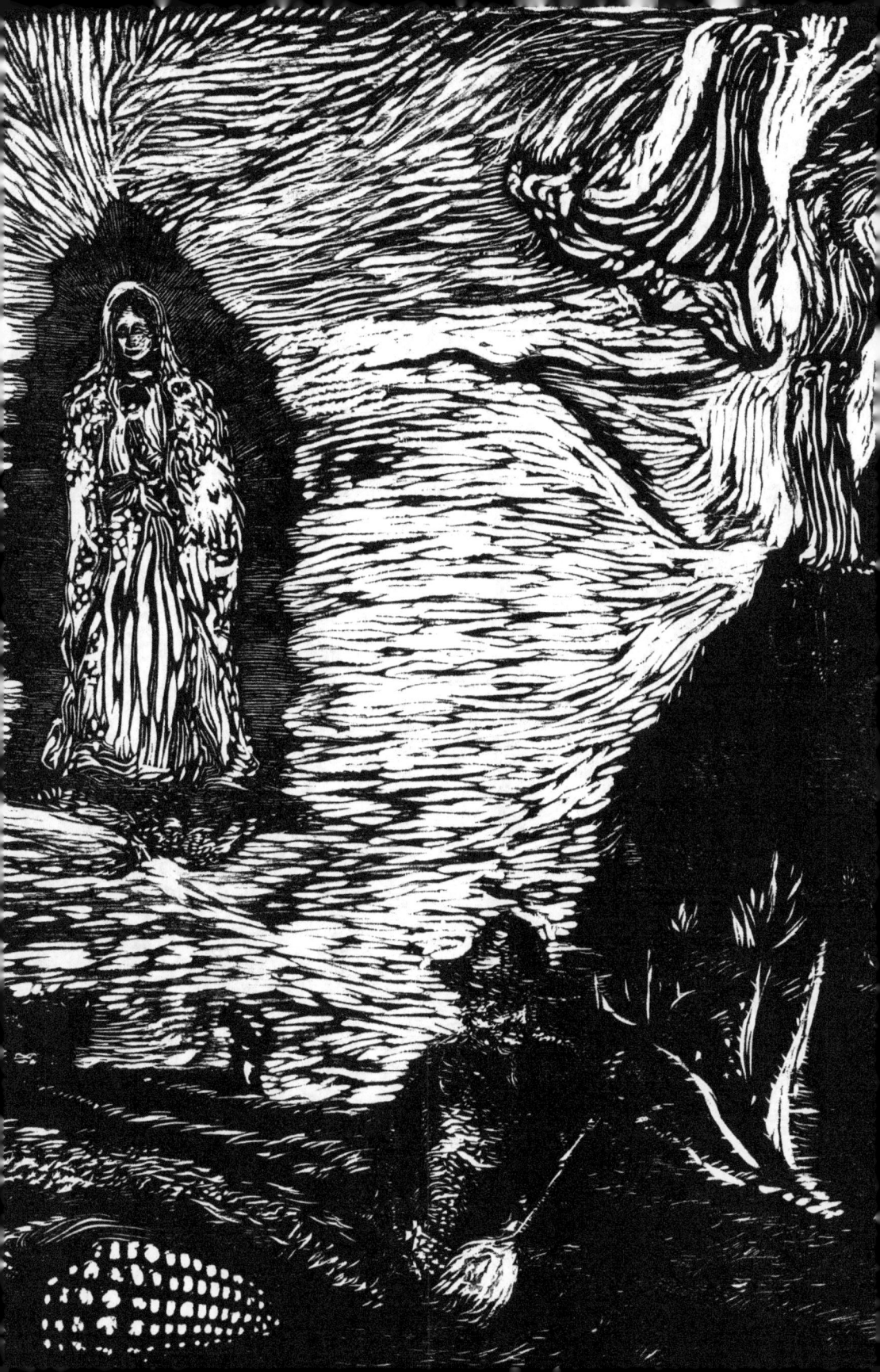

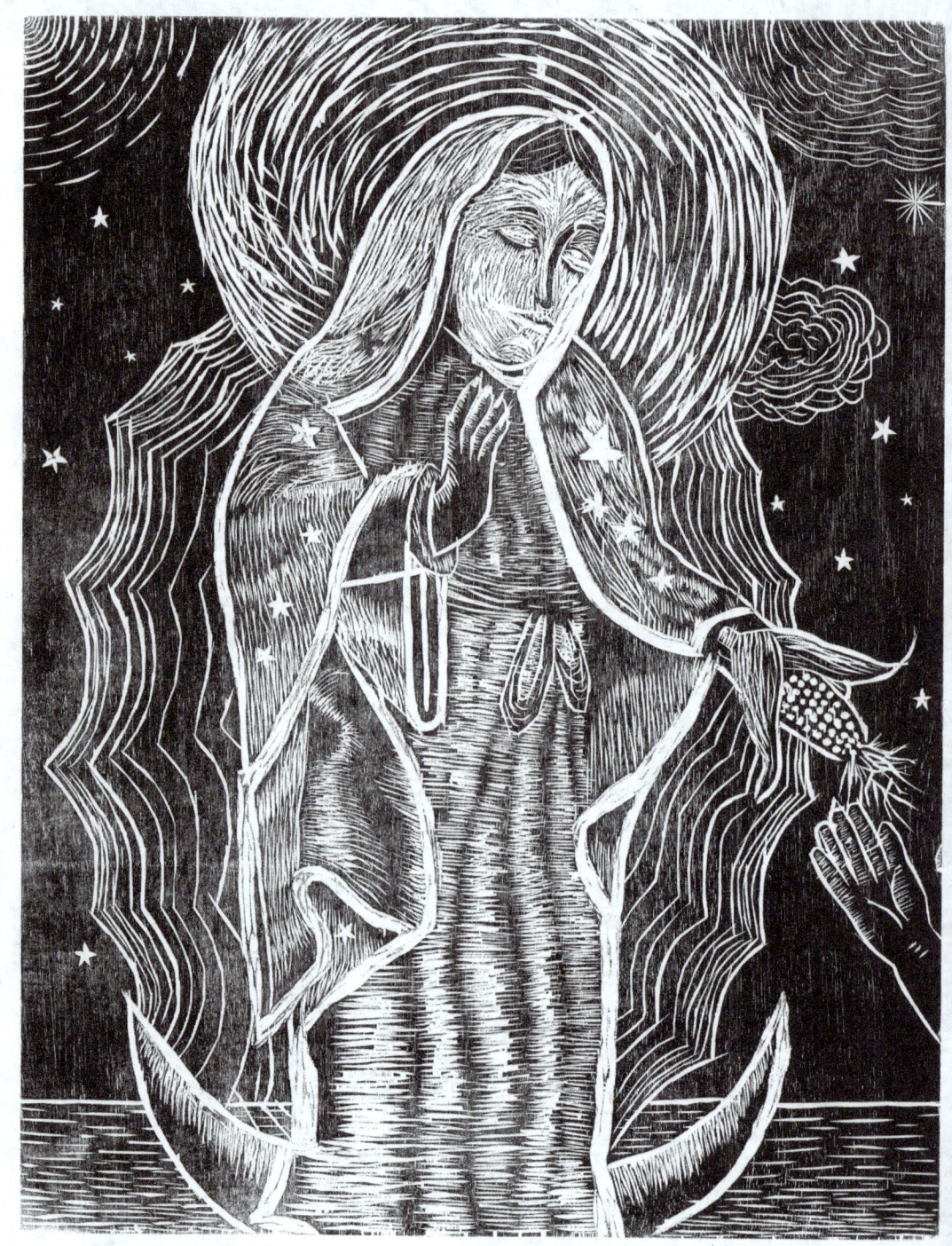

Virgin of Guadalupe, 2010, block print, 39" x 27 ½".
Woman on a White Cross, block print, 27 ½" 38 ¾". »
Previous page spread: *Virgen de Guadalupe*, 2006, block print, 27 ½" x 37 ¼".

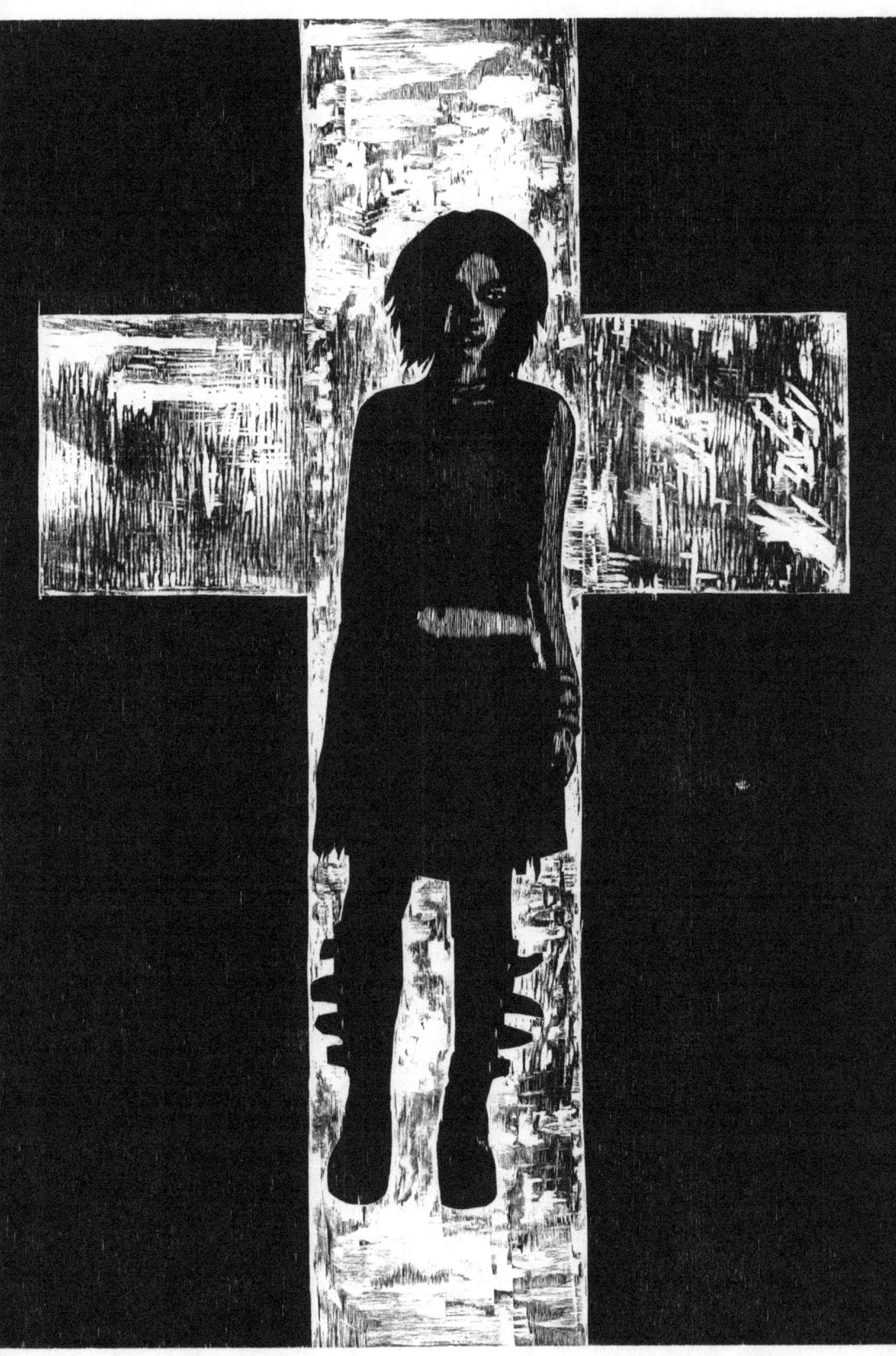

STAND UP, SPEAK UP

"We call on all artists who genuinely seek social transformation to organize to expand the creative movement of resistance and bring art to all sectors of society." —ASARO Manifesto

Buried Woman with Outstretched Hands depicts two hands reaching out from the ground as the stars overhead fall onto the mountainous desert landscape. Two strings of *papel picado* sway peacefully just out of the hands' reach. A face in the upper panels of these embroidered tissue papers looks out at the viewer. This action is further intensified by the eyes framing the face and staring forward. Below these panels three paper angels blow forward in a breeze wafting toward the viewer. As the woman raises herself out of the earth, the eyes crafted in the paper and propelled by the breeze invite the spectator to get up, stand up, and help pull this figure out of her unmarked grave.

Nacera en Oaxaca una Nueva Era (A New Era Will Come in Oaxaca) sends a similar message with indigenous symbolism. The central focus in this print captures a reclining, nude female birthing an ear of corn. Her lower body is framed by the serpent who releases her skeletal face from its mouth, while announcing a resurrection with its body. This figure, reflective of the cyclical motion between life and death, acts as an integral part of the Oaxacan landscape. The woman offers the people their primary sustenance, but she also reminds them of her power to kill. Reminiscent of the Aztec goddess Coatlique, known as a serpent-clad giver and taker of life, she calls to action those who might take her fruit. Her image is a symbol of indigenous permanency and resistance.

Dignidad: Lucha Resiste (Dignity: Fight Resist) indicates the pride in standing for the fruit the serpent woman bears for Oaxaca. The central figure in this piece emerges as a half-husked ear of corn among many others. Some below him "resist" and "fight." Others bring forth Molotov cocktails with corn tassel wicks. They all

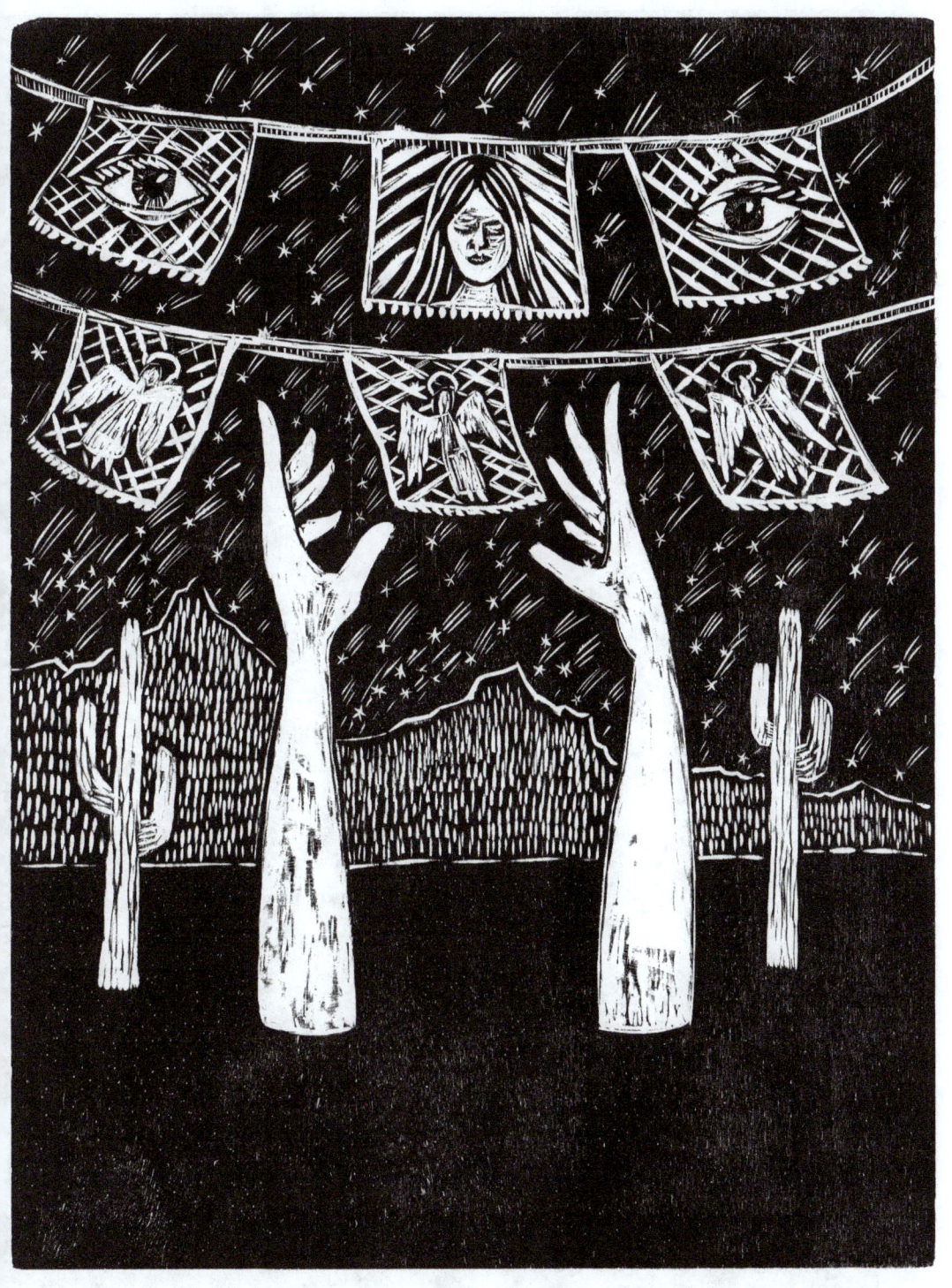

Buried Woman with Outstretched Hands, 2006, block print, 27 ½" x 39 ¼".

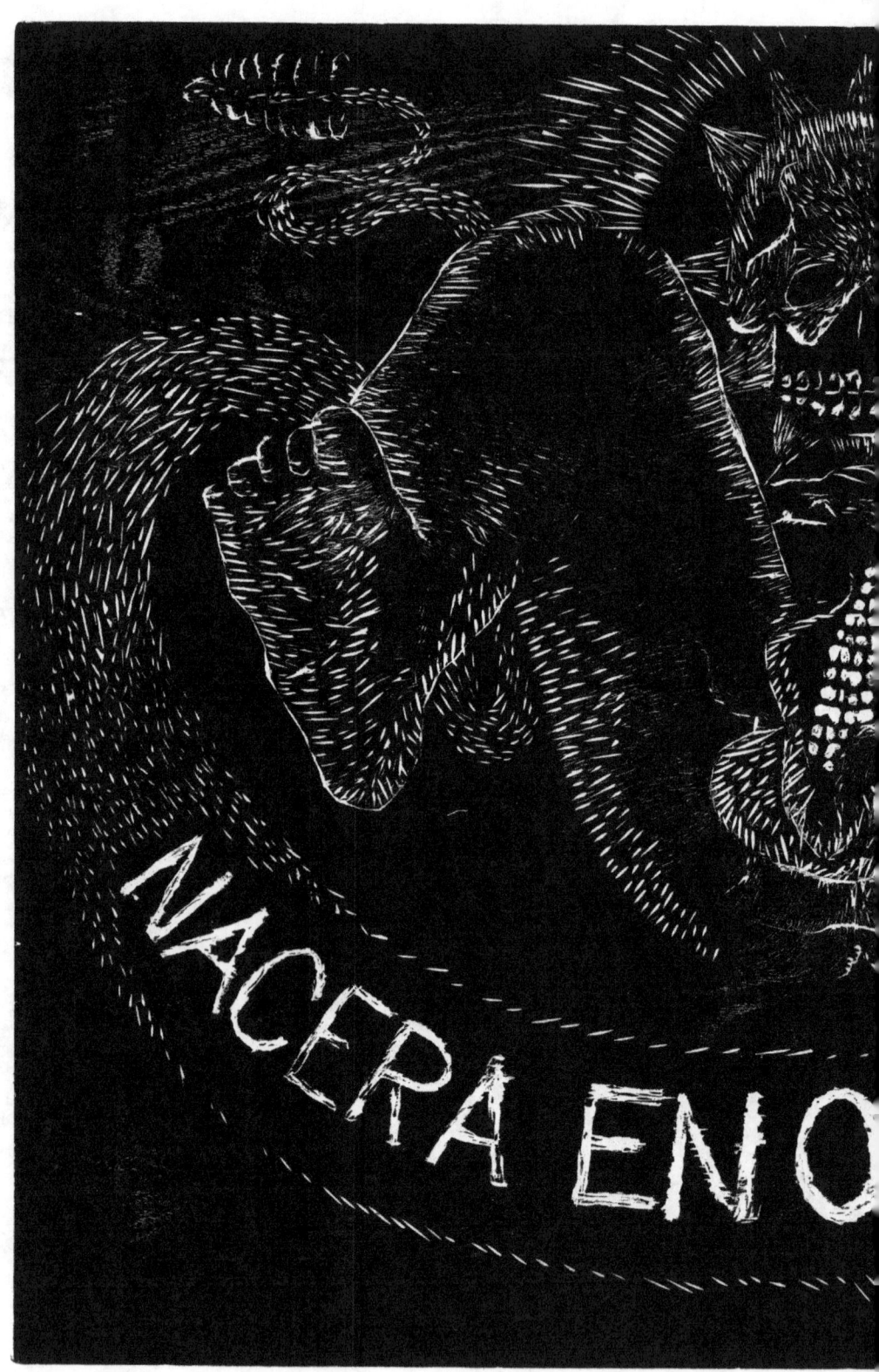

Nacera en Oaxaca una Nueva Era, 2010, block print, 39 ¼" x 27 ½".

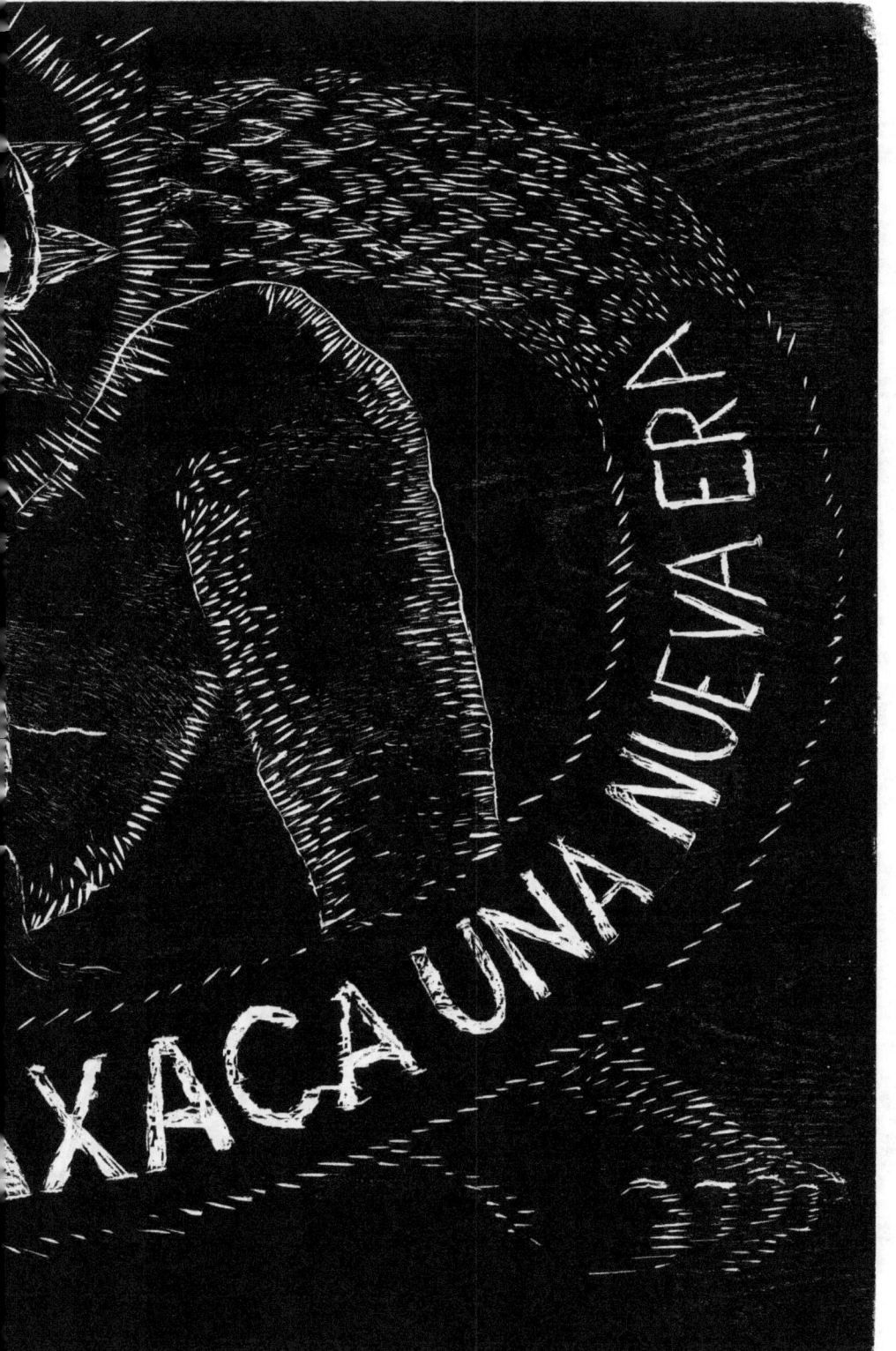

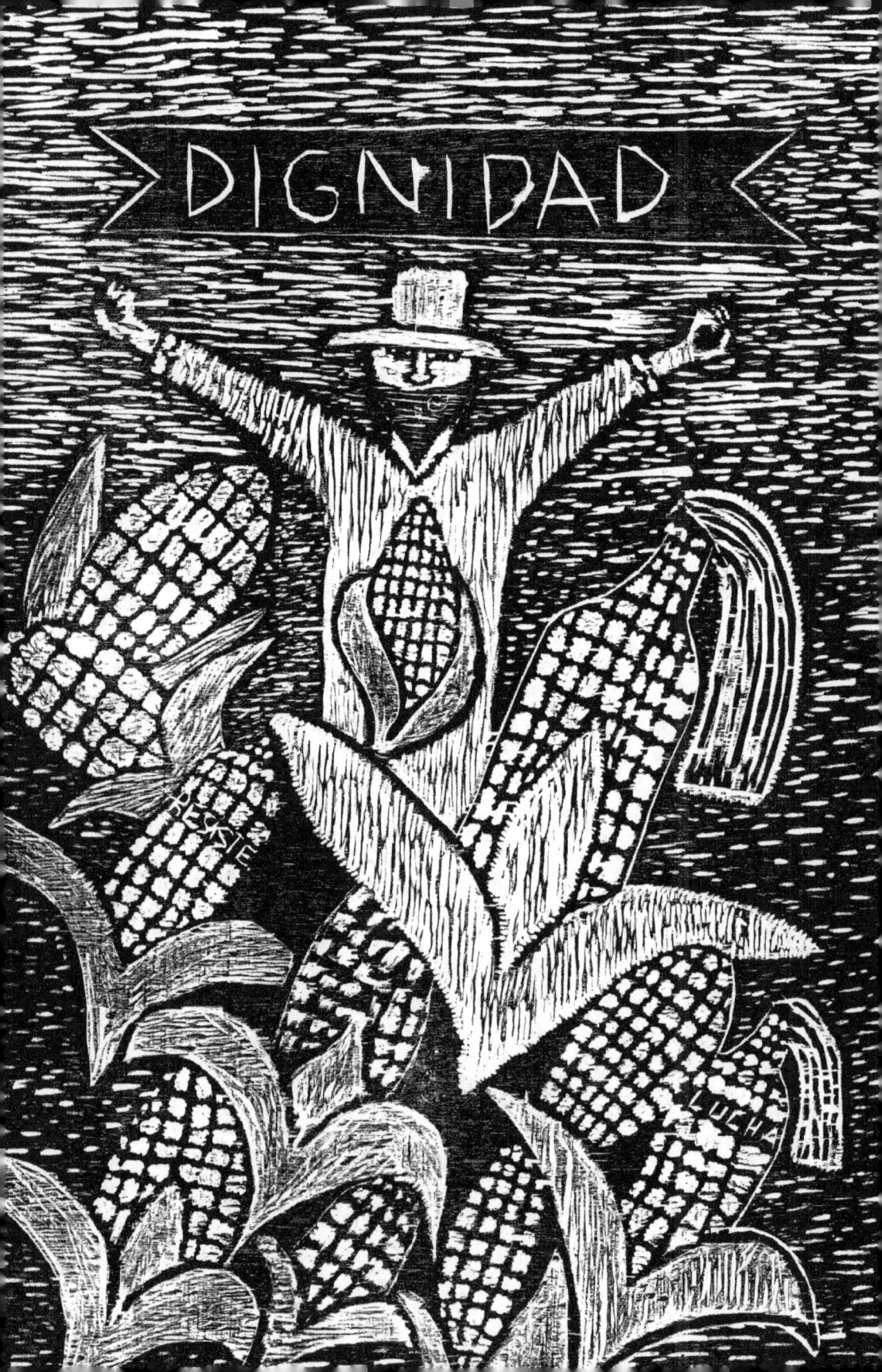

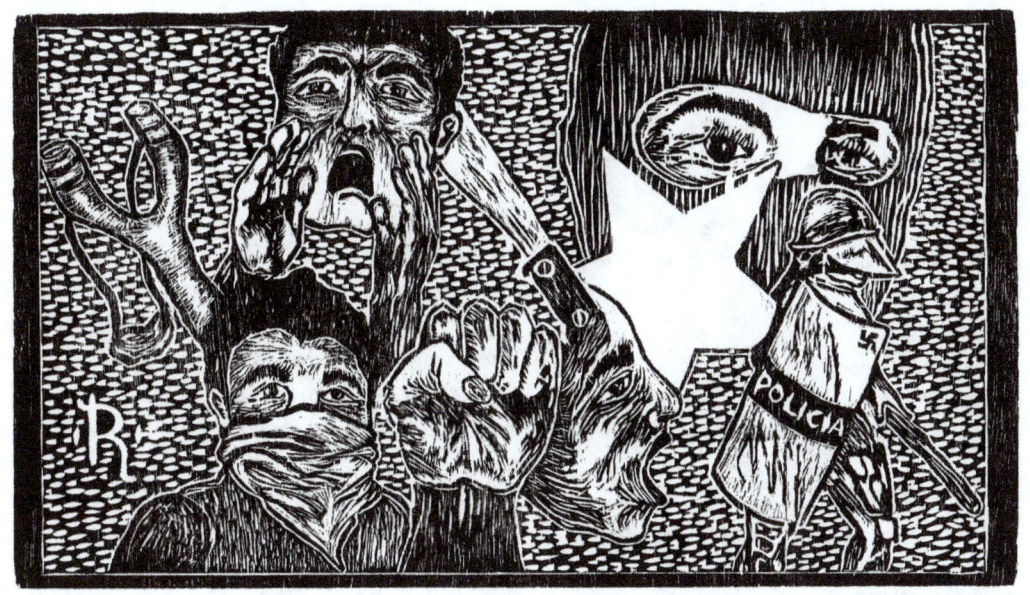

Policía, 2010, block print, 24 ¾" x 16 ¼".
« *Dignidad: Lucha, Resiste*, 2006, block print, 27 ½" x 39 ¼".

stand together, however, under the banner of dignity. The bandana across the central figure's face identifies him as a member of the resistance and his placement in the back high ground invites the viewer to stand with him, proud of their collective tie to this land and the fruit it offers them.

In each of these ASARO prints, the viewer's perspective originates from outside of the image, evoking an important connection between the artist and the viewer. These pieces invite viewers to stand up with the artists and participate in transforming the social reality.

"When we say *pueblo*, we're talking about the farm worker, the wage worker, the house-keeper, the student, etc. We are driven by them, to lift their morale, inspire them to keep fighting. We make graphic art for the people that are fighting. For those people who are asleep, we want to give them purpose—a desire to struggle and to take off their chains of exploitation." —Mario, ASARO

It is the essence of what ASARO's work is meant to accomplish. This final statement of ASARO's manifesto reflects their vision of art as a weapon for inclusion and their logo embodies this notion. The five-pointed red star in the barrel of the gun representing Oaxaca targets the viewer as the subject of the star and its mark.

Compositions that transpose the viewer into the scene accomplish this task as well. In *Presos Políticos Libertad* (Free Political Prisoners), the viewer is a prisoner

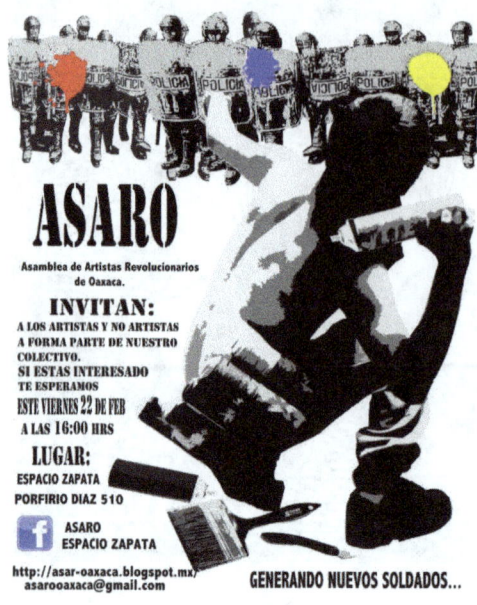

ASARO

Asamblea de Artistas Revolucionarios de Oaxaca.

INVITAN:

A LOS ARTISTAS Y NO ARTISTAS
A FORMA PARTE DE NUESTRO
COLECTIVO.
SI ESTAS INTERESADO
TE ESPERAMOS

ESTE VIERNES 22 DE FEB
A LAS 16:00 HRS

LUGAR:

ESPACIO ZAPATA
PORFIRIO DIAZ 510

f ASARO
ESPACIO ZAPATA

http://asar-oaxaca.blogspot.mx/
asarooaxaca@gmail.com

GENERANDO NUEVOS SOLDADOS...

ASARO Invita, 2008, color photocopy, 8 ½" x 11".

behind bars, watching two federal police in gas masks ready their clubs while helicopters fly overhead for reinforcement. There is no one else in the frame, but the police seem readied to protect the graffitied wall in their profile. References to other state sponsored attacks memorialize similar scenes in Tlatelolco, Acteal, and Atenco, where viewers, now prisoners to these backward scenes, have to get up and ask: why am I detained here and how should I respond? *El Indocumentado Carga el Bulto que el Legal no Cargaría* (The Undocumented Carries Baggage Legal Citizens Wouldn't) puts the viewer at the border fence, readied to climb on with all the "shit" one takes across that boundary.

In 2006 the Oaxacan people responded as a community united to speak up for themselves and for the teachers who had been needlessly attacked by police.

> "My sisters, my mom, my nieces and nephews and grandparents are all teachers. . . . I ran the risk to see how they were and in the heat of the moment. I saw how in the heat of the moment, people began to unite with each other." —Irving, ASARO

In the process they addressed a host of other issues and planned means for taking their public spaces back for their own communities. Replacing the hilltop auditorium version of the Guelaguetza performed for tourists with a community celebration of indigenous dance and song on the backstreets below the tourist scene set the stage. Other events followed, including several in which young people took to the streets with spray paint to manifest their grievances boldly on the walls of a UNESCO World Heritage Site.

The flier "ASARO Invita" (ASARO Invites) represents these scenes and reinforces their call to all artists. In the background of this image, a phalanx of riot police is lined across the top. In the foreground, an arsenal of painters' tools surrounds a kneeling individual. The shirtless figure in combat boots has his hand poised behind his head ready to pitch a can of spray paint as if it were a grenade. Splotches of colored paint indicate he has done so and that police were hit. The text invites both artists and non-artists to join their collective. Below the figure the text reads, "Generating new soldiers."

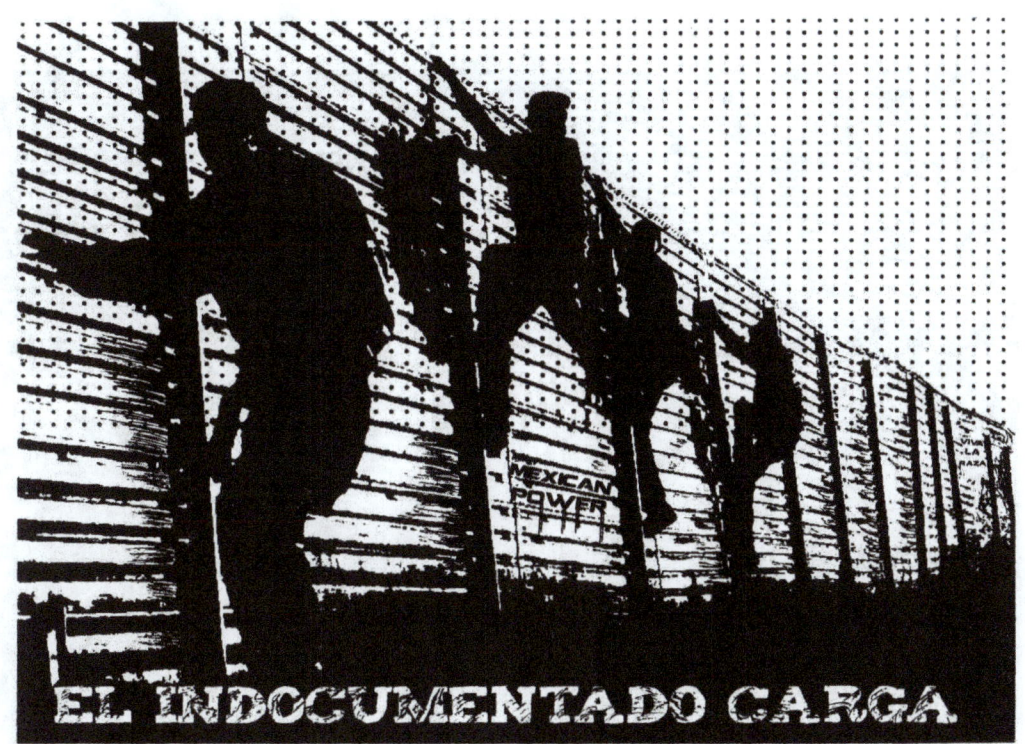

EL INDOCUMENTADO CARGA EL BULTO QUE EL LEGAL^NO CARGARIA

El Indocumentado Carga el Bulto que el Legal no Cargaría, 2011, screenprint, 9 ¾" x 8".

Democratic processes did merge out of the war that ASARO and other APPO-affiliated groups fought in 2006. Today ASARO works in a more politically stable environment, where they have notoriety—especially among young people—as artists committed to social action and education. They have also gained the respect of some government officials for their artistic excellence and their commitment to teaching young people about the power of art in the public space. The local government, now led now by a non-PRI affiliated governor who is from Oaxaca, recently began to sanction some of their work. In June 2013, ASARO was asked to paint murals on the walls of a central *mercado*. Currently, the Ministry of Education and Culture helps fund their youth workshops.

Despite disagreements between the new governor and APPO, governing forces are in active conversation with the community to create more political transparency and bring state-funded human rights violations to the forefront. ASARO's art plays an indispensable role in the formation of this discourse, giving ordinary people the courage to participate in their communities' transformations. Their Espacio Zapata also

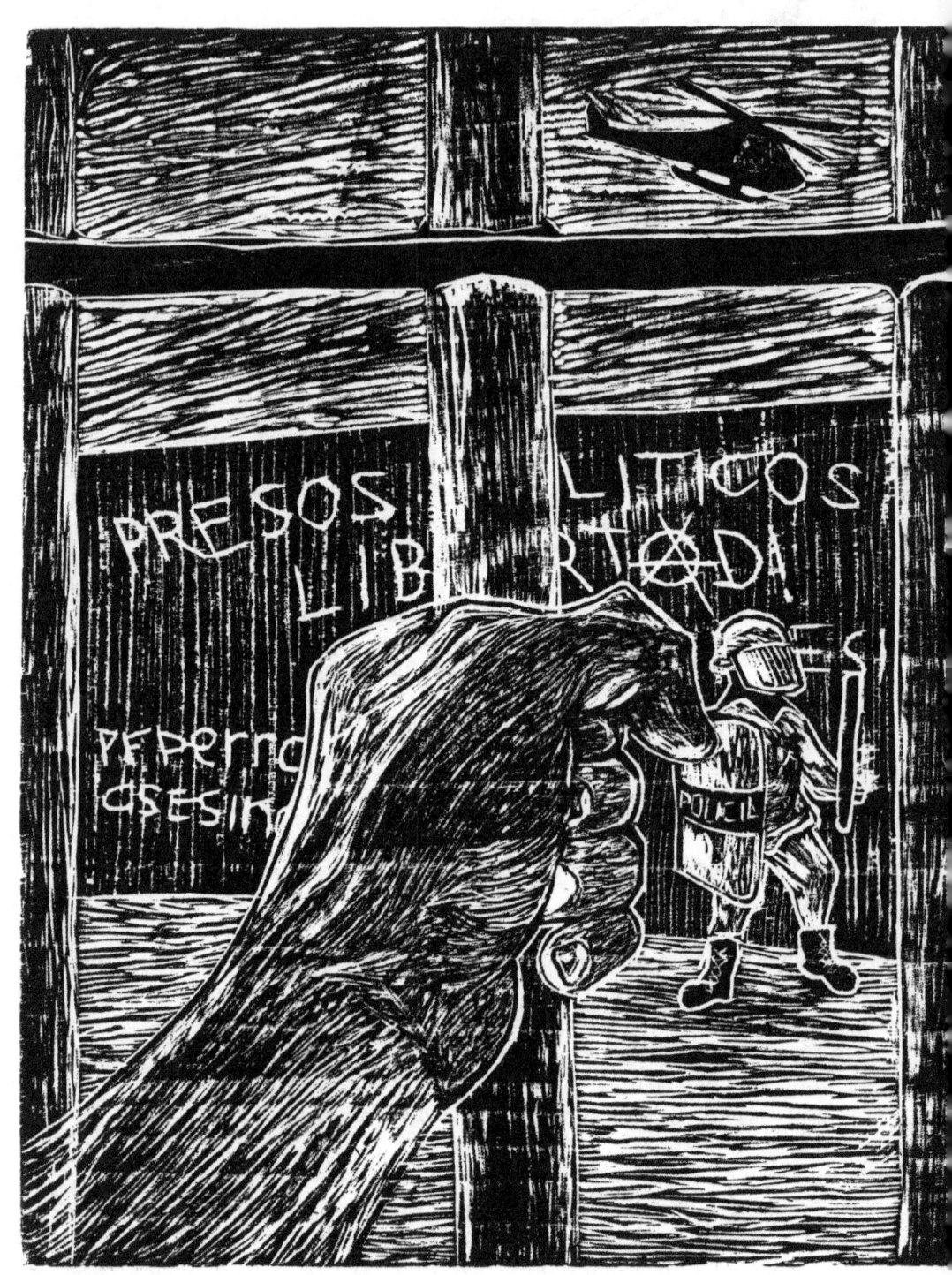

Presos Políticos Libertad, 2006, block print, 27 ¾" x 37 ½".

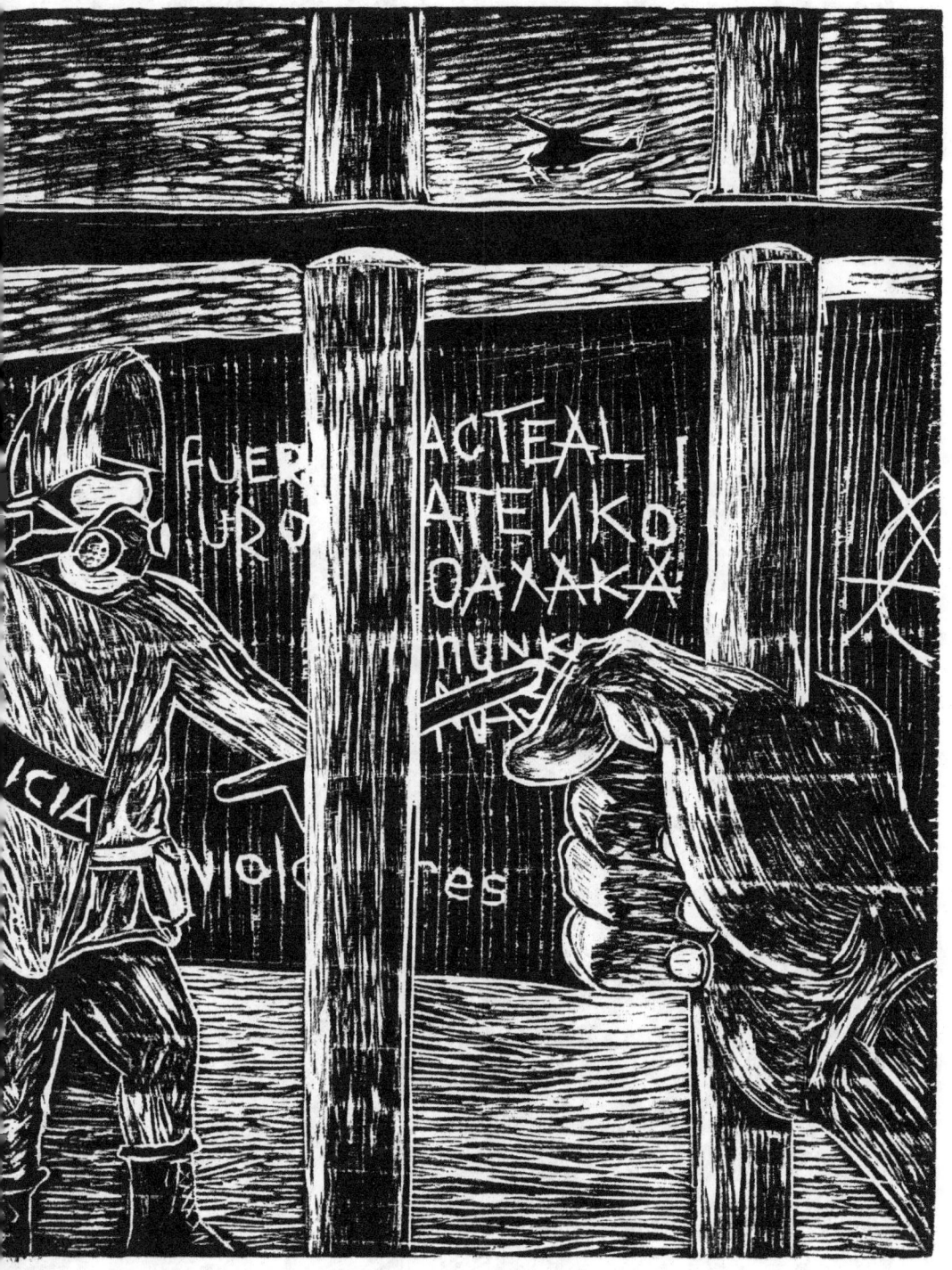

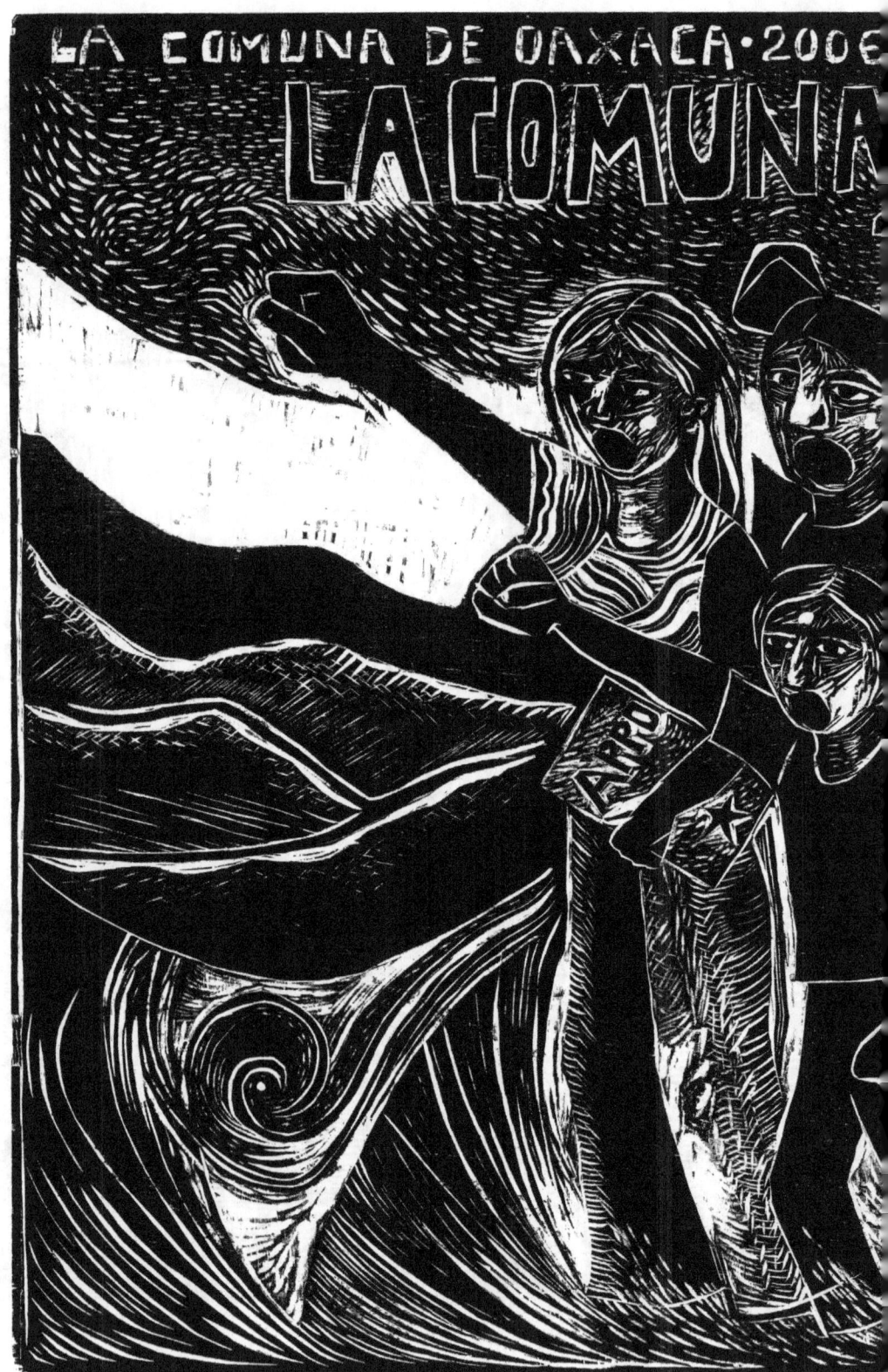

La Comuna de Oaxaca 2006, 2006, block print, 27 ½" x 39".

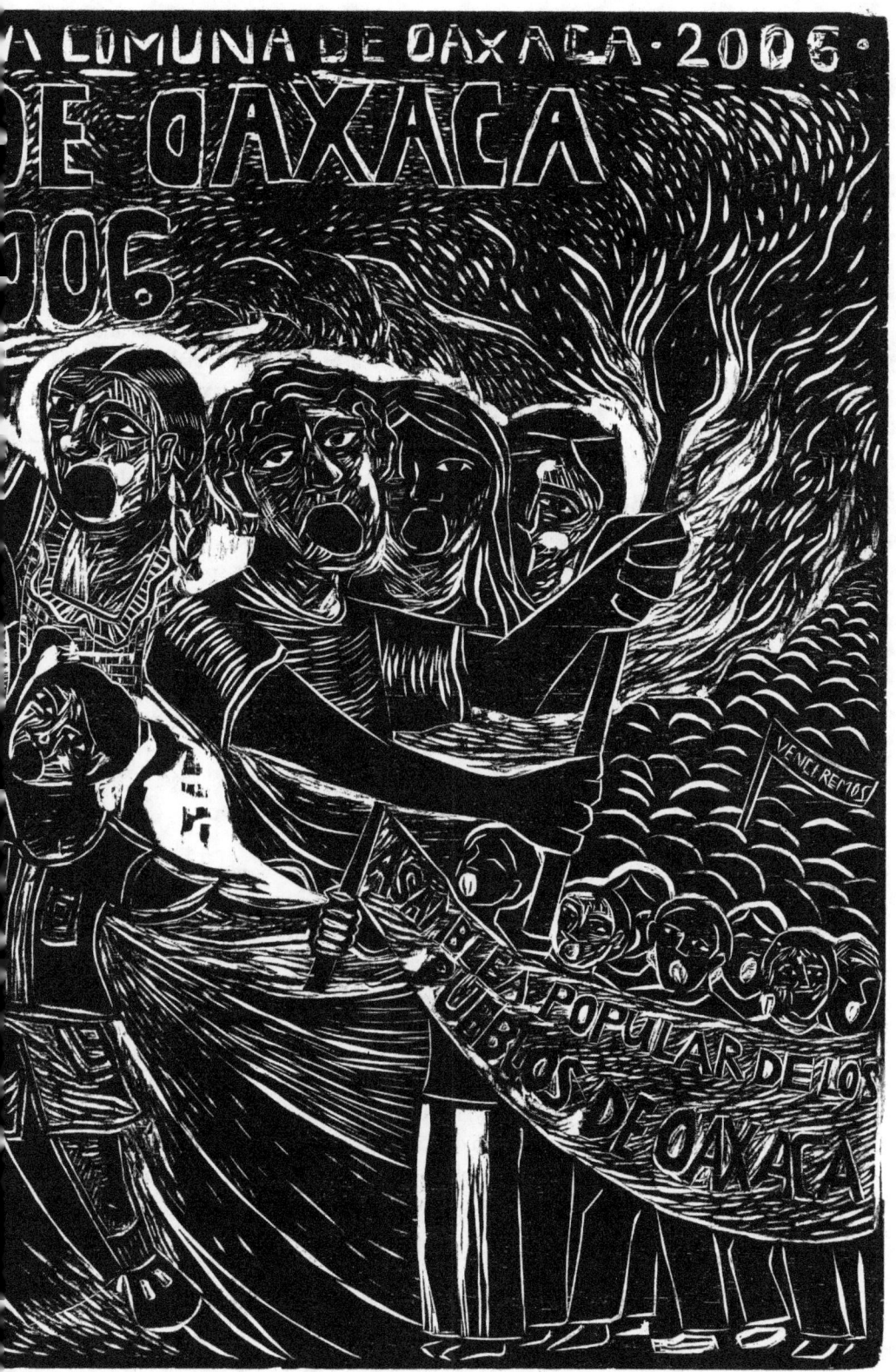

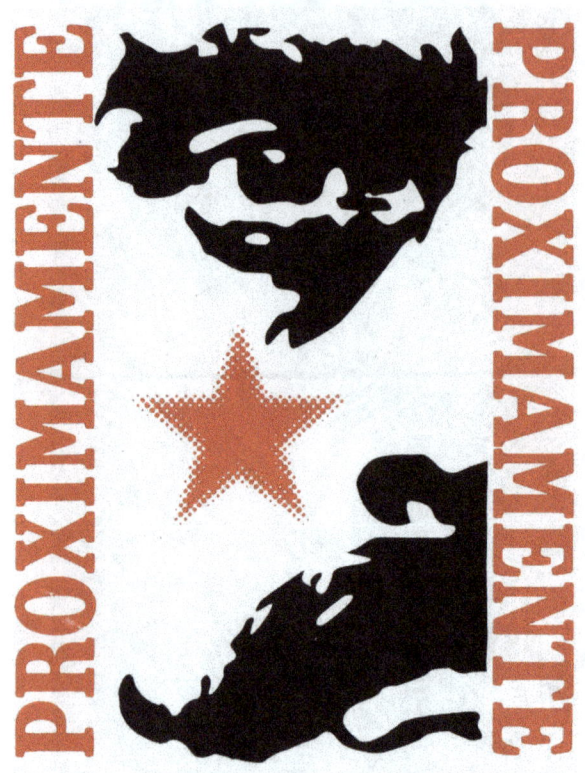

Proximamente, 2008, screenprint, 27" x 40".

lends space to creative projects outside of the arts. In July 2013, ASARO sponsored an initiative to collectively create a roof garden designed to teach local families how to grow in urban spaces and use it as a way to socially understand many of Oaxaca's native roots. This *sembrando conciencia* project, or growing/planting consciousness project, involves many who are not ASARO artists. Nonetheless their presence is integral to the space and the community.

"We use the same tactics that companies use to attack the city in order to sell things for consumption. We turn it around and say, all right then, here, consume change."
—Yescka, ASARO

In this sense, ASARO has become a fluid organization. People come and go. Some spray, some cook, some compost, and often community members come to drink a beer and talk with one another, surrounded by art and music. For ASARO, speaking is participating in an intervention as much as making sand sculptures that encroach on police phalanx or turning the blank walls of their city into storyboards. Sometimes it is printing, reprinting, and plastering physical and virtual walls with images that invite people to see what is hidden beneath the surface. At others, it is advertising and implementing events that bring differently talented people together in public celebrations of art, poetry, music, theatre, and communal learning. Sometimes it's just being in their space with other people enjoying the company. The important thing is the dialogue made possible through access to art and community.

ASARO continues to do graphic art with social content, giving workshops in various locations. It has opened the Espacio Zapata as an alternative workshop/gallery resisting the dominant aesthetic in the state, working instead to present social and political issues both in Oaxaca and the world, and building bridges with various individuals and organizations.

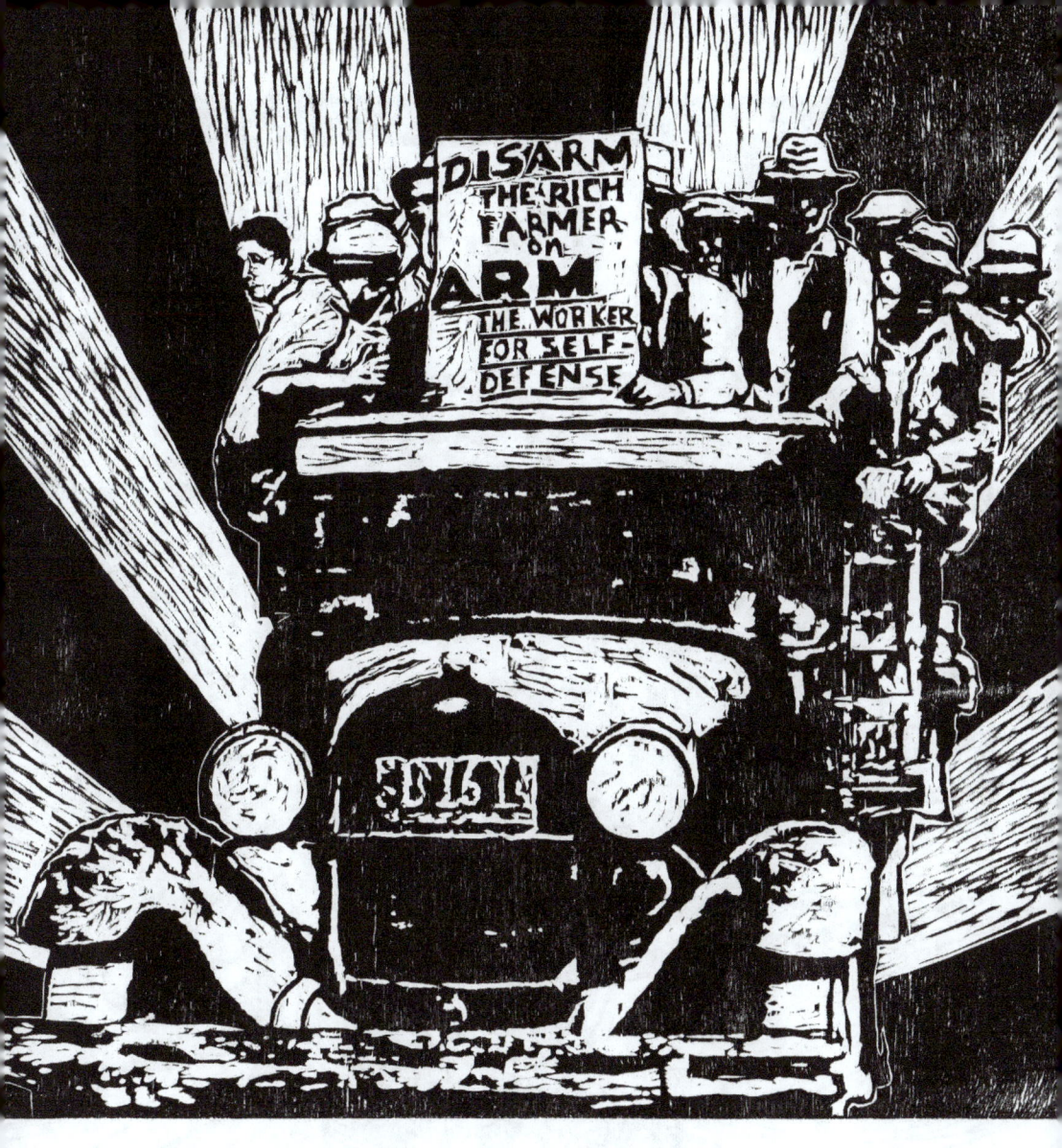

Disarm the Rich Farmer or Arm the Worker for Self-Defense, 2012, block print, 27 ½" x 28 ¼".

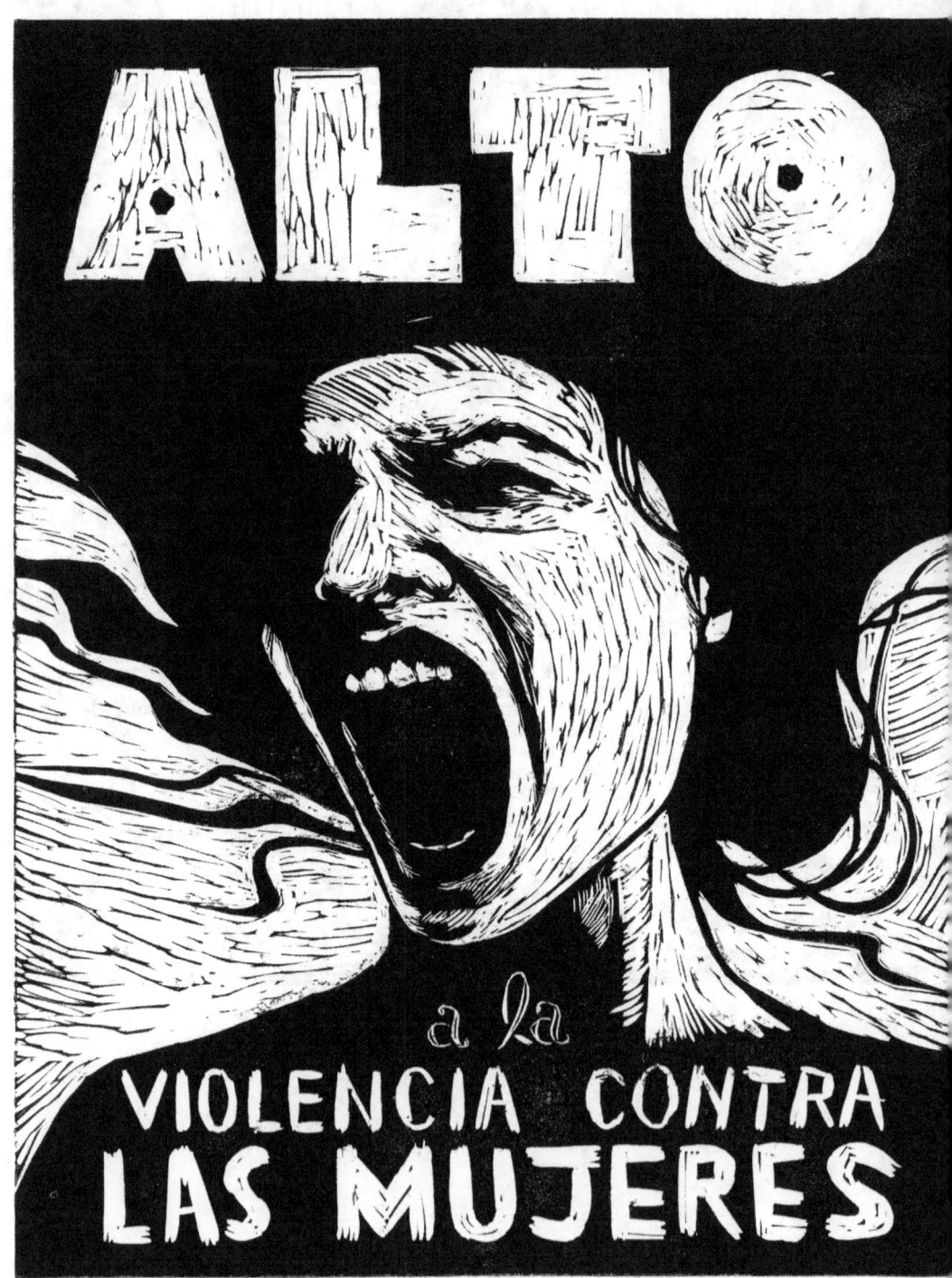

Alto a la Violencia Contra las Mujeres, 2010, block print, 18 ¼" x 22 ½".

ACKNOWLEDGMENTS

We are grateful for generous funding provided by the College of University Libraries and Learning Sciences at UNM. The careful eyes of Ramsey Kanaan, Craig O'Hara, and Gregory Nipper at PM Press and the thoughtful design of Josh MacPhee at Antumbra Design and the documentary photography of Itandehui Franco Ortiz have resulted in a book more impressive than we imagined. We also thank our friends, families, and communities as well as each other. Every chapter in this book reflects pieces contributed by each of us, enhanced by those in our personal and professional lives. We are especially obliged to the people of Oaxaca, particularly those at Café Atila, Taller Siquieros, and Proyecto Chicatana.

Some individuals and organizations deserve special mention for helping us get the ball rolling. They include: Mario Guzman, Cesar Chavez, Yescka, Irving Herrera, Ita, Chapo, and Line of the Espacio Zapata & ASARO; Beverly Karno, who turned us on to ASARO; Pauline Heffern, Sarah Kostelecky, Jacobo Baca, Fran Wilkinson, Sever Bordineau, Susan Awe, Wendy Pedersen, Kathleen Keating, Martha Bedard, Megan Jirón, and Micheal Hoopes in the libraries at UNM; and Mike Kelly and Claire-Lise Bénaud in the Center for Southwest Research. Patricia Covarrubias, Mayra Washington, Holly Barnett-Sanchez, Margaret Jackson, Leila Lehnen and Richard Wood in Latin American Studies at UNM have helped guide Mike in the formulation of ideas around ASARO. Jessica Mills, Wendy Wilson, Theresa Avila, Kim Romero-Oak, Camille Romero, Erika Romero, Kevin S. Graham, Flor Rodriguez-Graham, Alma Guadalupe Rodriguez, Electron Sanx, and Eduardo Vera have helped us express thoughts more clearly and deal with frustrations throughout this process.

This book accompanies an exhibit titled Getting Up Pa'l Pueblo: Tagging ASAR-Oaxaca Prints and Stencils at the National Hispanic Cultural Center (NHCC) in Albuquerque, New Mexico, and an online tagging component constructed by the Academic and Research Technologies team in the UNM libraries. Since the book would not exist without the exhibit we must also acknowledge the generous funding of the New Mexico Humanities Council for the exhibit; the thoughtfulness and support of Tey Mariana Nunn, David Gabel, and Richard Garcia at the NHCC; and generous contributions from the Latin American and Iberian Institute (LAII), the Southwest Hispanic Research Institute (SHRI), the College of Fine Arts, and the Center for Regional Studies at UNM. The exhibit is a memorial to Distinguished Professor of Art History, David Craven (1951–2012), whose infectious enthusiasm for Latin American art, theory, and popular movements is reflected in these projects.

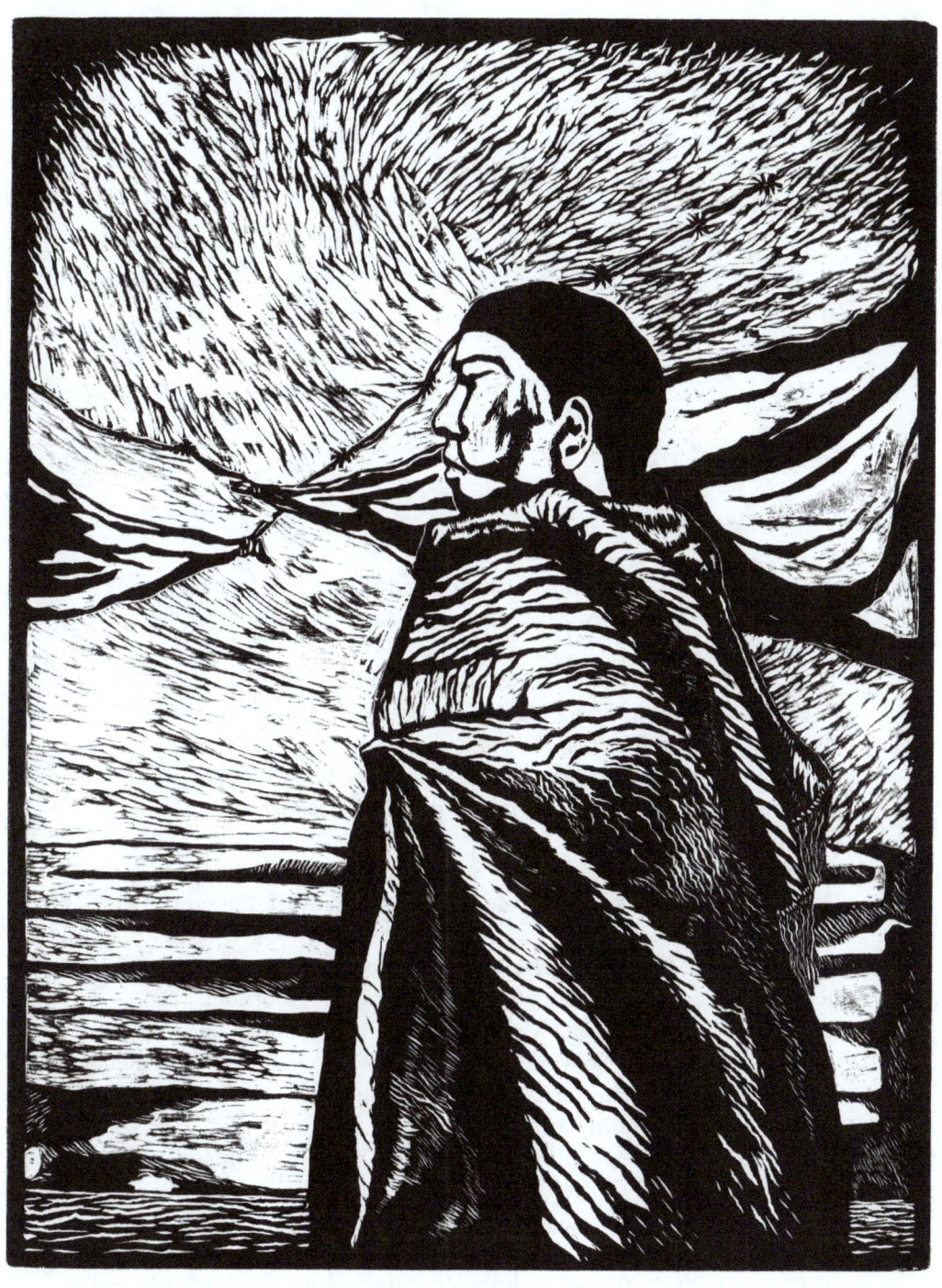

Indigenous Man with Sun, 2010, block print, 27 ½" x 39 ¼".

BIBLIOGRAPHY

Adler, Marina A. "Collective Identity Formation and Collective Action Framing in a Mexican 'Movement of Movements.'" *Interface: A Journal for and about Social Movements* 4 (2012): 287–315.

———. "The Role of Grassroots Organizations in the Promotion of Sustainable Indigenous Communities in Mexico." *International Journal of Humanities and Social Science* 2, no. 2 (2012): 235–48.

Aquino, Arnulfo. Imágenes de rebelión y resistencia: ASARO-Oaxaca 2006." *Discurso Visual: Revista Digital* 14 (2010). http://discursovisual.net/dvweb14/aportes/apoarnulfo.htm.

Arenas, Ivan. "Rearticulating the Social: Spatial Practices, Collective Subjects, and Oaxaca's Art of Protest." PhD dissertation, University of California, Berkeley, 2011.

ASARO. "ASARO Manifesto." *ASAR-Oaxaca BlogSpot* (updated June 2011). Accessed December 22, 2013. http://asar-oaxaca.blogspot.com.

Bénaud, Claire-Lise, and Suzanne M. Schadl. "ASARO: Claiming Space in Digital Objects and Social Networks," in *SALALM* #56 Preserving Memory: Documenting and Archiving Latin American Human Rights. Ed. Nerea Lamas (New Orleans: SALALM Secretariat: 2013).

Center for Southwest Research, University of New Mexico, Asamblea de Artistas Revolucionarios de Oaxaca Pictorial Collection, PICT 2010-005. http://econtent.unm.edu/cdm/landingpage/collection/asamblea.

———. Fernando Gamboa Collection of Prints by José Guadalupe Posada, 1888–1944, PICT, 000–428. http://econtent.unm.edu/cdm/landingpage/collection/joseguad.

Denham, Diana, and the C.A.S.A. Collective, eds. *Teaching Rebellion: Stories from the Grassroots Mobilization in Oaxaca*. Oakland: PM Press, 2008.

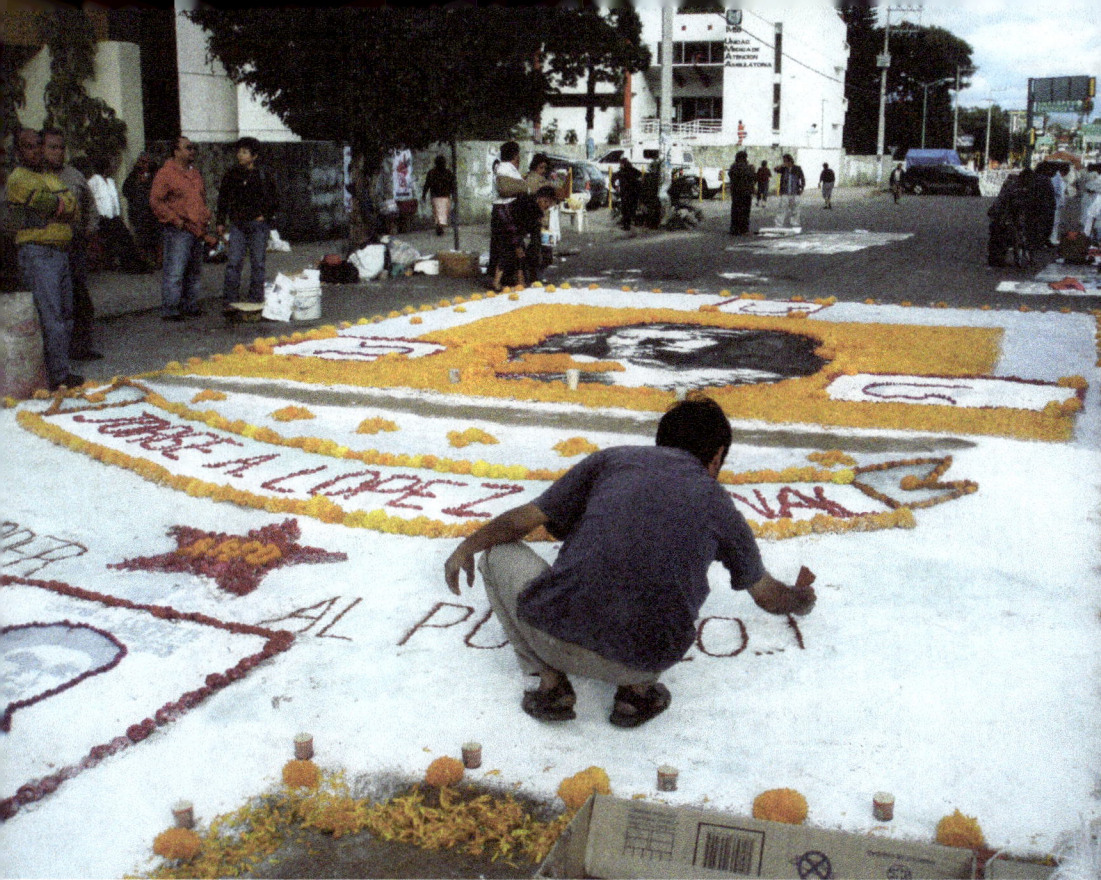

Memorial, 2007, sand sculpture.

Esteva, Gustavo. "The Asamblea Popular de los Pueblos de Oaxaca, APPO: A Chronicle of Radical Democracy." *Latin American Perspectives* 34 (2007): 129–44.

_____. "The Society of the Different, Part 2: We Are People of Corn: Life, Metaphor, Autonomy Oaxaca, Oaxaca, Mexico." *Motion Magazine* (April 2006). http://www.inmotionmagazine.com/global/gest_int_2.html.

Franco Ortiz, Itandehui. "El deleite de la transgresión. Graffiti y gráfica política callejera en la ciudad de Oaxaca," Thesis, Escuela Nacional de Antropología e Historia, Universidad Nacional Autónoma de México, Mexico City, 2011.

Frisari, Spartaco "Arte y movimiento en las calles de Oaxaca." *Desinformemonos* (June 30, 2011). http://desinformemonos.org/2010/07/arte-y-movimiento-en-las-calles-de-oaxaca/

Gibler, John. *Mexico Unconquered: Chronicles of Power and Revolt.* San Francisco: City Lights, 2009.

Híjar, Alberto. "Ideología, muralismo y muralismos." *Crónicas. El Muralismo, Producto de la Revolución Mexicana, en América* 14 (2011). http://www.revistas.unam.mx/index.php/cronicas/issue/view/2072/showToc.

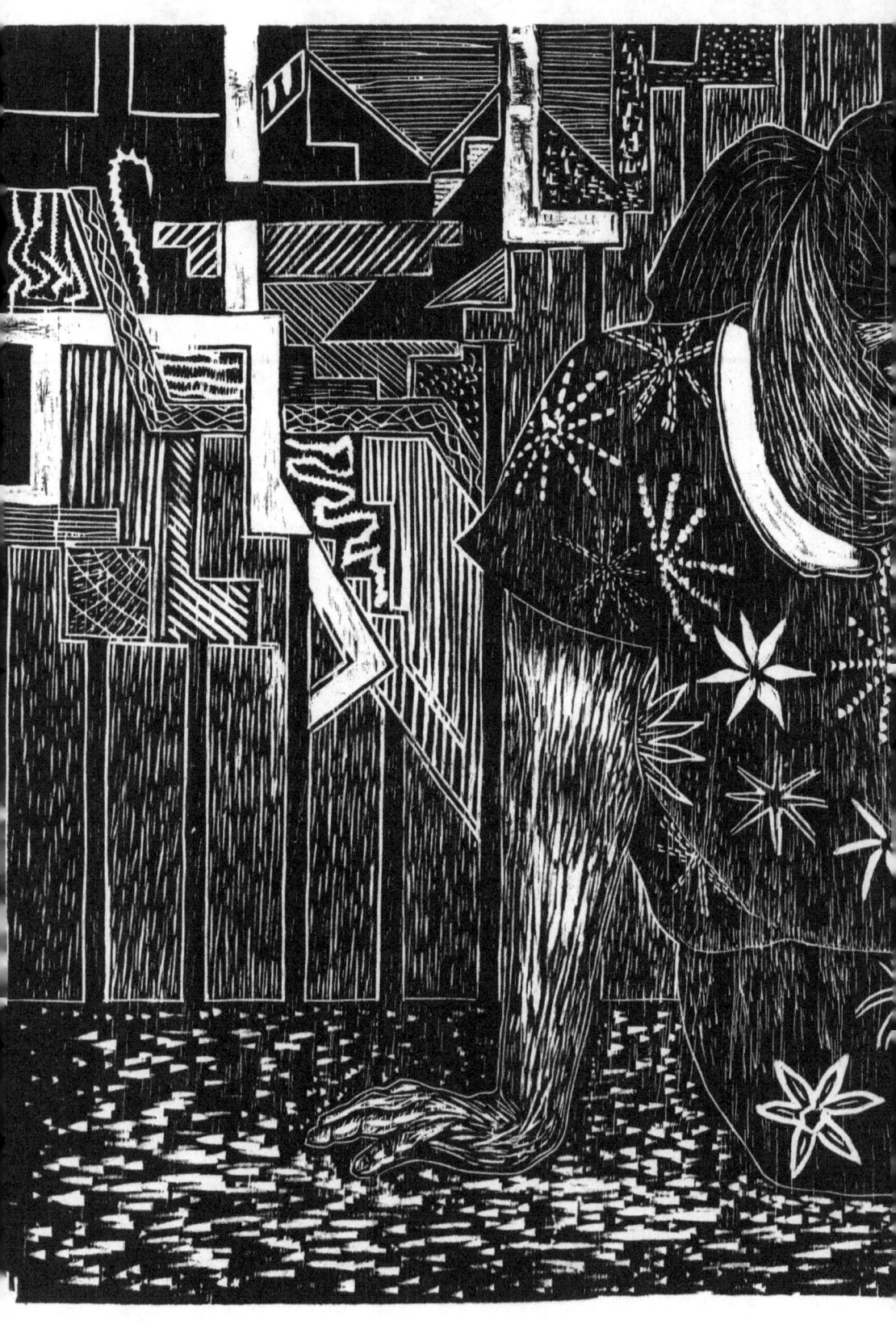

Indigenous Woman Sitting on the Ground, 2009, block print , 27 ½" x 19 ¾".

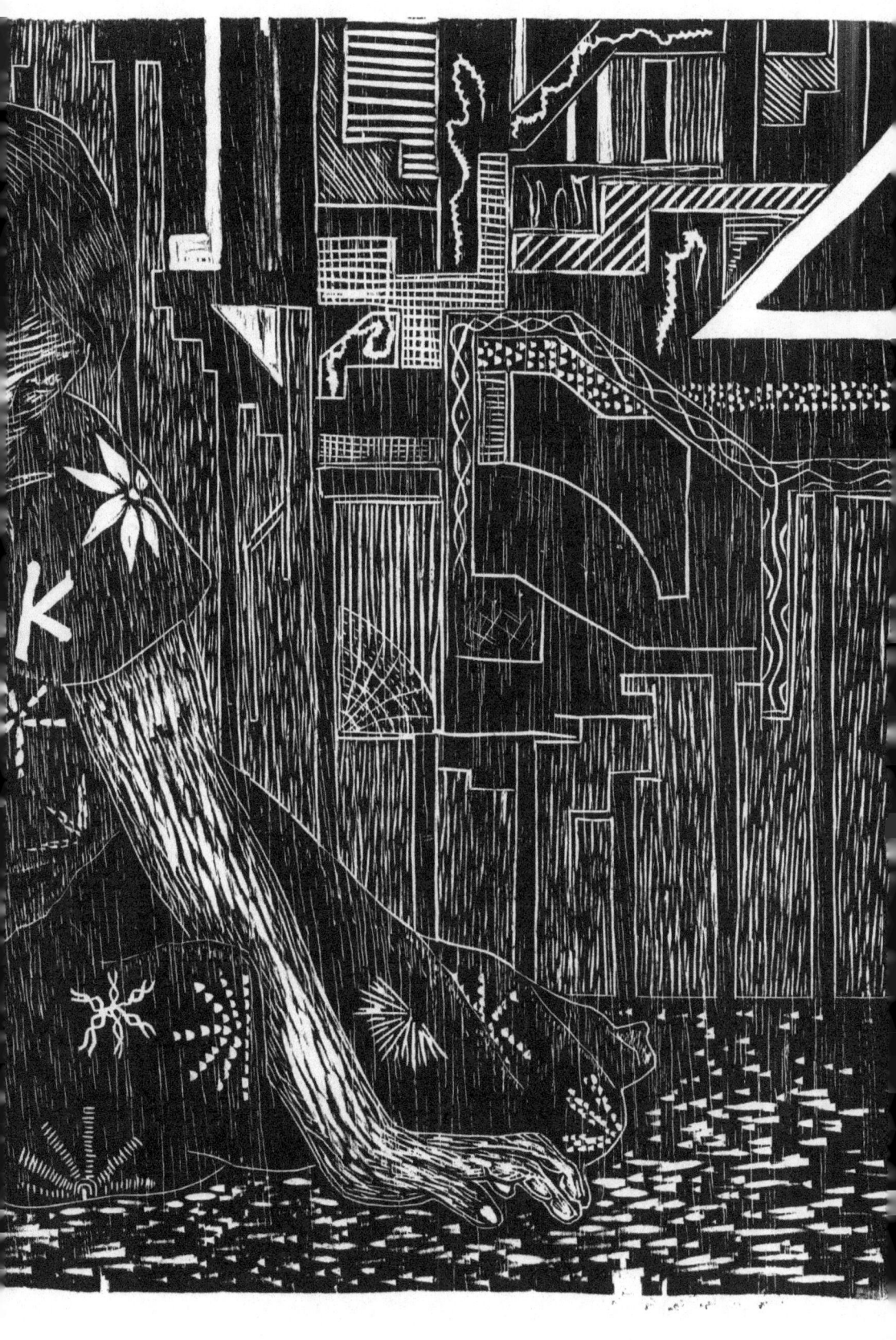

Kuper, Peter. *Diario de Oaxaca*. Introduction by Martín Solares. Oakland: PM Press, 2010.

Latin American Studies Association. *Violations against Freedoms of Inquiry and Expression in Oaxaca de Juárez: Report by the Fact-Finding Delegation of the Latin American Studies Association on the Impact of the 2006 Social Conflict* (2007) Accessed December 22, 2013. http://lasa.international.pitt.edu/members/news/files/LASA-OaxacaDelegationReport.pdf.

McCloskey, Kevin. "Dispatch from Mexico: Oaxaca's Vibrant Print Scene," *Printeresting* (September 12, 2012). http://www.printeresting.org/2012/09/12/dispatch-from-mexico-oaxacas-vibrant-print-scene/.

_____. "Oaxaca: 'Plaza of the Resistance,' Espacio Zapata & the ASARO Artists" *CommonSense 2: A Journal of Progressive Thought* 19 (March 2009). http://commonsense2.com/2009/03/politics-world/oaxaca-update/.

_____. "Mexico 2010 and an Update on ASARO of Oaxaca." *CommonSense 2: A Journal of Progressive Thought* 33 (February 2010). http://commonsense2.com/2010/02/politics-world/mexico-2010-and-an-update-on-asaro-of-oaxaca/.

_____. "Shinzaburo Takeda, A Japanese Master Artist in Mexico" *CommonSense 2: A Journal of Progressive Thought* 21 (May 2009). http://commonsense2.com/2009/05/art-culture/shinzaburo-takeda-a-japanese-master-artist-in-mexico/.

Meyer, Lois, and Benjamín Maldonado. *New World of Indigenous Resistance: Noam Chomsky and Voices from North, South, and Central America*. San Francisco: City Lights Books, 2010.

Nash, June. "The Fiesta of the Word: The Zapatista Uprising and Radical Democracy in Mexico." *American Anthropologist* 99, no. 2 (1997): 261–74.

Nevaer, Louis EV. *Protest Graffiti Mexico: Oaxaca*. New York: Mark Batty, 2009.

Osorno, Diego Enrique. *Oaxaca sitiada: la primera insurrección del siglo XXI*. Mexico City: Grijalbo Mondadori, 2007.

Rovingradio, "31st October—Political graffiti: Yescka, Oaxaca, Mexico" December 22, 2012. http://rovingradio.wordpress.com/2012/12/22/31st-october-political-graffiti-yescka-oaxaca-mexico/.

Saavedra, Edgar. "ASARO: Paradojas del Graffiti subversivo." *Mujeres* 6, no. 67 (2007): 45–46.

Secretaría de las Culturas y Artes de Oaxaca (SECULTA). "Clausura SECULTA los talleres artísticos, en comunidades rurales." March 5, 2013. http://www.culturasyartes.oaxaca.gob.mx/?p=5954.

Stephen, Lynn. "'We Are Brown, We Are Short, We Are Fat . . . We Are the Face of Oaxaca': Women Leaders in the Oaxaca Rebellion." *Socialism and Democracy* 21, no. 2 (2007): 97–112.

_____. *Transborder Lives: Indigenous Oaxacans in Mexico, and Oregon*. Durham, NC: Duke University Press, 2007.

Related Blogs and Social Networking Sites

http://www.myspace.com/revueltaculturalmexicana
http://www.myspace.com/asaroaxaca
http://www.myspace.com/tianguis_cultural
https://www.facebook.com/pages/ASARO-Asamblea-de-Artistas-
        Revolucionarios-de-Oaxaca/137205519697487
https://www.facebook.com/pages/ESPACIO-ZAPATA/136766426395176
https://www.facebook.com/guerilla.art.mx

14 de Juni No Se Olvida, 2007, street stencil and graffiti.
Following page: ASARO wheatpasting prints at the Festival de Puntos, 2011.

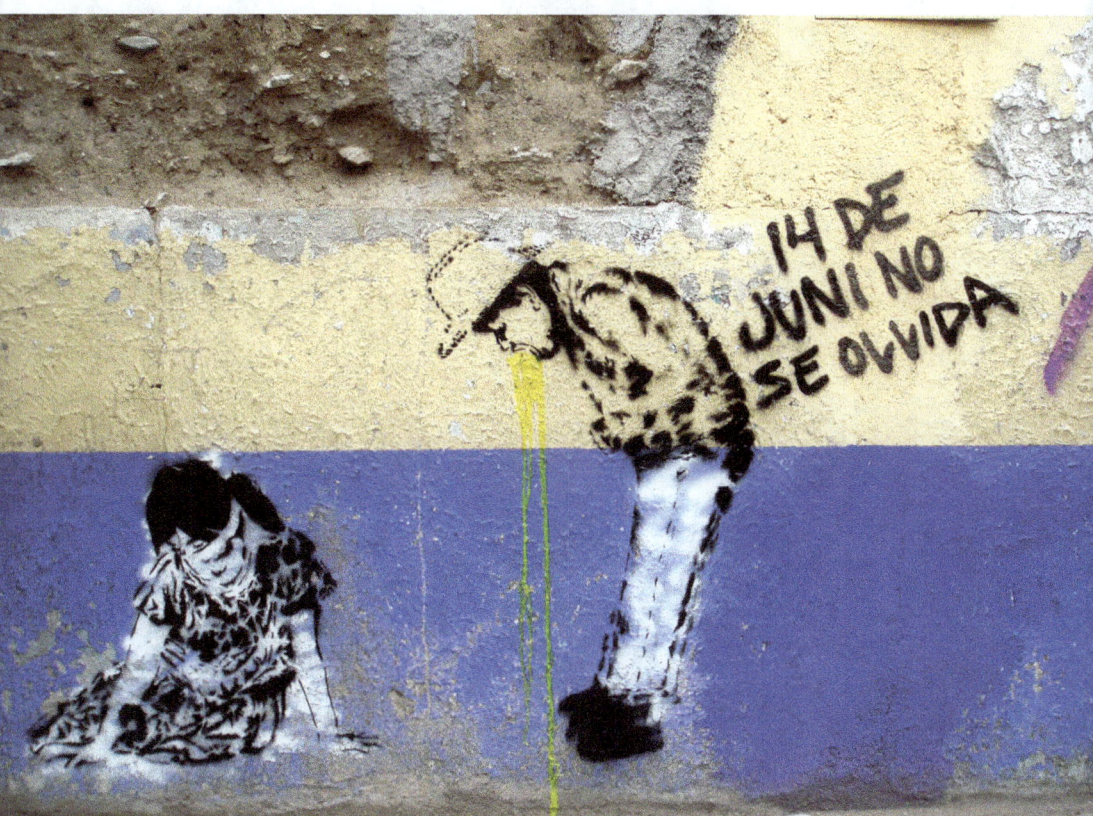

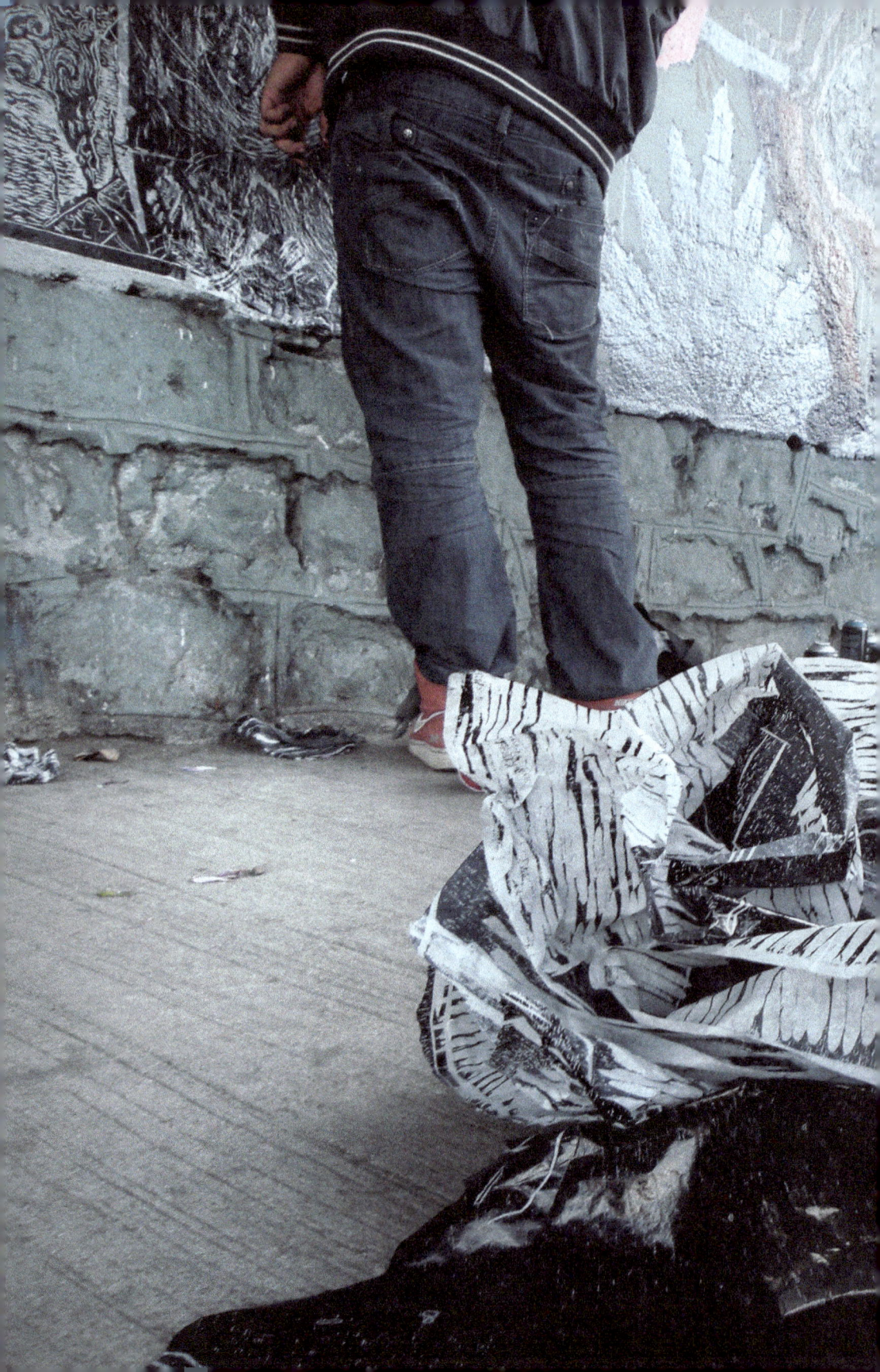

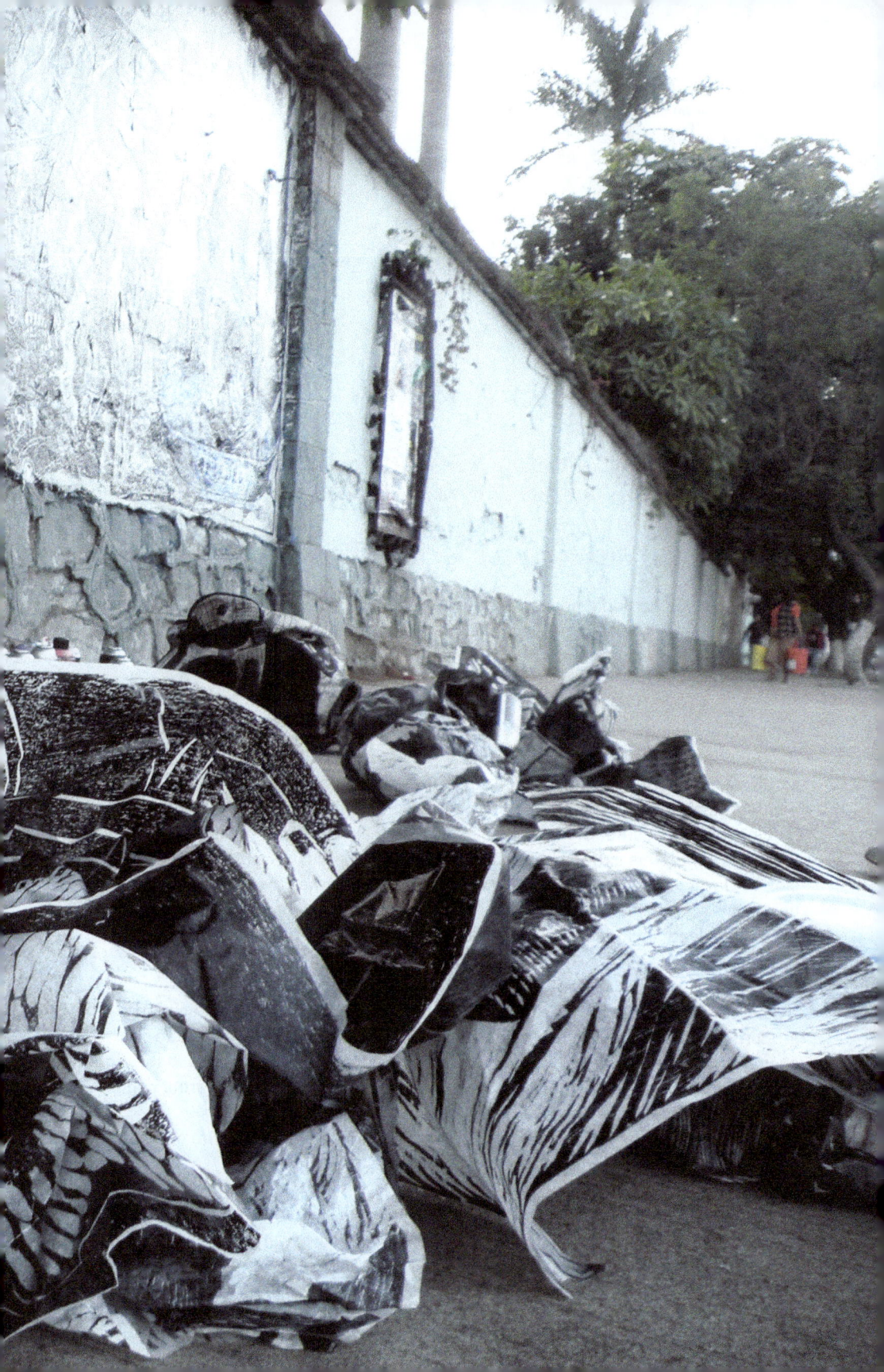

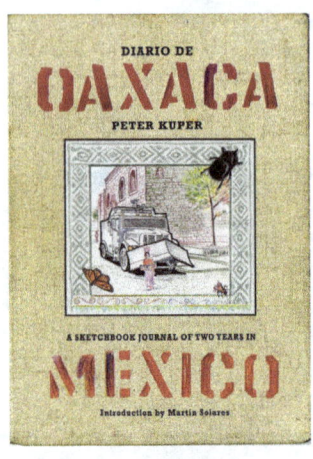

Diario De Oaxaca: A Sketchbook Journal of Two Years in Mexico
Peter Kuper, with an introduction by Martín Solares
ISBN: 978-1-60486-071-9
$29.95   208 pages

Painting a vivid, personal portrait of social and political upheaval in Oaxaca, Mexico, this unique memoir employs comics, bilingual essays, photos, and sketches to chronicle the events that unfolded around a teachers' strike and led to a seven-month siege.

When award-winning cartoonist Peter Kuper and his wife and daughter moved to the beautiful 16th-century colonial town of Oaxaca in 2006, they planned to spend a quiet year or two enjoying a different culture and taking a break from the U.S. political climate under the Bush administration. What they hadn't counted on was landing in the epicenter of Mexico's biggest political struggle in recent years. Timely and compelling, this extraordinary firsthand account presents a distinct artistic vision of Oaxacan life, from explorations of the beauty of the environment to graphic portrayals of the fight between strikers and government troops that left more than 20 people dead, including American journalist Brad Will.

Praise
"Kuper is a colossus; I have been in awe of him for over 20 years. Teachers and students everywhere take heart: Kuper has in these pages borne witness to our seemingly endless struggle to educate and to be educated in the face of institutions that really don't give a damn. In this ruined age we need Kuper's unsparing compassionate visionary artistry like we need hope."
—Junot Díaz, Pulitzer Prize-winning author of *The Brief Wondrous Life of Oscar Wao*

"Peter Kuper is undoubtedly the modern master whose work has refined the socially relevant comic to the highest point yet achieved." —*Newsarama*

"An artist at the top of his form." —*Publishers Weekly*

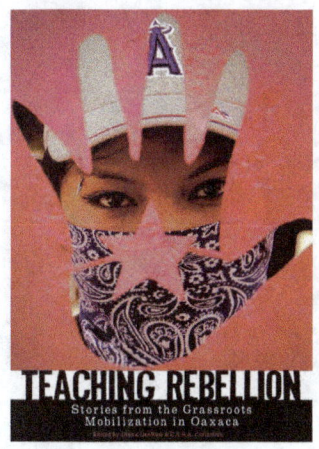

Teaching Rebellion: Stories from the Grassroots Mobilization in Oaxaca
Edited by Diana Denham and the C.A.S.A. Collective
ISBN: 978-1-60486-032-0
$21.95   384 pages

In 2006, Oaxaca, Mexico, came alive with a broad and diverse movement that capti-
vated the nation and earned the admiration of communities organizing for social jus-
tice around the world. The show of international solidarity for the people of Oaxaca
was the most extensive since the Zapatista uprising in 1994. Fueled by long ignored
social contradictions, what began as a teachers' strike demanding more resources
for education quickly turned into a massive movement that demanded direct, participatory democracy.

Hundreds of thousands of Oaxacans raised their voices against the abuses of the
state government. They participated in marches of up to 800,000 people, occupied
government buildings, took over radio stations, called for statewide labor and hunger
strikes, held sit-ins, reclaimed spaces for public art and created altars for assassinated
activists in public spaces. In the now legendary March of Pots and Pans, two thousand
women peacefully took over and operated the state television channel for three weeks.
Barricades that were built all over the city to prevent the passage of paramilitaries and
defend occupied public spaces, quickly became a place where neighbors got to know
each other, shared ideas and developed new strategies for organizing.

"Once you learn to speak, you don't want to be quiet anymore," an indigenous community radio activist said. Accompanied by photography and political art, *Teaching
Rebellion* is a compilation of testimonies from longtime organizers, teachers,
students, housewives, religious leaders, union members, schoolchildren, indigenous
community activists, artists, journalists, and many others who participated in what
became the Popular Assembly of the Peoples of Oaxaca. This is a chance to listen
directly to those invested in and affected by what quickly became one of the most
important social uprisings of the 21st century.

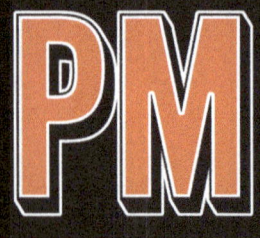

PM Press was founded at the end of 2007 by a small collection of folks with decades of publishing, media, and organizing experience. PM Press co-conspirators have published and distributed hundreds of books, pamphlets, CDs, and DVDs. Members of PM have founded enduring book fairs, spearheaded victorious tenant organizing campaigns, and worked closely with bookstores, academic conferences, and even rock bands to deliver political and challenging ideas to all walks of life. We're old enough to know what we're doing and young enough to know what's at stake.

We seek to create radical and stimulating fiction and non-fiction books, pamphlets, T-shirts, visual and audio materials to entertain, educate, and inspire you. We aim to distribute these through every available channel with every available technology—whether that means you are seeing anarchist classics at our bookfair stalls; reading our latest vegan cookbook at the café; downloading geeky fiction e-books; or digging new music and timely videos from our website.

PM Press is always on the lookout for talented and skilled volunteers, artists, activists and writers to work with. If you have a great idea for a project or can contribute in some way, please get in touch.

In the six years since its founding—and on a mere shoestring—PM Press has risen to the formidable challenge of publishing and distributing knowledge and entertainment for the struggles ahead. With over 250 releases to date, we have published an impressive and stimulating array of literature, art, music, politics, and culture. Using every available medium, we've succeeded in connecting those hungry for ideas and information to those putting them into practice.

Friends of PM allows you to directly help impact, amplify, and revitalize the discourse and actions of radical writers, filmmakers, and artists. It provides us with a stable foundation from which we can build upon our early successes and provides a much-needed subsidy for the materials that can't necessarily pay their own way. You can help make that happen—and receive every new title automatically delivered to your door once a month—by joining as a Friend of PM Press. And, we'll throw in a free T-shirt when you sign up.

Here are your options:
• $30 a month: Get all books and pamphlets plus 50% discount on all webstore purchases
• $40 a month: Get all PM Press releases (including CDs and DVDs) plus 50% discount on all webstore purchases
• $100 a month: Superstar—Everything plus PM merchandise, free downloads, and 50% discount on all webstore purchases

For those who can't afford $30 or more a month, we're introducing Sustainer Rates at $15, $10 and $5. Sustainers get a free PM Press t-shirt and a 50% discount on all purchases from our website.

Your Visa or Mastercard will be billed once a month, until you tell us to stop. Or until our efforts succeed in bringing the revolution around. Or the financial meltdown of Capital makes plastic redundant. Whichever comes first.

PM Press PO Box 23912 Oakland CA 94623 www.pmpress.org